This Book

Belongs To

Bobby Duncan

Some of My Best Friends Are Crazy

Baseball's Favorite Lunatic Goes in Search of His Peers

Jay Johnstone

with Rick Talley

Macmillan Publishing Company
New York

Collier Macmillan Publishers
London

Macmillan Publishing Company
866 Third Avenue, New York, NY 10022
Collier Macmillan Canada, Inc.

Library of Congress Cataloging-in-Publication Data
Johnstone, Jay, 1946–
    Some of my best friends are crazy : baseball's favorite lunatic goes in search
of his peers / Jay Johnstone with Rick Talley.
        p.   cm.
    ISBN 0-02-559560-1
    1. Johnstone, Jay, 1946–   .   2. Baseball players—United States—
Biography,   3. Baseball—United States—Anecdotes.   I. Talley,
Rick.   II. Title.
GV865.J63A3   1990   89-49153   CIP
796.357′092—dc20
[B]

Macmillan books are available at special discounts for bulk purchases
for sales promotions, premiums, fund-raising, or educational use.
For details, contact:

Special Sales Director
Macmillan Publishing Company
866 Third Avenue
New York, NY 10022

10 9 8 7 6 5 4 3 2 1

Printed in the United States of America

*To my wife, Mary Jayne, and my daughter, Mary Jayne Sarah,
to my parents, Jack and Audrey, and to parents-in-law
Bob and Mary Saunders.*

Contents

Acknowledgments

Sincere thanks to all who provided the experiences and fun we're sharing with you in this book, and to all the baseball fans across America who are laughing along with us.

Special thanks to Fred Weinhaus, president and general manager of WABC-Radio, who gave me the opportunity to do what I hope to do for the rest of my life: broadcast major league baseball games. Thanks to my super partner in the Yankee radio booth, John Sterling, who literally taught me how to broadcast a game. Appreciation, too, goes to the rest of our broadcast team— producer Chris Lentine and engineers Mike Maimone and Tony Sibilla—and to the Yankee front office gang who helped make my transition a lot easier: Dick Kraft, Arthur Richman, Jeff Idelson, Bill Squires, John Fugazy, Bill Emslie, Debbie Tymon, Annette Guardabascio, and all the rest of this terrific group.

Heartfelt thanks to the scruffy members of the Baseball Writers Association of America for helping me gather anecdotes and quotes; to my editor, Rick Wolff, for exploding a cigar in my face on the book jacket and giving me a bat with someone else's number on it; to Neil at Yolanda's in the Bronx for delivering pizza between games of doubleheaders; and to WABC-Radio sponsors Bill Liederman of Mickey Mantle's and Joe Healy of Runyon's.

Acknowledgments

Also, thanks to my illegitimate father, Tom Lasorda, who is always there when I need him; to the girls of the Los Angeles Dodgers Community Team: Michelle Fox, Laura Wallace, and Toi Crawford; to good friends Tony Capozzola, Mike DeStefano, Dave Baudouin, Harry Hindoyan, David Martin, Barry Stockhammer, Marc Reede, Vic Berelli, Ed Liberatore, Jerry Callahan, Ron Masak, Steve Rotfeld & Company, Charlie Gilb and all my pals at the L.A. produce market, and my New York roomies Dr. Archie (a.k.a. Dr. Robert Laboranti), Dr. Lou Cona, and Crazy Larry McTague.

Very special appreciation goes to my literary agent, Shari Lesser Wenk, who once again went far beyond the call of duty and to the edge of her sanity to assure publication of this book.

Finally, I would like to acknowledge the men and women of our country who have served to defend the American flag, especially those of my generation who left behind family and loved ones to serve in Vietnam. Too often we overlook what Old Glory really stands for and forget those who gave their lives to keep our nation free.

—*Jay Johnstone*

Some of My Best Friends Are Crazy

1

Crazies of the Nineties

As the Disney cartoon characters chain-danced past the National League dugout before the sixtieth All-Star Game last summer in Anaheim, chattering and joyfully waving, I couldn't help wondering what was in the minds of the millionaire ballplayers who observed, mostly stone-faced, from the bench.

Then I saw one of the players at the far end of the dugout grinning and waving back to Roger Rabbit.

Ahhhh, I thought. There is still some hope.

Maybe the Grand Ol' Game isn't dead, yet.

The man waving was Mitch Williams, left-handed relief pitcher for the Chicago Cubs. And as Roger, Goofy, Donald Duck, and friends continued on their merry way, twenty-four-year-old Williams moved forward, one foot on the top step of the dugout, as if he wanted to leap out to join this conga line of make-believe.

I would have.

But what Mitch almost did was good enough for me. It told me something.

It said that no matter how high the salaries may spiral, or how big the TV contracts get, or how many players enter the 1990s adorned with gold chains, briefcases, agents, attorneys, and headphones, there remains a constant: Major league baseball is still a little boy's game played by men.

1

And if you can't have fun, what can you have?

I had fun during my twenty seasons as a major league baseball player for eight teams, four in each league (Angels, White Sox, A's, Yankees, Phillies, Dodgers, Padres, Cubs). Through the years 1966–1985 (looks like something that should be etched on a headstone), I terrorized teammates, locked managers in their rooms, gave hotfoots to umpires, used the general manager's office phone for personal calls, donned a groundskeeper's coveralls to drag the infield, and occasionally climbed into the stands to visit with the customers.

Maybe that's why they called me Crazy Jay.

But somewhere along the way, I also collected 707 hits in the National League (.288), another 547 in the American League (.243), played in 1,748 games, chased down a whole bunch of fly balls, tripped on a few sprinkler heads (sometimes my Star Patrol Helmet radar got out of synch), and even hit 102 home runs.

And, having fun, I played with winners.

I had back-to-back .329 and .318 seasons with the Phillies in 1975 and 1976 (pitchers lost concentration when I talked dirty to them), and during the three-game playoff that we lost to the Cincinnati Reds in 1976, I set a NLCS hitting record (.778) with seven hits in nine at-bats. That '76 Philly team, incidentally, won 101 games en route to a pennant. When we won another division title in 1977, I hit .284; and in 1978, I went to the Yankees during the season and landed in the World Series.

With the Dodgers in 1981 we went all the way to a World Championship, beating the Yankees in six games, and I "timed my lunge" perfectly to hit a key two-run homer off Ron Davis in game four. Then, in 1984, I was part of the Cubs team that won a division title, the first championship of any kind on the North Side of Chicago since 1945.

But the numbers only explain the boring part of the game. Guys play baseball for one reason—to have fun. At least that's the way I played the game. And I believe that the teams who have the most fun do the most winning. And vice versa too.

The important bottom line: Laughter and winning often go hand in hand and I don't subscribe to the cynic's theory that teams loosen up only after they reach the top of the standings.

As I wrote in my first book, *Temporary Insanity*, laughter is conducive to winning. And if you don't go *Over the Edge* (title of my second book) once in a while, playing major league baseball can get awfully boring.

Why? Why can't a ballplayer just go out and do his job, call his stockbroker after the game, and drive his Porsche off into the night, 162 times a season, without partaking in any deviant behavior?

He can but he had better have nerves of steel.

I acted crazy to battle the pressure. I laughed to conquer fear of failure and I used the clubhouse as a stage to bring my teammates into the comedy.

Some ballplayers just don't get it. Ron Cey, for example, could never understand why I went into my carpenter's act and cut his spring training locker down to Penguin size. He just stood there and looked at this beautiful, baby-sized locker and shook his head.

But everybody else laughed and, believe it or not, people are still laughing on major league baseball fields and in the clubhouses. Sometimes even in the front offices.

That doesn't mean the game hasn't changed. Oh, how it has. It is *different*, folks, and as a Yankee broadcaster last season with New York radio station WABC, I certainly had a front-row seat to witness the differences.

For example, would Joe DiMaggio have worn a golden earring? Would Mickey Mantle have hired a nutritionist to accompany him on road trips?

Ballplayers of past decades had roommates on the road. No more. Today's player doesn't even have to sit next to a teammate on the plane, let alone room with him. It's all right there in the contract: A player is entitled to one open seat next to him on flights, in lieu of first-class accommodation.

Players of the sixties and seventies played in clubhouses so small they sometimes showered in shifts. The well-attended athlete of the nineties enjoys spacious clubhouses that feature TV lounges, weight rooms, Nautilus rooms, waiting rooms, managers' rooms, coaches' rooms, trainers' rooms, and doctors' rooms.

Yet more players go on the disabled list today than at any time in the history of baseball.

Money makes the difference.

We had September salary drives, today's player has a guaranteed, multiyear contract. The average player's salary of 1989 exceeded $450,000 and in 1990 was expected to top $600,000.

We worked during the off-season in second jobs, then punished our bodies in spring training to get back into shape. Today's financially secure players never get out of shape.

We ate french fries and drank milkshakes and juicy steaks when we could afford it, but also tried to pocket half of the meal money. They eat chicken and this year's designer fish.

We partied together. They have personal friends in every city and rarely go out in groups.

As rookies, we wanted to win jobs but treated veteran players with respect. Today's rookie walks through the clubhouse with his portable phone and isn't afraid to criticize management and teammates alike.

We caught the ball with two hands.

We cared first about the team.

More of us played with a burning desire. Baseball was all we had and all we wanted. I'm not so sure many of today's players even enjoy the game. Certainly they don't slide into second base or crash into the plumply padded outfield walls as if they do.

That doesn't mean we were *better* ballplayers but certainly we were different, and that's why I embarked during the summer of '89 on the mission of this book—in search of baseball's bizarre.

Had it disappeared? Had the hotfoots, naive rookies, pranksters, and practical jokers been replaced by a $1.06 billion television deal?

Was the game still fun?

I guess all you really need to know about Mitch Williams is that he takes a bowling ball with him on road trips.

I don't recall any ballplayers ever doing that.

Mitch says it helps loosen up his left arm, which has sometimes been known to send smaller projectiles at high speeds in unpredictable directions (in three minor league seasons he walked 407 batters).

Sometimes Mitch will bowl as many as fifty games in a single day. He even tried out the National Bowling Hall of Fame lanes, located across the street from Busch Stadium, when the Cubs visited St. Louis.

"It was ugly," said Mitch, describing his Hall of Fame lanes outing. "My high game was 140-something."

Many major league hitters would be happy to hit .140 against Mitch and certainly few "dig in" to try to take him deep. Example of a typical "Wild Thing" outing last summer: He walked two, hit two more, balked, and threw a wild pitch in the seventh inning against the Cincinnati Reds on May 21, yet *didn't allow a run.*

The inning: Todd Benzinger flied out; Jeff Reed was hit by a pitch but picked off first base. Mitch then hit Lenny Harris, wild pitched, walked pitcher Rick Mahler, balked the runners to second and third, then walked Chris Sabo. Joel Youngblood, however, flied out to end the inning.

By the end of the scoreless inning, Cincy manager Pete Rose was wearing a batting helmet in the dugout.

Said Wild Thing: "Just another day in the legend of Mitch Williams."

And as the Cubs continued their surprising 1989 season, the legend of Wild Thing grew: On Friday, August 4, Mitch recorded his twenty-eighth save when teammate Domingo Ramos made a game-saving dive on a Jeff King shot with two out in the ninth. The next day, King hit another shot off Williams, but this time it went off the reliever's ear and, despite Mitch's protests, he was removed from the game. Two days later, just two outs from his twenty-ninth save, manager Don Zimmer removed a downcast Williams from the game—and one day later, during batting practice, Wild Thing cracked a bat over his knee, then later pitched two scoreless innings to get save number twenty-nine.

Zimmer's reaction to Williams's unpredictability: "How many

times have you seen it? How would you like to have your life depending on it? Stick with me and you won't have any hair. But I don't get uptight about it. I expect it.''

"If Mitch were a nightclub act," said Dodger announcer Vin Scully one night during a typical Wild Thing appearance, "they'd introduce him as 'the always exciting Mitch Williams.' ''

"But Mitch is *fun*," said Zimmer. "He's been fun ever since he joined this club.'' (He was obtained from Texas in a trade that sent outfielder Rafael Palmeiro to the Rangers.) "He's a fun guy to be around and not just when he's pitching well.''

Teammate Rick Sutcliffe on Mitch: "I pitch like I'm sitting in an easy chair and he pitches like his hair is on fire.''

Says outfielder Andy Van Slyke of the Pirates: "If everybody pitched like him I'd quit.''

Early during the 1989 season Williams asked the Wrigley Field organist to play the music to the sixties classic "Wild Thing" whenever he entered a game, but pitching coach Dick Pole felt it underscored his control problems (which it did), so the organist began to play "Thriller" instead.

The nickname of "Wild Thing" stuck, however, and Mitch is certainly hyper enough to fit it.

I can relate to that. I would wander around the ballpark and talk to fans hanging over the walls. Mitch does the same thing. Says Mitch about himself: "I'm a little different.''

He has a tattoo of movie cartoon character Speedy Gonzalez on his right calf. ("My dad has Tasmanian Devil and Yosemite Sam tattoos. My brother has Gumby and Pokey. Our family has never been accused of being all there. That's why I was glad I was traded to the Cubs. Some of my relatives thought a Texas Ranger was a cop.'') And he tries to get through a baseball season by shaving only four or five times.

Why Wild Thing? The idea came to Williams like a giant flash in the night after he saw the movie *Major League*. He identified with actor Charlie Sheen's portrayal of a young, flaky reliever who enters the game with fans singing "Wild Thing.''

Mitch also related to the baseball movie *Bull Durham*. "When

I first saw Nuke Laloosh [the pitcher] I thought they were doing the story of my life,'' said Williams.

Indeed, some opponents are suspicious of Williams's celebrated ''wildness.'' Pirate manager Jim Leyland suggests that Mitch gets away with throwing brushback pitches without penalty because umpires chalk it up to wildness.

Mitch just shrugs and says: ''I didn't walk all those guys in the minor leagues on purpose.''

Adds sportswriter Frank Luksa of the *Dallas Times-Herald*: ''Williams has walked more people than a seeing-eye dog.''

As you may have guessed, I'm a Mitch Williams fan.

For two reasons.

Not only because he knows how to have fun (''My sense of humor comes from my dad, who always said there was no better medicine than laughter: With all the trouble in the world, life's too short to spend it moping around'') but because of Mitch's dedication.

He is often the first man to reach the ballpark and certainly I can relate to that. If Mitch and I were playing on the same team, we'd probably run into each other at McDonald's at dawn before an afternoon game.

And, despite his intensity, Mitch has apparently come to grips with one of baseball's harsh realities: that some days you're going to blow games instead of save them.

''You can't save them all,'' said Mitch, during the heat of the Cubs' pennant drive in 1989. ''It's an occupational hazard.''

Spoken like a man who knows about hazards. When Mitch Williams was a small boy, he climbed onto the roof of his house, only to hear his father order him down.

''So I dove off,'' recalls Williams, ''and Dad caught me.''

Mitch comes off the mound with the same reckless abandon and, so far, has suffered no crashes worse than Will Clark's base hit to win the National League Championship Series.

Mitch Williams isn't alone. There are others. And as we enter baseball's final decade to usher in the twenty-first century, consider some of the Crazies of the nineties. They may average a half-million dollars a year in salary but they're still *baseball players* and maybe that says it all.

Join them for some fun:

It's pitcher Roger McDowell of the Phillies spraying Wrigley Field bleacher fans with a hose.

And rookie reliever Kenny Rogers standing up to represent the bullpen whenever Texas Ranger fans do the wave.

It's Cincinnati pitcher Danny Jackson using a bat to demolish his Riverfront Stadium locker, claiming later it was the work of termites.

And teammate Kent Tekulve presenting Jackson with a punching bag to use for any future outbursts.

It's Darrell Evans of the Atlanta Braves recalling the triangular spacecraft he and his wife saw hovering over a neighbor's home.

And Wayne Tolleson of the Yankees with his own close encounter. Even though his team was scheduled for another game in Cleveland on Monday, Wayne checked out on Sunday, missing by only one day.

It's Dan Gladden of the Twins sending a $104 room service breakfast to teammate Al Newman at the Grand Hyatt in New York. Not original, but effective.

It's Steve Bedrosian of the Phils pouring a bucket of water on manager Nick Leyva after his first managerial victory.

"I thought they only did that in football," said Cubs announcer Harry Caray.

"At least they could have heated up the water," said Leyva.

It's Mark (Mr. Gadget) Davis of the Padres saving weird toys and water pistols. Example: model of a left-handed baseball player with a hot dog in his mouth and mustard on his shirt.

And Reds' reliever Rob Dibble with a license plate that reads "I Pitch."

It's Cleveland pitcher Greg Swindell, on the day he pitches, biting off a fingernail and keeping it inside his cheek during the game. He tried gum in college but it didn't work, and he's afraid he'll swallow tobacco.

And the Baltimore Orioles taking infield practice without a ball—shades of the House of David barnstorming teams of years past.

It's Gerald Perry of the Braves going 123 at-bats without an RBI, with teammates wearing small pieces of black tape on the bills of their caps in memory of his last ribbie.

And Vance Law of the Cubs getting a shaving cream pie in his face during a TV interview.

It's Mets minor league pitcher Todd Welborn "dipping" dirt into his cheek instead of chewing tobacco and explaining, "I don't like tobacco because it causes diseases. Dirt is free and nobody bums it off you."

And Jerry Reuss bringing a good luck Sammy Doll (named for White Sox pitching coach Sammy Ellis) into the dugout.

It's Atlanta outfielder Geronimo Berroa missing a routine fly ball and later finding a garbage can in front of his locker with an attached sign: "Try This."

And Roger McDowell keeping a snake named Larry in a cage above his locker at Vets Stadium, then holding a private ceremony for Larry when he passed away.

It's left-hander Mark Davis leaving shoes in front of San Diego rookies' lockers with inscribed messages on them.

And Tom Brunansky of the Cardinals suckering teammate Joe Magrane into thinking he was supposed to pose for a *Gentleman's Quarterly* magazine spread.

I think you're getting the idea. The Crazies are still out there and you're going to meet them in coming chapters.

First, though, have you ever wondered what it would be like to be an announcer for a major league baseball team?

For the New York Yankees?

Stay tuned.

2

Did I Really Say That?

At last count, there were fifty-five of us in major league broadcast booths.

Ex-jocks.

Or, as Howard Cosell once described former ballplayers who become radio and television sports announcers:

"Men without intellect, without training, without my background at law, without the spontaneity of articulation that I possess."

I plead guilty. The only thing I know about law is how to chase down deadbeats who don't pay their bills at my auto parts business. Intellect? Howard probably has me there, too, even though I've written more books than him.

But I wonder what degree of "spontaneity of articulation" we'd get from Haaawaaaaaaad if somebody put Capsolin (heat balm) in his undershorts? I did it once to pitcher Dave Goltz in the Dodger clubhouse and he later got so spontaneous he almost drove his car off the freeway.

Training is something else. Most ex-jocks walk into broadcast booths with little or none, hoping that their on-the-field background will overcome any fear of the microphone or lack of announcing experience.

11

That's the fault of the broadcast industry. But radio-TV execs think nothing of throwing a former ballplayer into the fire and watching him roast. After all, if it doesn't work they can always fire him and hire another.

Because of this lack of training, many players-turned-announcers don't understand when they're saying something right or wrong and seldom is there someone to tell them. As ex-Tigers pitcher Mickey Lolich, part-time color commentator for Detroit's Class AA team in London, Ontario, said when asked about his progress:

"I haven't been caught yet with a hot dog in my mouth when I was supposed to be talking."

I was lucky. Before joining WABC radio as Yankee commentator last season alongside play-by-play man John Sterling, I had done some radio and television work in both Chicago and Los Angeles, as well as hosting the syndicated cable TV show *Lighter Side of Sports*.

Besides, my first major league roommate twenty-three years ago was Jimmy Piersall. I figured that prepared me for anything.

Nevertheless, I wasn't exactly ready for what happened on March 3, 1989, the afternoon of the first Yankee exhibition game to be broadcast on WABC radio from West Palm Beach, Florida.

Sterling baptized me.

Here's a guy, my partner, who had previously announced Braves games for superstation WTBS, so naturally he knew a lot of people from Atlanta, the Yankee opponent that day. So we show up at the ballpark early and start shooting the breeze with sportswriters and players on the field. Next thing I know it's like 12:45 P.M., the game is scheduled for 1:05 P.M., and we're sitting in the lounge having a sandwich and a Coke.

"Hey, John," I said, "isn't it getting a little late?"

"Oh, yeah," said Sterling, "I guess we should mosey on up to the booth."

We walk into the booth nine minutes before air time and people are going nuts. The producers thought we were lost. The director of sales was screaming. And here we are with no notes, no lineups, nothing written down, and *it's my first game.*

"Don't panic," says Sterling, "we'll get there," and for the next nine minutes we're feverishly writing down the lineups, locating statistics, and testing the headsets.

"Thirty seconds," somebody yells, and I'm thinking, "Are they serious? What am I doing here?"

"Fifteen seconds!"

"Five, four, three, two, one . . . you're on!"

"Hello, everybody, this is John Sterling and Jay Johnstone and welcome to Yankee baseball. It's a beautiful day in West Palm Beach for this first spring training game between the Yankees and Atlanta Braves and the starting pitchers are . . ."

Just like silk, he was. I'm sweating, and Sterling, the pro, is loving it. Finally, he throws it to me and I mumble something I can't remember and we're off and running.

Then, after about two innings of smooth sailing, I turned around to face all the WABC folks who had been nervous and said:

"And tomorrow we're showing up *seven* minutes before game time. How do you like that?"

Joe Torre, who announces for the California Angels, said last season after Oakland's Curt Young threw a brushback pitch past the Angels' Glenn Hoffman:

"Is that called dustin' Hoffman?"

That's clever.

Ralph Kiner, who announces for the New York Mets, ushered out the eighties by saying:

"All of the Mets' road wins against L.A. this year have been at Dodger Stadium."

That's careless.

Then there was Kathleen Sullivan of CBS *This Morning,* who asked Baltimore manager Frank Robinson how his team was getting along without Eddie Murphy.

That's dumb.

There was even a broadcast type who approached San Francisco's Will Clark at the 1989 All-Star Game and said, "Kevin, can you explain . . ." before Clark yelled, "Hold it," making a timeout sign with his hands.

"Wrong color," said Clark, "wrong muscles, wrong guy."

Moral: It's nice if you can be clever in the announcing booth, but it's even more important that you pay attention. As Tony Kubek, who in 1989 did double duty broadcasting for the Toronto Blue Jays and NBC, said: "You've got to maintain a level of concentration in the broadcast booth more intense and over a longer period of time than you do as a player."

Presumably, if you concentrate, you don't say what Jerry Coleman said during a CBS radio Game of the Week when the count reached three and oh on St. Louis outfielder Tom Brunansky:

"You never want to come right down the middle on three and oh," said Coleman, "no matter what the count."

Then there was Harry Caray of WGN in Chicago, who said indignantly during a Cubs broadcast:

"I'm really upset about Mike Ditka trading Ed McMahon."

We all make mistakes and if I stick around long enough in this new career, somebody will probably accumulate a list of my bloopers and label them "Jaybirds."

So far, with me, it's not things I wish I hadn't said. It's how I said them. Sometimes, during times of excitement, everything I learned in English grammar seems to depart my brain, and later I'll think, "Did I really say that?"

I'll complete a thought as I'm talking, for example, and it just doesn't come out right. I guess that's what makes Vin Scully so special. Everything he says seems to come out eloquently. I've never really said something I didn't want to say, but sometimes my mind races so quickly that my tongue gets left behind.

But I've been careless, too. Once last season I told WABC listeners that Gary Sheffield was hitting for the Milwaukee Brewers when Glenn Braggs was actually at the plate. I went into a long spiel about Sheffield's youth and potential and I was talking about the wrong guy. But what can you do? You just go on.

One other time, drawing upon all my twenty years of major league experience, I suggested that it would be a great time for the Yankees to turn a double play. Brilliant thinking. There were already two outs.

You really do have to pay attention. Listeners don't want to hear that the ground ball went to shortstop. They want to hear the *name of the shortstop* as he throws to first base.

It all comes second nature to my partner John Sterling, of course, who can recount exactly how earlier scoring went in a game without ever looking at his scoresheet. I haven't been able to master that. Hey, I'm just now learning to read my own scorekeeping. Sometimes my scorecard looks like a checklist from the Jet Propulsion Laboratory in Pasadena. And I'm sure I'm not the first to use "WW" as a scorekeeping device.

"WW?"

Wasn't Watching.

I think it was Paul Hornung who once said about former Green Bay Packer teammate Max McGee:

"He has the perfect face for radio."

I'm sure I qualify for that definition, as do a number of other former-ballplayers-turned-announcers. We may not be beautiful, but we're everywhere. When Nolan Ryan faced the Yankees last season, he found he had pitched against more New York broadcasters (Bobby Murcer, Tom Seaver, Lou Piniella, Tommy Hutton, and Yours Truly) than players in the current Yankees lineup. The only Yankee hitter he had previously faced was Steve Sax. But he still beat the Yanks, 6–2.

Another who has a face for radio but nevertheless has made it big on TV is former catcher Bob Uecker, a.k.a. "Mr. Baseball" from his commercial success. He has gained considerable popularity due to his Lite beer commercials and his regular role on the TV sitcom *Mr. Belvedere*. He also serves as a regular announcer with the Milwaukee Brewers and is easily the most recognizable personality traveling with the team.

Example: While riding in the front seat of the team bus headed for Yankee Stadium, Uecker noticed a worker sitting in the back of a panel truck stopped in traffic in front of the bus. The man, only a few feet away, was pointing into the bus and although nobody could hear him, the players could read his lips as he screamed, "You're Bob Uecker . . . You're Bob Uecker." Finally, the guy leaned forward in the truck to tell the driver, who promptly got out, walked around to the back of the truck, looked into the Brewer bus, then disgustedly reached around and pulled the panel door shut on the guy in back.

Uecker was funny before he got famous and he remains funny. When the Brewers were flying into Los Angeles International Airport one evening, their chartered plane got caught in the wash of a 747 landing in front of them and did a half-barrel roll before the pilot righted it and made a safe landing.

Uecker, seated on the aisle, immediately leaned out and whispered to the stewardess:

"Go tell the captain I don't like that. Tell him not to do that anymore."

Torre, a former major league player and manager who has become one of the very best television commentators in the business, once said, "I'm still waiting to wake up one day and find there's more to it than there really is," and I know what he meant.

Being a baseball announcer, particularly an analyst, is easy. I'm serious. Once you master the routine, you can simply be yourself and have fun. That's when "announcing" becomes the easiest part because you're just talking about what is happening on the field. Unlike television, when you talk to a radio listener you become his eyes. You tell him what you see, what it means, and how you felt about it, and you can have some fun doing it.

It's not brain surgery.

The difficult part for me, in the beginning, was the preparation—coming to the ballparks early, studying scouting reports, talking with other broadcasters and writers, and learning about the strengths and weaknesses of unfamiliar players in the American League.

Take American League MVP Robin Yount of the Brewers as an example: He's a fastball hitter, likes the ball out over the plate, but he'll use the entire field. With two strikes, he shortens his swing. He may go the other way with the pitch but has enough power to hit it out.

With a pitcher, you learn what he throws and what he throws best. Does he have a curve and slider? Split-fingered fastball or split-fingered change? How has he done during the last few weeks?

I DIDN'T SAY THAT . . . KINER DID!

On Bruce Sutter's career-ending arm injury:
"He's going to be out of action for the rest of his career."

On relief pitcher Steve Bedrosian, after trade from Phillies to Giants:
"All of his saves have come during relief appearances."

When Bobby and Barry Bonds were about to become the all-time father-son home run champions:
"They will surpass the father-son tandem of Buddy Bell and Yogi Berra."

When *Kiner's Korner* cameraman caught Roger McDowell leaning against the stands to inform his pregnant wife he had been traded from the Mets to Phillies:
"And it so happens," said Kiner, "Len Dykstra's wife is also pregnant and she, too, will now be coming to the Philadelphia Phillies."

On form or off? Is he healthy? The "book" on players changes from series to series and it's my job to study the book.

Spring training is just that every year for announcers. Because all the managers are looking at so many different players—sometimes guys wearing number 88 that you've never heard about and will never hear about again—it becomes a guessing game in the broadcast booth.

We had a guy last spring play a sensational game and we had no idea who he was.

We finally just gave him a name, José something-or-other.

I mean this guy played a helluva game—great catch and throw from the outfield in the ninth inning—but he's wearing some number that isn't on anybody's scorecard and we didn't know who he was. But since he was a Latin player, we called him José something-or-other and said he was a "phenom" who we were sure everyone would be hearing about in the future.

Maybe you have heard about him but I still don't know who the guy was.

Sure, it's fun. I'd be lying if I said it wasn't. But it isn't so much fun when the rain comes into the booth and makes the ink run on your scorecard; or when it's forty-four degrees and you're wearing socks over your boots in the broadcast booth to keep from freezing because nobody wants to close the windows because they'll lose the crowd noise; or when you spill coffee onto your media guide and scorecard and before you know it, you've written "WW's" all over the margins.

But it's fun when you're doing those live commercials (we've got so many on sold-out WABC broadcasts that sometimes we say things like ". . . and this thirty-second bathroom break will be brought to you by Scott Tissue"). Often we're so busy with John's play-by-play and commercials that I may not have time to say more than "Uh" or "Yes" during a half-inning. Maybe that's why the New York tabloids haven't been printing Jaybirds like they print Kinerisms. Maybe I haven't given them enough complete sentences yet.

Sometimes I'll be handed a twenty-second commercial to do in nine seconds. No way, so I just eliminate things and it always makes the sales people nervous. At other times I'll just ad lib through the copy and that makes people nervous, too. But if you can't have fun, why do it?

I use a headset, Sterling uses a pod, which is a microphone that he's forever knocking over. He'll turn one way, "thump thump" goes the pod, and I'll say, "Did it again, huh, John?" on the air. Or he'll turn and his earpiece will fall out. He usually loses it about three times a game. And one time last season I turned to get something, forgetting my headset was on, and pulled all the controls off the table, sending our engineer into near-apoplexy.

But one day I'll get it right. After all, I was only a rookie.

The toughest part of my job is criticizing a play or player, perhaps because it's so easy to do.

That may sound like something Yogi Berra would have said but I think you know what I mean.

Example: I've never seen a routine grounder. All the time you hear announcers talking about routine fly balls or routine grounders but what does that mean? The ball could hit a dirt clod, or a seam in the artificial turf, or have overspin on it.

There's nothing routine about anything ever done in baseball and I try to bring that into perspective.

Yet, with our eyes in the sky, we do see ballplayers fail to hustle after fly balls. We see grown men making $1 million a year fail to run to first base. And you have to describe what you see.

Tim McCarver, a former teammate with the Phillies and now a successful broadcaster with the Mets and ABC network, once said about being a critic: "Your praise is nothing unless you can objectively criticize. And there are problems along the way . . . some of the guys who are still playing expect a degree of protection from somebody who's been there. And you owe them no more than fairness."

Former players, then, walk a fine line as announcers. Some never cross it. Unlike baseball writers or columnists, we're "ex-players" and although we're down in the clubhouse, associating with players and talking their language, we are also now expected to "report" on the radio.

It would be too easy, however, to sit upstairs and say to a radio audience, "How can he miss that ball?" I know how he missed it because I've missed them myself. So sometimes you have to bite your tongue and remember just how difficult the game of baseball can be.

Seldom, though, do I socialize with players. I'm part of their lives, yes, but now I'm on the other side of the fence, too. So far,

I've had no serious confrontations with players, Yankees or otherwise, but I've got to figure it will happen. It goes with the job.

Am I a homer—an announcer who unabashedly roots for the Yankees? I hope not, because I don't work for them. I work for WABC, that powerful New York radio voice managed by Fred Weinhaus.

But who's kidding whom? Obviously there is a tendency to want the Yankees to do well and I'm sure fans can hear it in my voice. A couple of times last season, for example, I made the mistake of saying "we" and "us" instead of saying "Yankees." In some cities, of course, that's standard. Harry Caray of the Chicago Cubs has been saying "we" for years, no matter where he worked, and I'm convinced his popularity with the listeners is connected to his "I'm just a fan, too" approach to the profession.

Harry, though, is a legend who has been announcing baseball since 1945 and last summer received the Ford Frick Award during Hall of Fame ceremonies at Cooperstown, New York. He can say whatever he wants. Sometimes he'll be standing by a batting cage and young players from the visiting team will come up to introduce themselves and shake his hand.

That hasn't happened to me, yet, so I guess I'll learn to say "the Yankees need some runs," instead of "Hey, let's go! We need some runs." Sterling is helping. He wrote the words "WE" and "US" in big, bright, black-and-red letters in our booth last season. John is real subtle.

I also caught some flack last summer for criticizing the official scorer in Kansas City, who made an awful scoring call on a ball hit by Rickey Henderson up the middle. The guy gave second baseman Frank White an error even though he ran full blast behind the bag to knock down the ball and absolutely had no throw.

So big-mouthed me, I not only knock the scorer on the air, I write him a note that read: "I don't know who the official scorer is, nor do I care, but if I was Rickey Henderson and I hit a ball like that and didn't get credited with a base hit, we'd have to discuss it tomorrow."

Then I signed it and pinned it on the press room bulletin board.

Well, I caught heat because some radio critic from the New York *Daily News* wrote that I had threatened to kick the scorer's ass in the note. I never did anything of the kind, so I threatened to sue the rag, and everybody at WABC thought it was great because my name was in the papers.

I guess that's how it works in Big Apple Show Biz but the simple fact remains: The KC scorer made a horseshit scoring call. (P.S.: He changed it to a hit the next day.)

WABC's Fred Whatshisname (vice president and general manager Fred Weinhaus), incidentally, is an interesting character. He keeps saying things like, ''For a guy with no talent, no ability whatsoever, I can't believe I hired you as a broadcaster.'' That's just his way of being one of the boys, right?

Certainly he was on our side when George Steinbrenner told him we had to wear neckties in spring training. Mr. Whatshisname stood right up to Manager George and said, ''First of all, nobody sees radio announcers in the booth so why should they wear ties? I'm not going to have my announcers wearing ties if they don't want to wear them. And, secondly, when George Steinbrenner signs the paychecks, he can tell the announcers what to wear. Until that time, he can butt out.''

Or something like that.

One piece of advice I would like to offer any newcomers to the Ex-Jock Brigade of Broadcasters in 1990:

Don't say anything on radio or television if you're not prepared to follow through.

My buddies Jim Rooker and Tom Paciorek learned the hard way.

Paciorek, broadcaster for the White Sox, ended up losing his curly locks. Rooker, who announces for the Pirates, got sore feet. Both because they had big mouths.

Paciorek should have known better. He's the same guy who, when being platooned by manager Tony LaRussa as a Sox player back in 1984, lost his cool and said to a reporter: ''Tony couldn't manage a fruit stand.''

"That was a dumb thing to say and I regretted it," said Paciorek.

But Tom made another mistake on May 19 of last season when he vowed to "shave his head" if the lowly White Sox ever won eight games in a row. At the time, the comment didn't get much attention. After all, how were the Chisox going to win eight in a row?

But I didn't forget. Neither did some of the Chicago players and sportswriters, and when the Sox streak reached seven, I was telling everybody on the Yankee network about it.

Paciorek couldn't back out. The Sox won again and there was Tom, first getting a burr haircut from a pretty girl, then donning a wig.

"It was the most publicized haircut since Elvis Presley went into the Army," said Sox player Steve Lyons.

"I didn't do it for publicity," lamented Paciorek.

But he got it and hey, it was one of the highlights of a slow season on Chicago's South Side. Trivia follow-up: Tom Paciorek played eighteen seasons in the big leagues for the Dodgers, Braves, Mariners, Chisox, Mets, and Rangers, lifetime batting average .283, but did you know that his brother, John, holds the major league record for highest career batting average (1.000)?

Outfielder John Francis Paciorek played one game for the Houston Astros in 1963 and went three for three, scored four runs, and had three RBIs. You could look it up.

Rooker was watching the Pirates beat the Phillies, 10–0, after a half-inning last season when he innocently said: "If we lose this one, I'll walk back to Pittsburgh."

Oops. The Bucs were beaten, 15–11.

"I felt secure until about the sixth or seventh inning," recalled the ex-Pirate pitcher, "then I broke into a cold sweat."

Rooker eventually turned his gaffe into a positive, collecting donations for his 315-mile walk following last season and turning over the proceeds to Bob Prince Charities, founded by the late Pirate broadcaster to benefit several Pittsburgh-area charities.

Rooker was accompanied on his "Rook's Unintentional Walk" of twelve days by a support crew in a motor home.

"It could have been worse," said the forty-seven-year-old Rooker. "I could have said it in Los Angeles."

Postscript: Later last season, the unpredictable Pirates did it again, jumping ahead of the Cardinals, 10–0, in St. Louis. That's when Rooker's announcing partner, Lanny Frattare, tested Jim by saying, "If we lose this game . . ." but Rooker didn't take the bait. "If we lose this game," said Jim, realizing how far it was from St. Louis to Pittsburgh, "our road record will be 11–23. There's room in my mouth for only one foot." The Pirates won, 12–4.

I like radio stations that get involved.

Example: It was sponsoring San Francisco station KNBR that ran a contest to give Giants sluggers Kevin Mitchell and Will Clark their nickname "Pacific Sock Exchange." Other fan entries: Clarksky and Hutch, Lumber Jocks, Captains of Crunch, The Dudes of Destruction, Thriller and Killer, and Seek and Destroy. Also, my favorite, Great Pair of Knockers.

Then there was the promotion by Toronto radio station CJCL, sponsored by a grocery chain, in which a selected listener could win money if a Blue Jay player hit a grand slam homer in a selected inning. In 1987 the prize was $10,000, and in '88 it was $25,000, but nobody won. So in 1989, the station increased the prize to $50,000 and what happened? Three players—Lloyd Moseby, Pat Borders, and Junior Felix—hit homers with the "bags full" in the right innings, costing the friendly grocer $150,000.

Another station, WCCO in Minneapolis, which sponsors Twins games, caught some attention last season by interviewing the *entire population* of the state's smallest town, Funkley, Minnesota (population seventeen) and inviting the residents to a game. While all seventeen Funkliers were watching the Twins, incidentally, their town was being guarded by the sheriff, who is not a resident of Funkley.

More good deeds: Jacques Doucet, the Expos' French-language radio broadcaster (CKAC), started a series of French lessons for fourteen Expos players on the road, teaching them pronunciation of the alphabet and counting from one to ten. Also, Rene Cardenas of KWKW, the Dodgers' Spanish-language radio outlet, volunteered his time last spring to give L.A. sportswriters Spanish lessons so they could better relate to players. It did not help them, however, in communicating with Eddie Murray.

Another radio personality, Chet Coppock of WLUP in Chicago, helped former Chisox relief pitcher Kevin Hickey find a job. Hickey, desperate for work since leaving baseball in 1983, admitted his plight during a talk show conversation with Coppock. Chet promptly made some phone calls and Hickey landed a job as doorman/maitre d' at Ditka's restaurant.

One station that did not endear itself to the baseball hierarchy was KZOK-FM in Seattle, which in 1989 kept playing a parody of Mariners' owner George Argyros to the melody of "The Mighty Quinn." So angered was the Mariner front office that the team pulled eight thousand dollars in advertising from KZOK, prompting disc jockeys Kent Voss and Jim Kimmel to play the parody even more.

Why were Mariner officials so miffed? Maybe because the refrain used throughout the song said *George Argyros is a mighty schmuck*, and also called him a "bonehead." The song also chided Argyros for trading "Jeffrey Leonard for a pregnant gnome."

Some teams have no sense of humor.

My favorite announcer story of 1989: Utilityman Rey Palacios of Kansas City has the ability to hold a baseball inside his mouth. Don't ask me how, the guy just has a big mouth and will probably end up being an announcer someday. But when he demonstrated his talent on cable TV in Texas last season before a game between the Royals and Rangers, announcer Norm Hitzges called his bluff.

He tossed a football to Palacios and asked him if he was a two-sport athlete.

*   *   *

Two can play that game, though. When a TV reporter approached George Bell of Toronto for his thoughts about Blue Jay manager Jimy Williams getting fired, Bell replied: "If you want to ask me a question like that, ask me loud enough in front of the whole team."

So the enterprising reporter did and Bell replied, "No comment."

How long will I remain a baseball announcer? That's a question I can't answer. That I played in the major leagues for twenty years with my talent was amazing enough. Who knows, maybe I'll get bored and do like my former Yankee compatriot on TV, Lou Piniella, who said: "I was a player, coach, manager, general manager, manager, scout, and now a broadcaster. I think I'll go to medical school and try being a trainer." Instead, Lou-Lou returned to managing with the Cincinnati Reds.

I do know this. I'll improve in the broadcast booth because of confidence. Herb Score, the one-time great pitcher who has gone from analyst to play-by-play man in his twenty-seven years with the Cleveland Indians, says: "The big thing is learning to relax and letting things flow. And it doesn't happen in one or two years. It takes several years."

As Paciorek says: "The toughest thing I had to do was put legitimate sentences together and not sound like Elmer Fudd or Porky Pig."

Dddddddddaaaaaat sounds easy enough.

3

Free Spirits, Flakes, and UFOs

It has been almost eight years since Darrell Evans and his wife, LaDonna, saw the flying saucer hovering above a neighbor's house in Pleasanton, California.

It's such an old story that Darrell doesn't talk about it much anymore, except to say, "I don't know what it was, or what it means, but it was there."

Most people believe Darrell. After all, it's not like *Jay Johnstone or Bill Lee or some other certifiable spaceman said he saw a flying saucer.* Darrell is respectable and well-read and grew up in Pasadena, California, where his father was a supervising mechanic at the Jet Propulsion Laboratory, that city of scientists which, among other things, sends you picture postcards from Neptune and Mars.

So when Darrell and his wife, both veteran sky-watchers, tell about an extraordinarily clear June night and a noiseless unidentified object hovering perhaps only a hundred feet above the deck of their home, who is to scoff?

"It was shaped like a triangle," said LaDonna, later, when interviewed by Ron Fimrite of *Sports Illustrated*. "The lights were bright and white, not at all like the lights on an aircraft. The fuselage was charcoal gray, kind of opalescent. It looked like steel. The fuselage sloped down to a windowless dome. There was no sound at all.''

''LaDonna wanted me to get a camera,'' said Darrell, ''but I said no, I just wanted to watch. It was so strange. It was as if they wanted us to see them. It was if they had singled us out. At least, I wanted to think that. I guess I'd always hoped there'd be something like this, something that would come in peace. I think we knew from the start what it was.''

''It would be vain of us,'' said LaDonna, ''to think there was no one else in the universe.''

The Evanses, who watched the UFO for perhaps twenty minutes, told only a few close friends and did not go public with the sighting for almost two years. As LaDonna said, ''It's not the sort of thing you bring up with people you've just met.''

Nor does Darrell joke about it now. It has never been a frivolous subject with him, nor has the fact that his career took a powerful upsurge after the sighting. Indeed, one year later Darrell had his best season in a decade, hitting thirty home runs for the Giants, and soon afterward became a free agent and signed a $2.25 million, three-year contract with the Detroit Tigers, with whom he played in the 1984 World Series.

I am envious because I have never seen a flying saucer, although I did hang around one spring with Bo Belinsky.

But I do wish Darrell and LaDonna Evans had made personal ''contact'' with their hovering craft, because I have a suspicion that it was manned by some of my pals.

Maybe Mickey Hatcher and Greg Minton as copilots, Larry Andersen and Jerry Reuss navigating, Steve Sax and Dave LaPoint manning the rear turret guns?

If they weren't there, you can be sure they wish they had been. Certainly they are all qualified.

Consider Hatcher, all-everything utilityman for the Los Angeles Dodgers, who once played linebacker at Oklahoma. Two seasons ago he hit .368 with two home runs in the World Series but, afterward, was totally ignored by Madison Avenue when heroes were sought for product endorsements. Mickey's reaction?

"I don't think anyone could find me. I live in Apache Junction, Arizona, and only the Pony Express knows how to find my house."

Hatcher, seen in various poses during the 1989 season (wearing dry ice under his cap; wearing a catcher's mask in the Dodger Stadium dugout), is a free spirit in every sense. Mickey's spontaneity, however, put him on the disabled list and cost him considerable playing time last season.

What happened: Three teen-aged kids who had been drinking beer were strolling past Mickey's L.A. apartment one night when one said, "Hey, that's where Mickey Hatcher lives." At that, another ran to the window and banged so hard the glass shattered. Hatch, who was standing just a few feet away bidding a friend goodbye at the front door, immediately gave chase. But as he chased the frightened, scampering teens up the street incline, thirty-four-year-old Hatcher pulled a hamstring muscle.

"Unbelievable," said Hatcher, who spent the next fifteen days on the DL. Mickey, though, did not press charges once the culprits were caught.

"But I lectured them," he said. "I told them that next time somebody might put them into jail and that down at L.A. County, they like to see young guys. I think they got the message."

In a Dodger season of few giggles, Hatcher provided the biggest on a May night on which he pitched. Mickey was called upon by manager Tom Lasorda to work the ninth inning of a 12–0 loss to the Cardinals. Actually, infielder-outfielder Mickey had volunteered, since the Dodger bullpen was a shambles. And when he started warming up, hundreds of fans raced from their left-field pavilion seats to lean over the bullpen railing and watch.

What ensued was not art. Hatch sprinted to the mound, hit Tim Jones with his first pitch, then balked and walked Denny Walling and Tom Brunansky to load the bases. Going to his curveball, however, he got Jose Oquendo to bounce into a double play ("I wanted to swing before he hit me," said Jose), giving up the only run of the inning. He then walked Milt Thompson but got Tony Pena on a line drive to the right fielder.

It was the only inning all night in which the Cardinals didn't get at least one hit (they had nineteen). Hatcher, though, was unhappy with his performance, slamming his glove as he entered the dugout.

"I've waited ten years for that chance," he said, later, standing in front of a locker decorated with a rubber chicken, fright mask, beach ball, tarantula, Mickey Mouse balloon, and oversized toothbrush, "and I had good stuff in the bullpen, too, except for the one changeup I threw over the fence. My big problem out there was that the umpire [Jim Quick] was squeezing me. I needed one more inning because I was beginning to find the strike zone. I'll do better next time."

There was no next time, but a few days later when the Cubs came into Dodger Stadium, Chicago reliever Mitch Williams sauntered up to Hatch and said: "I told you throwin' strikes wasn't as easy as it looked."

Dan Quisenberry of the Cardinals could also have given Hatch some advice on the vicissitudes of a relief pitcher. After striking out the side last season, Quis couldn't remember the last time it had happened: "Eighth grade, I think. It was Whiffle ball. There was one seven-year-old kid. We were using his house so we had to let him play."

Quis, having spent most of his career in the American League, also made his third major league plate appearance last season after 616 games. He promptly displayed a Mel Ott batting style, but after grounding out, said: "I wasn't sure if I was lifting the right leg. Besides, I thought they were in a zone defense and they were playing man-to-man."

What is it with pitchers? Remember when Pascual Perez played with the Braves and ran out of gas on the freeway because he couldn't find the exit ramp to Atlanta–Fulton County Stadium, earning him the forever-nickname of Perimeter Perez? Well, he's got a brother (Melido) with the White Sox and the two of them wager cows and pigs over total victories.

But I don't think they use a bookmaker.

*   *   *

Then there is twenty-six-year-old pitcher Randy Johnson, traded last season from Montreal to Seattle. The only reason Randy couldn't have been in Darrell Evans's spacecraft is that he's too tall (six-ten).

How tall? Pirates coach Rich Donnelly says, "He's so tall, when he comes to a set, he can *tag* the runner at second base. They don't have a pickoff play. He just *reaches over and tags you!*

This story also makes Randy a true Cadet: During an exhibition game last spring in West Palm Beach, then-Expo Johnson had to have his roomie, John Trautwein, explain who Henry Aaron was. Then, after learning that Aaron was a home run hitter, Randy asked: "Why isn't he in the lineup today?"

Another Generation Gapper: Tom Candiotti of Cleveland, when asked to explain his home pitching record of 13–2 during the 1988 season, said: "Maybe it has something to do with the ghost of Bob Feller."

I hope somebody then told him that Feller was still alive.

Minton, Myers, and McClure. How would you like to manage a major league team with that 3M trifecta in your bullpen? Actually, two of them, Greg Minton and Bob McClure, performed last summer for Angels manager Doug Rader, who deserved them, while the third, Randy Myers, was once again an effective stopper for the New York Mets before being traded in the off-season to the Reds.

Myers is your normal left-handed relief pitcher who wears camouflage-print t-shirts under his uniform, reads magazines about the Foreign Legion, and shops at military surplus stores.

"He is unlike anyone else in the game, or anyone you're likely to meet in your life," says Mets catcher Barry Lyons, who has spent his share of afternoons and evenings in the Mets' bullpen with Myers.

"You laugh at him because he's different," says former teammate Wally Backman. "Nothing personal, but he's crazy."

Crazy? I can't buy that and neither can the remarkably strong Myers, who doesn't see anything unusual about grabbing the clubhouse boy and hanging him upside down. It is true that Myers has also been known to lift weights during a game because he says it pumps him up, and he *always lifts* after a game, whether he has pitched or not.

In the bullpen, Myers is known for his conversation. He is fascinated by guns and weapons and, according to ex-teammate David Cone, "can tell you 109 ways to kill a person." Perhaps that's why Myers decorates his locker with a poster of a bare-chested blonde draped with bandoliers and cradling a machine gun.

Ho hum. Just another southpaw.

Another one is Dr. Rott, aka Bob McClure of the California Angels. This five-eleven lefty even has a Dr. Rott license plate for his truck and for ten years has been compiling notes on the "art of rotting." McClure and his best friend, Dave Downing, plan to write a book about the subject of inactivity. They even have a patent on a line of inactive leisure wear. After all, contends McClure, isn't "rotting" the real national pasttime?

McClure's Definition of Rotting: *Getting parallel; the art or science of doing nothing while looking as if you are doing nothing.*

"We want to erase the guilt people seem to have about relaxing," said McClure, in a *Los Angeles Times* interview last summer. "Too many of my friends could not rott—it's always spelled with two T's, by the way—without guilt. They felt they had to be doing something constructive."

So McClure came up with a rotting system. You move up in rott degrees, sort of like karate, from green level to black level, and so forth, until you reach the level of master rotter. Then you get a black robe with gold tips. But it isn't easy, as McClure explains:

"Let's say your first day is Saturday. If you get up on the couch and watch football all day and don't leave, except to go to the bathroom or to go to bed at night, you've accomplished a minor rott. If you return and make it through Sunday, it's a major rott. Then, if you make it all the way through *Monday Night Football*, that's a coma rott. And, if you can hang out all the way to *Thursday Night Football*, six full days, that's a death rott. There have been only two documented death rotts, by myself and Dave."

McClure insists there are also rott maneuvers, such as:

The prenatal rott: "You have your back to the TV and peek at it over your shoulder. This is a good one when you just can't lie on one side any longer."

The sailor rott: "Your eyes are at half-mast. This is a good one when you're in the second stage of a major rott."

The possum rott: "One eye is buried in the pillow and the other is open just enough to let the light in from the TV."

The Angels reliever also talks of the tier rott (one guy lies on the floor below the guy lying on the couch) and such maneuvers as group rotts and rott-a-thons.

McClure does not move around a lot in the bullpen.

Minton was once fined one hundred dollars for hang-gliding; and, upon coming home late at night, has been known to hit golf balls from his back lawn onto neighbors' roofs. Also, he once dived into the shallow end of a hotel swimming pool from a second-story balcony.

Moon Man Greg, however, will forever be remembered in baseball lore as the guy who hijacked the team bus. Indeed, if ever there is a wing at Cooperstown for free-spirited acts of brilliance (and why shouldn't there be?), Minton is a shoo-in.

It happened in Houston during the 1982 pennant race when Greg was pitching for the Giants, who were two games out of first place and staggering. Or, as Minton later phrased it: "Everybody's posterior was real tight. Mine was a little looser."

So he boarded the team's chartered bus at the Shamrock-Hilton hotel, saw the keys in the ignition, and thought "Why not?" even though he had never driven a bus before. After stripping a few gears, he somehow maneuvered a few miles to Gary's Hats and Boots shop, where he bought a pair of boots, then completed the trip to the Astrodome.

Minton arrived at 4:50 P.M., ten minutes before the team bus was due. By 5:10, nobody else had shown up. Finally, by 5:25, teammates who had grabbed taxis started to straggle into the clubhouse.

"Moonie," said Giants general manager Tom Haller, "is what I heard true?"

"Depends on what you heard."

"The bus. Did you steal it?"

"I was just trying to loosen up the team."

"Then why don't you loosen up your wallet."

The boots cost Minton $75, the bus ride cost him another $120, and the Giants finished third, two games back.

But, what the hell. He tried.

Some ballplayers, like Jerry Reuss, are sneaky quiet in the club-house. He'll sit around and not say anything and the next thing you know your shoes are glued to your helmet and he's sitting there like a Bible salesman.

Others are chatterers. For example, here's what Pirate Mike LaValliere says, with fondness, about one of his teammates, Andy Van Slyke: "When we have a closed-door meeting we want to tape his mouth shut. He always has to put in his two cents worth and it isn't worth two cents."

Andy can't help it. He just likes to talk and sportswriters are thankful. Their notebooks are filled with his one-liners, such as this comment about Candlestick Park:

"Sir Isaac Newton wouldn't be a very good outfielder in this park. The gravitational pull is disrupted."

Okay, Andy. And what about the fact that you once suffered from dyslexia?

"I always knew I saw things differently than most people. I'd be better off if my name was Bob Harrah. Sometimes I think the count is two and one when it's one and two. There are some games we actually lost that I thought we won."

It was Van Slyke who gave us: "The biggest adjustment from the minor leagues to the majors is learning how to spend forty-five dollars in meal money in a single day."

Imagine this conversation: At Van Slyke's curiosity about Greg Harris of Philadelphia wearing a unique glove to allow him to throw with either hand, third baseman Randy Ready of the Phils said, "He's amphibious" (meaning ambidextrous).

"Amphibious?" asked Van Slyke. "What's that mean, that he can pitch underwater?"

*   *   *

Don't ask me why people in baseball say some of the things they do. They're just being themselves and the words come out. Former Orioles outfielder John Lowenstein, for example, once recommended moving first base back a foot to ninety-one feet. Why?

"To eliminate close plays."

And after John Kruk of the Padres allowed a runner to score on a sacrifice fly because he had forgotten how many outs there were:

"It was just stupid, a gastric disturbance in the brain area."

And after Houston shortstop Craig Reynolds tried his hand at pitching last summer for the first time since 1986, giving up four runs, Pirates pitching coach Ray Miller said:

"Craig just isn't effective on a thousand days rest."

So where is the confusion? I understand what those guys meant. Life in the big leagues is as simple as described by Toronto Blue Jays rookie Frank Wills, who said, upon being called up last May:

"The game is played with a round bat and a round ball, the players run around the bases, and what goes around comes around."

Right.

Steve Lyons, infielder for the White Sox, showed me last season that he had his priorities straight. Explanation: Pizza Hut had a promotion where free pizzas were given to ticket-holders at Comiskey Park any time the Chisox held opponents scoreless. Well, on this particular night the Sox were throwing one of their rare shutouts and Lyons could hear the fans shouting "pizza, pizza!" when he hurried a throw. Result: Lyons was assessed with an error as the Cleveland Indians scored a run they probably would have scored, anyhow. Said Lyons: "When I heard the fans crying for pizza I had to give it a shot. The error was worth the risk."

Lyons, incidentally, is nicknamed Psycho. I'll let him tell you why: "Mostly because of my baserunning escapades when I was with the Red Sox. I guess the most memorable came in 1985, my rookie year.

"We're down by a run with one out in the tenth inning against Texas and I singled, but when they tried to pick me off first, they threw the ball away and I ran to second. Marty Barrett then hits a flare into right field and George Wright makes a dive for it. I couldn't tell, though, whether he caught it or not because of the slope of the field, so I was all the way to third base and decided to go back to second. After all, I didn't want to get doubled up if he did catch the ball. Well, on my way back into second I see Barrett coming and we both end up sliding into second at the same time. Now he hops up, looks at me and says 'What the hell are you doing here?' So I turn around, run toward third, and Wright throws the ball *between the third baseman's legs, through the pitcher's legs backing up the play, and into the dugout.* Marty and I both scored on the play and we won, 2–1.''

Psycho claims he tried to keep a no-prank profile in the Chisox clubhouse last year because he remembers what happened when he was in Boston.

"Things were getting a little out of hand with the practical jokes and finally Yaz (Carl Yastrzemski) had enough. So he just started around the clubhouse cutting pant legs off guys' suits. Man, guys were coming in off the field and their pants were six inches shorter! So I was just hoping last year, especially when Jerry Reuss was around, that things wouldn't go that far because we didn't have that many guys on the White Sox who could afford to buy new pants.''

As a player, I never subscribed to "low profile" behavior in any clubhouse. You never had to ask if Jay Johnstone was around. But, as previously stated, *today's players are different.* They're facing *some* of the same pressures we faced (although job security often isn't one of them) and their performance is often threatened by the boredom of a long, long season. Sometimes, though, they just can't pull the trigger to give themselves release.

Consider Cincinnati pitcher Jose Rijo, also known as Chicken Rijo. He planned a great stunt last season, but then didn't pull it.

Rijo told teammates that if he threw a complete game against the Dodgers in Los Angeles, he'd pay to have a taxi enter Dodger Stadium immediately after his last pitch. Rijo's plan: He would enter the taxi in full uniform somewhere down the left-field line and ride in comfort back to the team hotel. I guess Chicken Rijo figured this was a safe gesture inasmuch as he hadn't thrown a complete game in eighty-five previous tries.

You know what happened. Rijo shut out the Dodgers (didn't everybody?) but reneged on calling the taxi.

Why? Chicken said he couldn't be sure his wife, Rosie, would be able to catch a ride, and that may be the worst excuse I've ever heard.

Imitations are always popular within the clubhouse. The Yankees' Steve Sax, for example, can recite *Caddyshack* as well as Rodney Dangerfield. Ex-Dodger Mike Marshall can do a great imitation of Kirk Gibson's limping home run trot. Cardinal outfielder John Morris has former teammate Jack Clark's swing down pat.

And when clubhouses are loose, there has always been the danger of losing one's clothes, or at least having them altered. It's a wonder some of today's more tight-assed players haven't requested private areas with padlocks to hang their clothes. Maybe that comes with the next basic agreement.

When the Cubs were hot last summer, for example, a mystery tailor kept altering the street clothes of hitting heroes. Dwight Smith hit a three-run triple and later found his silk shirt emblazoned with Cub insignias and his name and number (18) in white tape. One night later, Shawon Dunston's purple shirt was tape-altered to read "Magic" with Earvin Johnson's number 32.

I'm surprised somebody didn't get fined, considering the lack of humor usually found within the Cubs clubhouse. Talk about serious. It's no wonder they haven't won a pennant on the North Side since the end of World War II.

Not that manager Don Zimmer doesn't know how to relax. But there aren't many giggles when general manager Jim Frey is in the neighborhood. I once wrote that he was the only manager I ever played under who didn't think I was funny.

"And he's right," said Frey.

Actually, Jim is an astute baseball man who has done a remarkable job of keeping the Cubs in a contending position (Dallas Green also played a role before departing, as his scouts signed most of the current Cub talent), but I guess Frey and I will always differ on having fun.

Frey and Zimmer, for example, banned hotfoots.

Can you imagine? Hotfoots have been a part of baseball since the game began and to *put a ban on them* was totally asinine. Frey even fined four members of the Cubs five hundred dollars each for sliding on the tarp during a rain delay at the first Cubs night game in 1988.

"I was one of them," said pitcher Al Nipper, after being traded from Chicago. "It may not have been the smartest thing to do but it was entertaining for the fans who had to sit in all that rain.

"If you can't have fun, what's the fun in playing? You've got to blow off steam somehow. But having fun isn't allowed around here [on the Cubs]."

Frey, who takes the position that clubhouse pranks only get people hurt, replied: "I didn't see Nipper do anything funny or hear him say anything funny."

Someday, though, I'm going to make Jim Frey smile. I just haven't figured out how, yet. Within the shadow of the ballpark, that man doesn't laugh.

What would I have done if somebody had invoked a "no hotfoot" rule when I was playing?

I would have used a blowtorch. I'd get the hairspray and just melt their shoes to the chair. That's what we used to do to rookies who acted too cocky and showed a lack of respect. We'd take their shower shoes, which are mostly plastic anyhow, then light a can of aerosol hairspray, turning it into a blowtorch, and just melt their shoes right to their chair. The first rule in a baseball clubhouse is to never get mad, anyhow. You just get even.

Back to the frivolous future: Pitcher Mike Krukow of the Giants can work such miracles with analgesic balm that I wonder why he hasn't tried doctoring a baseball with it. For that matter, maybe he has.

Mike takes the real hot stuff, Capsolin, and puts it right under the flaps of some unsuspecting guy's shower shoes, so your toes slide in there and the stuff gets in the crease of your toes. Then you start to burn and you can't make it stop.

Krukow, of course, has been in the forefront of continuing one of the National League's great traditions: The painting of the horse's balls in Chicago.

From my first book, *Temporary Insanity,* comes this background, verbatim:

"At the corner of Belmont Avenue and Sheridan Road in Chicago stands a statue of General Phillip Sheridan, hero of the Civil War. The Gutzon Borglum sculpture, erected on July 17, 1924, depicts General Sheridan, mounted on a rearing horse, in combat. Riding high above the busy intersection and an island of grass (a dog walker's haven), General Sheridan is ostensibly rallying his troops during the battle of Shenandoah Valley, 1864."

The good general's original horse, I feel relatively sure, did not have orange testicles. But the one in Chicago does during baseball season.

They are, in baseball clubhouse parlance, "The Horse's Balls of Chicago."

Every National League team, you see, when visiting Chicago to play the Cubs, travels from the hotel to Wrigley Field by bus. And every bus driver takes the same route—north on Outer Lake Shore Drive, exit at Belmont, right turn at Belmont and Sheridan on the Inner Drive, then north to Addison Street. Every bus passes the statue of General Sheridan. Every team peeks at the horse's balls.

It's tradition, and superstition.

Sometimes it's good luck to see the balls. Sometimes a player will deliberately not look, in hopes of breaking out of a hitting slump. Different players treat the tainted testicles in different ways.

And why are they painted? That's tradition, too. Different teams—most recently and prominently, the San Francisco Giants—use "painting of the balls" as initiation for rookies. Sort of a trial by paintbrush.

Krukow tells rookies how he and Bruce Sutter, when rookies with the Cubs, got full of beer one day at the Cubby Bear Lounge, and painted the horse's balls blue. Then he tells them that it doesn't matter if you get caught, because the cops just take you down to the neighborhood precinct and let you sign a book, sort of a *Who's Who* of baseball heroes who have painted the horse's balls over the years.

There is no such ledger, of course, but the rookies buy it every time. And each summer that the Giants (and a few other teams, such as the Pirates and Reds) come into Chicago, the horse's balls get painted.

There have been feeble attempts to stop such desecration of the horse's private parts, both by Giants management and by columnist Mike Royko of the *Chicago Tribune* (Royko wondered what would happen if the Giants ever got near the Statue of Liberty), but I suspect the tradition will survive.

Actually, if the City of Chicago really wanted to protect General Sheridan's horse's balls, I suppose a simple solution would be for the bus company that transports teams to Wrigley Field to travel a different route.

And get caught in traffic.

To my knowledge, the American League does not have a tradition to match the decorating of General Sheridan's horse. Maybe the Yankees should come up with one, like an annual visit to Alcatraz when the team plays in Oakland. The only problem there would be getting everyone back.

Unfortunately, most "initiations" have disappeared from baseball. You just don't see them much, anymore, and maybe it's because so many rookies today are so rich. They walk into the clubhouse with all the gold chains, portable telephones, and matching luggage to match their attitudes. Hey, I'm so old I can remember when they sat in the corner until somebody sent them on an errand. Not that I wasn't brash, in my own way, but I still respected the veteran players.

Today's youngsters don't respect the veterans like they should. Hey, it's just like a fraternity. It is a fraternity of a select group of men talented enough to play baseball in the major leagues. Today's rookies, however, are more than just egotistical, which I don't mind. What I *do* mind is the disrespect. Look at what twenty-year-old Gary Sheffield did in Milwaukee. He came into town, started criticizing management and called some of the pitchers a "bunch of girls" for not protecting him when opponents threw at him. I'm just surprised some of his own guys didn't throw at him in batting practice before he was finally returned to the minors for more seasoning. Gary may have been popular with all those kids dealing in "future" baseball cards, but with that attitude he couldn't have been too popular with other ballplayers.

To repeat: One of the major differences between ballclubs of today and those of earlier years, before free agency: *Togetherness.* Players often don't play together long enough to get to know the names of other guys' wives. Also, they don't spend enough time *together* away from the ballpark. Even on the road, everybody goes his own way and it does make a difference with the personality of a team.

As talented as the Mets were in 1989, for example, they struggled most of the season trying to find themselves. Also, after Roger McDowell and Len Dykstra were traded to the Phillies for Juan Samuel, something seemed to be missing.

"All the characters left," said McDowell, who continued his lunacy with the Phillies. "You can have players with a lot of talent, but you also need people to get more into the game than just RBIs."

Back to rookies and how to treat them: After their first major league hit, put Band-aids on the ball. Then type up a fake note telling them to report to the team physician with a sperm specimen. You'll be surprised at how many fall for that one. Another sure-fire winner: Send the kid a note telling him where to appear for a TV interview or endorsement session. He'll show up every time, but there are never any cameras waiting.

One favorite with Tom Lasorda and the Dodgers in spring training: Send for a rookie, or perhaps a new player who just joined the club that season, and tell him to pack his bags because he's been traded or cut.

When Lasorda told Pedro Guerrero one spring he had been traded to Cleveland I thought Pete was going to cry. So Lasorda sent him to see General Manager Al Campanis, who said, "Pete, what day is this?"

"What difference does it make?"

"What day is it, Pete?"

"I dunno, why?"

"Today is the first day of April, Pete."

"So?"

"April first, Pete. Don't you know about April Fool's Day?"

"Ooooooooh," said Guerrero. "I love you."

Speaking of love, have you heard Kurt Bevacqua's Miss Tampa Tarpon story?

It happened more than twenty years ago, when Bevacqua was playing in the Cincinnati organization for the Tampa Tarpons of the Florida State League and, as young players are wont to do, he made the acquaintance of this beautiful young girl who had been honored as Miss Tampa Tarpon.

Bevacqua was smitten and asked Miss Tampa Tarpon if perhaps they could "date" and she said yes, giving him the address of her home and telling him what time to pick her up.

Kurt showed up on time, suitably dressed in sports coat and tie, and was mightily impressed with the home of Miss Tampa Tarpon. It was a large estate home in a very distinguished neighborhood and upon entry, Kurt found himself meeting her very distinguished parents.

Nervously, while awaiting an appearance by Miss Tampa Tarpon, Kurt asked for directions to the bathroom and received them.

It was a large, gorgeous bathroom with white shag rug, wall-to-wall.

But, to Kurt's dismay, there was no toilet tissue, a discovery he didn't make until already seated and finished.

What to do? Should he summon the very distinguished parents of the very beautiful Miss Tampa Tarpon and ask for toilet tissue?

Ahhhh, an idea.

Shedding his coat, dress shirt, and tie, Bevacqua then removed his white t-shirt, tore it into shreds, and used it as a substitute for toilet tissue.

He then threw the shredded pieces of shirt into the toilet bowl and flushed, only to gaze in horror as the toilet backed up and sent dirty water overflowing.

All over the gorgeous, white shag rug, wall-to-wall.

Now what to do?

Bevacqua put on his shirt, coat, and tie and walked to the first-floor bathroom window, opened it, climbed out, and disappeared into the night.

Well, what would you have done?

4

The Fans and the Ballparks—Nothing Nutty Here, Right?

At the north end of Bobby's 3 saloon in Vero Beach, Florida, can be found two plaques with the inscriptions: "In Honor and Deep Appreciation to Tirack and Headgear."

Appropriately, these handsome plaques have been inset into the bar in front of two stools on which two men can be found during most of the month of March, any year.

Their real names are Edgar (Headgear) Maly and John Tirack (pronounced tie-rack) and they are baseball fans.

And it is for their unflagging devotion to The Game that they have become living, honored legends, although certainly proprietors Bobby McCarthy and Bobby (Whataguy) Kost are also appreciative of the business that has been generated at the north end of their saloon over the years.

The word "fan" is derived from "fanatic," which, according to my computerized dictionary, means "someone excessively enthusiastic or devoted; a person who manifests extreme and often uncritical ardor, fervor, or devotion in an attachment."

Without such fans there would not be major league baseball.

Consider Headgear and Tirack.

Headgear, sixty, works for a state liquor store in Pittsburgh, Pennsylvania. Tirack, sixty-seven, is retired in Pittsburgh. They are close friends and have been traveling to Vero Beach, Florida, spring training home of the Los Angeles Dodgers, for twenty-four years. Usually they stay four weeks and they seldom miss an exhibition game at Holman Field, sometimes also traveling cross-state to Tampa or Bradenton. Their annual trek usually costs them about four thousand dollars each.

Why Vero Beach? Because Tirack, once a minor league umpire (Mountain State League), struck up a close friendship with ex-Dodger Johnny Podres when he pitched in the minors. They have since also become friends with Dodger pitching coach Ron Perranoski.

"Mostly," says Headgear, "we just love baseball."

There are Headgears and Tiracks everywhere—bleacher bums, season-ticket holders, bugle-blowers, executives who skip work, fan club presidents, kids, yuppies, octogenerians, exotic dancers, and so forth—approximately 55 million, annually, who pay an average daily cost of twelve to twenty-two dollars, depending on their city, to follow baseball. And if they're not at the ballpark, they're listening on radio or watching TV.

They support us. Without them, I wouldn't have a job. Neither would the ballplayers, and they shouldn't forget it.

It was forty-one degrees in Chicago on April 7, 1989, and there were three guys wearing gorilla suits on the left-field bleacher walkway at Wrigley Field.

Where else but a ballpark can you wear a gorilla suit in the middle of the day and be considered normal? Besides, it kept them warmer than the players on the field.

Steve Lyons of the White Sox was standing in the on-deck circle in Yankee Stadium when a woman leaped out of the box seats and gave him a kiss.

"She said one of her friends promised her a thousand dollars if she would do it," said Lyons.

Was his wife, Lynn, watching on TV back in Chicago?

"I'm sure I'll get a phone call tonight."

Lyons has the right attitude about fans. He was once spotted sticking his head out of a visitors clubhouse window to *ask fans for their autographs*.

I can relate to that because my favorite game, as a player, was playing "Let's Make a Deal" with fans, trading them baseballs or autographs for hot dogs, peanuts, or pizza. After I wrote my first book, while still playing with the Dodgers, I took a carton into the audience at Dodger Stadium before a game and sold twenty books. Hey, who says books should only be sold in bookstores?

Because of proximity, Wrigley Field fans have always developed unique relationships with players, even the visitors.

"If you can take the initial abuse," says relief pitcher Roger McDowell of the Phillies, "you can win them over. But it takes about two years."

For years, fans on Chicago's North Side have made a ritual of arriving early for batting practice and, sometimes, extracurricular activities. Example: Last summer some of the New York Mets, never favorites in Wrigley Field, took turns throwing baseballs at the Wrigley Field scoreboard, trying to get the balls into the small, open slot where scoreboard keepers stick numbers for runs scored in the ninth inning. Friendly bleacher fans (have times changed or what?) accommodated the players by shagging the balls bouncing off the scoreboard and throwing them back to participants Lenny Dykstra, Bob Ojeda, and teammates.

This wasn't exactly Jimmy Piersall firing a fastball off Bill Veeck's exploding scoreboard at Comiskey Park, but it was entertainment. Anyhow, both Dykstra and Ojeda were the only Mets to "score" with their scoreboard-tossing, each holding his arms aloft like a referee signaling a touchdown. And was there a name for this pregame game?

"Yeah," said Dykstra, "twenty bucks."

Unfortunately, and perhaps that word isn't strong enough, the days of watching early batting practice at Wrigley Field are over. The Cubs announced during 1989 that the gates will no longer be opened until ninety minutes before game time.

Why? Because no longer do the Cubs hold back twenty thousand seats for game-day sale as previous owner Philip K. Wrigley always did. Nowadays, 91 percent of Cub tickets are purchased in advance and management figures those fans don't arrive early enough to watch BP, anyhow. So, for just a few hundred fans, why open the park so early?

Next thing you know Cubs management will be telling bleacher fans they have to keep their shirts on. Even the girls.

Wrigley Field fans think nothing about giving advice or arguing with a manager.They're so close to the game they figure it comes with the price of the ticket. One day last summer during a game manager Don Zimmer got into a heated debate with fans behind the Cubs' dugout, not realizing that WGN-TV's creative director, Arnie Harris, was showing it to everybody at home. The argument? Fans wanted Zimmer to order Dwight Smith to bunt with nobody out and a man on first base in the eleventh inning. Instead, Zim let him hit away and Smith bounced into a double play. Now the fans were really all over Popeye (my favorite nickname for Zimmer) but he got the last laugh. Curt Wilkerson singled, pitcher Les Lancaster doubled him home, and Zim was forgiven.

Then there was the afternoon last summer when members of the cast of an updated version of the play *Bleacher Bums* converged on the right-field bleachers at Wrigley Field to "research their roles." They picked a good day for new scenes: One fan set a beer on a ledge and accidentally knocked it down onto the head of a blind man standing in a concession line. Another young fan was given two beer showers in honor of his birthday.

I think Harry Caray calls it fun at the old ballpark.

Baseball fans are irrepressible. Example: There is a standing policy throughout baseball press boxes—No Cheering. Baseball writers sometimes secretly hope a particular team wins (usually they're rooting for whichever team will finish the game quicker so they can finish their stories), but no matter what, *no cheering*.

Now that you understand the ground rules, consider this scene: Giants versus Cardinals in Busch Stadium, and as San Francisco's Ernest Riles gets thrown out stealing, a man wearing a Cardinals cap and jacket bursts into cheers.

Duffy Jennings, SF's publicity director, immediately turns to the man, glares, and says:

"This is a working press box, pal."

"You could have fooled me," said the fan. "When you can't cheer for your own team, something's wrong."

"Do you work here?" asked Jennings.

"Any time I'm in the state of Missouri, I'm working," said Governor John Ashcroft.

"Oops," said Jennings.

My opinion: They still should have booted the Governor out of the press box, but who was going to do the booting?

Gregg Olson, American League Rookie of the Year last season with the Baltimore Orioles, offers this insight on fans:

"I was in the post office and a guy said, 'Nice game last night.' I look down and I'm wearing a blue shirt, no orange. I'm only a rookie. I'm supposed to be unknown. I've only been here a month and three weeks."

But the "fan" knew him. They don't miss much.

Yankee fans don't miss anything.

I'm serious. They are the most knowledgeable in the game. Not merciful, but knowledgeable. Play badly and they'll boo. Ask Steve Balboni, who incurred the wrath of New Yorkers last spring when he was struggling. Every time he looked into the stands, somebody was screaming or pointing a finger at him. Then one day against Frank Viola (then with the Twins), Balboni jacked a grand slam homer into the spectators and, for a few moments, he was a hero. Fans stood cheering and demanding that he come out of the dugout for an encore but his teammates, who had also heard all of the booing, wouldn't let him.

Yankee fans, though, are big-time knowledgeable. They know when to applaud great plays and when to criticize poor ones. You can't say that about fans everywhere. Some of the beach people in San Diego still cheer pop flies.

In New York, though, if you hit behind the runner the effort is recognized. And when there are two strikes on a hitter, you can count on Yankee fans to be on their feet, cheering for the third one. They've also adopted from Wrigley Field bleacher fans one of my favorite displays of loyalty: Whenever the visiting team hits a home run, the fans will throw the ball back onto the field. They're doing it in Yankee Stadium, too, and it's a wonderful expression of disdain for the enemy.

Then there are Dodger fans. They appreciate what's going on but don't get involved. For them it's entertainment, not religion. Remember that dramatic home run by Kirk Gibson to win game one of the 1988 World Series? If you ever get a chance to view the videotape (which the Dodgers used as a promotional tool throughout 1989), take a look over the right-field pavilion of Dodger Stadium as Gibson's home run lands. There you will see an endless string of taillights of automobiles leaving the parking lot. But they all heard Vin Scully describe the home run on their car radios and they'll all tell their grandchildren they were there.

An "incident" at Dodger Stadium usually means an usher couldn't intercept a beach ball. An incident in Yankee Stadium could mean somebody was trying to throw a bomb from the upper deck. Sometimes the fights get so bad they have to carry out the security guards. And, almost always—whether in L.A., New York, Cleveland, Chicago, or wherever—unruly behavior in the audience can be traced to the sale of beer. That's why I like the rules at Dodger Stadium: No sales after the seventh inning and no beer vendors. If you want a beer, you have to go get it and each customer is limited to carrying away just two. At the Oakland Coliseum, they use a different kind of safeguard. All vendors must check the ID of every customer, prompting one senior citizen in a long beer line to say: "I'm flattered. It's the first time I've been carded in forty years."

Whatever it takes.

All you need to know about Red Sox fans is the way they treated Wade Boggs on opening day last spring. He's the only guy I ever knew who got a standing ovation for cheating on his wife.

His teammate Roger Clemens, meanwhile, was getting booed.

Why? Because he had made disparaging remarks about Boston's baseball fans. All Boggs had done was receive national publicity for his affair with Margo Adams.

"Clemens dumped on the fans and Boggs didn't," said one Bo-sox fan, upper-deck patron Ken Magrath, who was quoted nationally. "You know what they say about Red Sox baseball: It's not life and death. It's more serious than that."

Fans represent the lifestyles and mores of their cities. In Anaheim, where it costs more to park your car (four dollars) than for a ticket to the game (three dollars general admission), they're not sure whether their team is contending for a pennant or not, but it sure is a nice evening for fun (Angels officials estimate every home game is interrupted at least nine times by beach balls on the field). In Milwaukee they tailgate and in St. Louis they bring their families and picnic baskets from as far away as Arkansas and Oklahoma. Philadelphia is like New York. They appreciate good baseball but if it's bad, look out. They can be vicious. I've always said that if the game got rained out in Philly, the fans would go to the airport to boo bad landings.

All fans want a winner to cheer. In Minneapolis they need decibel counters—inside their dome it sounds like a jet taking off. It's the only ballpark in America where a guy could make a fortune with an earmuff concession. On opening day of the 1987 World Series in Minneapolis, twenty thousand earmuffs were sold. Toronto fans are going to set all kinds of attendance records in their new Skydome and they'd do the same in Montreal if the Expos would quit breaking their hearts.

I wish I could say the relationship between players and fans was all love, but that wouldn't be true, either. Sometimes it can get rough out there. In Philly in the mid-seventies, for example, fans were throwing such things as panties, bras, and popcorn at me and I survived. As a rule, though, I'm against fans throwing *anything* onto a playing field.

Security and control of beer sales is the answer. Otherwise, you'll have White Sox fans throwing slats from the left-field bleacher seats (as they once did) and Yankee fans throwing knives (as they did at Wally Joyner of the Angels) and Cub fans throwing ball-bearings (as they once aimed at Pete Rose).

Throw all the beach balls you want, folks. But let's be cool with the ice balls and lug nuts.

As Lonnie Smith of the Atlanta Braves said: "Sometimes it's like the fans think we're purposely going out there to lose. We're not. We're trying."

On the other hand, it was Tom Lasorda of the Dodgers who said: "I can get truck drivers who try. Give me some guys who do."

Many fans have the same attitude. But they shouldn't be throwing cigarette lighters, as they did toward Andy Van Slyke of the Pirates last season when he was hitting .272. Attached to the lighter was a note that said: "Use this to light a fire under you."

In Houston, some fans were escorted out of the Astrodome for displaying signs unfavorable to Astros owner John McMullen. The signs said, simply: "McMullen Stinks." Other fans cheered the signs and pelted a security guard with cups of—you guessed it—beer.

Honestly, sometimes I wonder why something more serious hasn't happened at a ballpark. As John Kruk said after having a particularly ugly day playing outfield for the Padres (before his trade to Philly): "I'm just glad they don't allow guns in the stadium. If there was a sniper in the park, I'd be dead."

John was only kidding, of course, but is the day coming when you may have to pass through a metal detector on your way into the ballpark?

Players react differently to heat from the fans. When the Orioles were losing a doubleheader to the Red Sox at Fenway Park last season, spectators near the Baltimore bullpen were shouting, "Choke, choke."

"You should know," shouted Orioles bullpen coach Elrod Hendricks, "you live here."

Then there was Bruce Hurst of the Padres, a devout Mormon who replied to an especially abusive fan in Houston:

"Aw, go wash your car."

*   *   *

Some fans would rather write than shout.

Mike Krukow of the Giants got a letter from some guy who wrote, "You're through. Why don't you just quit?"

"I wrote back something nasty," said Krukow. "I never sent it but I felt better."

Doug Sisk, who labored for the Mets during the mid-eighties, recalls getting a "fan letter" with a prescription enclosed. Some lady had actually gone to a pharmacy for the prescription and had attached a note that said: "You're having a bad year, Doug, and so is your crazy friend Jesse Orosco, and we're not too happy with you."

Sisk then checked out the prescription and it was for cyanide.

"P.S.," said the note, "I'm not giving you my name or address because you and Orosco might come over and blow up my house."

Matt Merullo, twenty-four-year-old catcher with the White Sox, got a letter from a woman who thought she was his mother.

That's right. Mother.

It turns out that she had given up her baby, who was born on the same day as Merullo, so she sent Matt a picture of herself and her husband.

The guy looked exactly like Matt.

Nevertheless, he had to disappoint the lady because he had a mother of his own and knew her quite well.

Another concern of the major league ballplayer: Fatal Attraction.

Steve Lyons of the White Sox recalls getting a nineteen-page letter from a woman fan who took every letter in his name and turned it into a long poem. She wrote about his piercing blue eyes and flashing smile, sent along her phone number, and asked if Lyons was married. That's when Steve began to worry.

So he had the letter traced and discovered the lady was eighty-one years old and living in a nursing home.

So what do you do about an eighty-one-year-old who has a crush on you?

Lyons told her he was married.

*   *   *

There are ballparks and there are ballparks.

You're so close in the press box at Tiger Stadium that you can see the numbers on the players' shoes, and when they foul balls back, you duck. At Fenway Park, Boston, the announcers are located so high they just guess on balls and strikes.

Kent Hrbek of the Twins hit an opposite-field home run at the Metrodome and credited the air-conditioning with blowing it out. In Los Angeles, the weak-hitting home team wondered if the backdrop in Dodger Stadium might be the problem. Consequently, a section of bleacher seats was blocked off from fans. It didn't help.

In Cleveland, pitcher Doug Jones of the Indians labeled Municipal Stadium "a museum of unnatural history," and teammate Joe Carter said about the ballpark and city: "This is almost the twenty-first century but around here it sometimes doesn't seem like the twentieth century. History is great, but come on." There was also a threatening evening in Cleveland when the grounds crew failed to put the tarp on the field. And, sure enough, there was a massive downpour that forced the cancellation of batting practice.

"You'd think with a stadium by the lake," said umpire Rich Garcia, "they'd put a tarp on the field." The groundskeeper said he had received an incorrect weather report. Meanwhile, in Atlanta, many Braves players were blaming the field for seventy-four errors in their first seventy-nine games, yet 1989 was the first season they had a full-time groundskeeper at Atlanta–Fulton County Stadium.

Atlanta wasn't the only place blaming the ballpark. In Chicago, where the White Sox are building a new stadium, shortstop Ozzie Guillen was saying about old Comiskey Park:

"This is the worst ballpark in the major leagues. The worst. It's an awful place."

Hey, guys, don't pick on the groundskeepers. I'm on their side. They put in horrendous hours when nobody notices. So do the clubhouse workers. How about this one: After the Triple A Richmond Braves and Toledo Mudhens played a doubleheader last season until 1:55 A.M., the players went home. But clubbies Tex Drake and Steve Barden stayed to shine shoes and wash clothes until 6:00 A.M., and that's not an unusual story. Even at the major league level, clubhouse workers sometimes spend the night at the ballpark after a late return from a road trip. I've done it myself.

Clubbies lead different lives from anyone else in baseball. The clubhouse is their kingdom but seldom do they leave it—with the exception of Yosh Kawano, who has been the home clubbie with the Cubs since the beginning of time. One thing about Yosh: When the Cubs are in the thick of a pennant race you can forget the dirty laundry. Yosh can be found wearing his white t-shirt and sailor cap sitting in the Chicago dugout.

Jim Muhe, visiting clubhouse manager for the Dodgers, has a unique list pasted inside his own locker: He has served seventeen father-son combinations in his major league clubhouse over thirty seasons.

Those major league fathers and sons: Yogi and Dale Berra, Maury and Bump Wills, Vernon and Vance Law, Tito and Terry Francona, Gus and Buddy Bell, Marty and Matt Keough, Dick (Ducky) and Dick Schofield, Bobby and Robbie Wine, Bobby and Barry Bonds, Bob and Terry Kennedy, Ozzie (Osvaldo Jose) and Ozzie (also Osvaldo Jose) Virgil, Sandy and Roberto Alomar, Julian and Stan Javier, JoJo and Mike White, Freddy and Gary Green, Bobby and Mike Adams, Don and Tommy (ex-bullpen coach) Zimmer.

"You only see that in a visiting clubhouse," says Muhe, about his unusual roster. "I guess it's my claim to fame."

And how about those crews who work at stadiums that serve more than one professional sport? Example: After the San Diego Padres and Atlanta Braves finished a baseball game last August, Jack Murphy Stadium manager Bill Wilson and his twenty-person crew worked all night to prepare for an NFL exhibition game. So what had to be done? The pitching mound had to be leveled, foul poles and pipe-rail outfield fences had to come down, as well as the backstop net and the dugouts. Also, goalposts and thirty-second clocks had to be put up. Most difficult was moving the field-level stands from third base to the outfield, with seventy holes being dug so the steel pipes could be dropped into concrete.

Then all the teams and customers had to do was show up.

Somebody even wondered last season if the grounds crew at Dodger Stadium did anything "special" to prepare the pitching mound for same-night performances by Orel Hershiser and Frank Viola. After all, it was the first-ever matchup between defending Cy Young Award winners (Viola had to get traded to the Mets to make it possible), so wouldn't the groundskeepers do something special, like maybe import some dirt from Egypt or something?

"Right," said first-year groundskeeper Matt Seymour. "We had a guy from Cairo shave dust off the pyramids and send it over." For the record: Viola won that rare matchup, 1–0.

Ballparks, I suppose, do make a difference. But what else has to be done for the modern-day player? Should all stadiums have a shoeshine man in the dugout? Cellular telephones under the bases so guys could call their brokers during dull periods?

"I guarantee that when we get our new ballpark," says Guillen of the Chisox, "the team attitude will be better. We will want to show up. We will play a lot happier. You come into the Comiskey Park clubhouse and it's so small you can hardly move around. You can barely see the game from the dugout, the bullpen is far away, the batting cage is real bad, and the equipment room isn't even a room."

There you have it, folks. White Sox players believe they have been losing because of their old ballpark. Has anybody told them they have a modern park in Seattle?

One thing I don't like about new stadiums: The dugouts are so far apart they've taken away the art of bench jockeying. So have the stadium organists who play so loudly between innings that nobody can hear across the field. How can you put the craps on some guy in the other dugout if he's two miles away and the loudspeakers are blaring organ music? It's different, of course, in Fenway Park or Tiger Stadium or Wrigley Field. But in the new parks the dugouts are so far away you need binoculars to see who you're playing or maybe a fax machine. You could be jumping up and down and screaming every obscenity in the book at the enemy dugout and those guys would just smile and wave, because they couldn't hear you. You might as well send them roses.

Also, I'm glad I'm not paying for somebody's new ballpark. The costs are unbelievable. Who knows how much it will finally cost taxpayers for the San Francisco Giants to escape the horrors of Candlestick, if they ever do. And in Minneapolis, the Metrodome commission was investigating the feasibility of a third deck, adding fifteen thousand more seats. It would mean raising the Teflon roof at a cost of $25 million.

One place where they're not building a new ballpark is on the North Side of Chicago, where the Tribune Company has done a spiffy job with Wrigley Field (but why can't you get rid of that Torco sign, guys?).

The Wrigley Field ivy was as green as ever during the 1989 season and still able to gobble up baseballs. It's true that the late Bill Veeck helped plant that ivy fifty-three years ago (and when is *he* going to get into the Hall of Fame?) and, as legend has it, former Cub Hank Sauer once stored pouches of tobacco in the stuff. Another former Cub, Jose Cardenal, always claimed he hid baseballs in the ivy, in case he needed a spare during an emergency. I was just glad the stuff gave a little whenever I crashed into the wall. It's not the same as foam padding but it helps, even if it does stick you.

Anyhow, Tony Gwynn of the Padres lost a ball out there last summer and said, afterward: "It was a weird feeling. I pulled the vines back to look for the ball, then I kicked the vines, and finally it rolled out. I guess I didn't look long enough. I didn't want to see something crawling out at me."

There have been some changes at Clark and Addison. They've got new skyboxes (average lease price: fifty-five thousand dollars a year) and there's a new press box located so high the media guys are claiming nosebleed.

Anyhow, Harry Caray, who's about seventy-three or eighty-three years old, decided he didn't want to use the golf cart the Cubs made available, so he walked up the ramps some, then started using the golf cart, too. Said Harry about the upper-deck press box location: "It's as close to Heaven as I'm going to get."

For the record: Wrigley Field is the only NL park without a press box elevator. Milwaukee and Minnesota are the only AL parks without one.

Whitey Herzog, manager of the Cardinals, has the answer for Wrigley Field, anyhow. He thinks they should tear down the place.

"It's a nice, old park," said Herzog. "There used to be a lot of nice parks like Wrigley but they've all been demolished."

So much for sacrilege. Besides, newer doesn't always mean better. Example: The Big Owe, which is what they call Olympic Stadium in Montreal. It has become the biggest, costliest joke in Canada because, somehow, they never have conquered the retractable roof. The stadium has been plagued by cost overruns since its 1976 debut at the Olympic Games, and the price tag has since reached $1 billion, give or take a few million. They didn't get the hundred-ton fabric dome installed until three years ago and even last season, with everybody laughing, it was almost unmanageable. Said one Montreal sportswriter: "It was supposed to be retractable in forty-five minutes and they've got it down to twelve hours."

This kicker, too: Montreal doesn't open the roof if there is a fifteen-mile-per-hour wind or 30 percent chance of rain. Also, it's closed on weekends and holidays because government employees operate it and they don't work on weekends and holidays. Said Expos publicity director Rich Griffin: "If we ever make it into the World Series, the dome will probably be closed because October is the government's month off."

Meanwhile, over in Toronto, they have been bragging about their new SkyDome, which cost *only* $500 million. After all, their retractable roof works!

Ellis Clary, veteran scout for the Blue Jays, said about the SkyDome: "I'd like to rent this place out. It would be a good place for deer hunting."

Clary, a native of Valdosta, Georgia ("I live so far in the boondocks I have to go hunting to walk toward town") usually has something "down-home" to offer about any subject. If he isn't baseball's wittiest man, he's a close second. He once gave a scouting report on Cubs second baseman Ryne Sandberg and said: "I found his weakness. He can't slide into the wind."

There is no wind when they slide under the SkyDome roof. But when it's open, look out.

"You've got to pray for rain when you play in Toronto," said Detroit's Keith Moreland. "It's like playing in a totally different stadium when the roof is back. Candlestick Park on its worst night can't match this place."

Some players theorize the wind comes from two tunnels underneath the thirty-one story stadium, which carry team buses and other vehicles. Their word for the dome: Architorture.

"I felt like I played in two different places," said Texas catcher Jim Sundberg after working out with and without the SkyDome roof.

"I was kind of hoping they'd have retractable fences," said Blue Jay pitcher Mike Flanagan.

"The biggest joke was when Toronto fans gave the roof a standing ovation when it closed," said Brewers pitcher Chris Bosio. "I thought they'd made some kind of big trade or something. In the United States, fans would never react like that."

I really enjoyed the SkyDome when the Yankees visited Toronto. It looks like a turtle and that alarm bell with the roof could drive me nuts, but I wish I could have played there. Any time you've got artificial turf and a padded fence to crash into, you've got my kind of ballpark. I think it will definitely be a hitters' park—375 feet in the power alleys, 328 down the line, and the ball will carry. At that, though, it's not the hitters' park that old Exhibition Stadium was, but some players were glad to see the move. Kansas City pitcher Bret Saberhagen, who had an 0–3 record and 12.86 ERA in the former Blue Jay home, bid the old park farewell by saying: "I hope they bomb the place."

The SkyDome is something else. When Blue Jays relief pitcher

Duane Ward walked into the clubhouse and saw marble-topped, angular card tables arranged in a circle, he said, "We're knights of the round table." So what happens when some future Toronto manager decides there will be no more card playing in the clubhouse? Maybe they can use the marble-topped table area as a reading room.

My favorite feature of the SkyDome: stainless-steel cuspidors, complete with running water, in the dugouts. Ralph Houk, one of the great tobacco spewers, would have loved it. Also, the stadium has a health club and the SkyDome Hotel, which opened last fall, with 350 rooms, 70 of them overlooking the outfield. Some of the rooms with a view of the game cost more than one thousand dollars a night. There is also "the world's longest bar" in the center-field club level, a Hard Rock Café in right field, a roof-level running track, and an abundance of bathrooms.

And remember the "gull problem" at old Exhibition Stadium? Seagulls loved the place. They would swoop down on the ballpark in the seventh inning (sometimes sooner) to devour any food left in the aisles. It was at Exhibition, too, where Yankee Dave Winfield once drilled a gull with a throw between innings and was arrested and charged with cruelty to an animal.

Now the new concern: Will the gulls also invade the SkyDome? There was actually a master plan to hire a falconer to keep five falcons in the building—three on duty and two on standby—to discourage gulls, pigeons, and starlings from trying to settle, mess up the roof machinery, and cause a health hazard with their droppings. So far, though, the falconer himself is only on standby, eyes trained upward.

Another SkyDome feature: the biggest wide-screen center-field TV (Sony) scoreboard in baseball. Also, closed-circuit TV in the dugout that allows a manager to watch his pitchers warming up in the bullpen.

I suppose if you're going to be biggest and best you have to have the biggest and best scoreboard images—but how about elsewhere in baseball where they don't have electronic displays? Consider the Everett, Washington, Giants of the Class-A Northwest League, who offer a less-sophisticated type of entertainment.

Every sixth inning they send out Jim Averill, thirty-five, known as The Walker, wearing pink shorts, flying goggles, rainbow suspenders, and a derby hat, and he races a fan around the bases. Averill, the son of Hall of Famer Earl Averill, starts at second base, walks toward third, then goes home. The fan is allowed to run but he must start at first base.

At last count, before his pink shorts split, Averill was winning 80 percent of the time.

Final thought on the SkyDome: I sure wish I had one of those McDonald's concessions. It's the first ballpark I've ever seen with a big-name fast food franchise and somebody is going to make a fortune. For that matter, nothing is cheap about the SkyDome. Jumbo hot dogs cost $6.50 and draft beer sells for $3.30. Outfielder Pat Sheridan of Detroit took a look at the concession price list and said: "Well, I guess you can ask your kids, 'Do you want to go to a ballgame or to Europe?'"

Actually, there has been something of a revolution in the ballpark food industry. In Montreal Stadium you can buy muffins, a selection of Chinese dishes, and smoked meat sandwiches. In Baltimore they've even gone kosher—pastrami, turkey, corned beef, salami, kosher dogs, and tuna sandwiches. In Philadelphia they're selling egg rolls and pork fried rice, in Anaheim you can buy fish and chips, at Wrigley Field they offer potato skins, in Cleveland they had a major controversy between dueling mustard companies, and in San Francisco they're hustling yogurt and vegetarian hot dogs, whatever that means.

Okay, okay. But sushi, too?

Abner Doubleday would throw up. Who wants to eat raw fish at a baseball game? Whatever happened to hamburgers and hot dogs? Why don't they just serve chili beans to fans behind home plate, with instructions for them to all belch when the home team is at bat and send home runs over the fence. That makes as much sense as eating sushi.

I'd rather pay a visit to the Manhattan delicatessen owner who offered free, one-pound salamis (a seven-dollar value) to anyone showing up with a ticket stub from a Mets game won by pitcher

Frank Viola. It was a great promotional stunt, but when Viola pitched the Mets to a 13–1 victory over the Cardinals at Shea Stadium, Abe Lebewohl, owner of the Second Avenue Deli near Tenth Street, was swamped. By 8:30 P.M., even before Abe got back from the game, seven hundred of the one thousand salamis on hand had been given out to fans who produced valid ticket stubs from the game. Abe gave the others rain checks but what will he do in 1990 if Viola gets hot and wins twenty-five games?

He'd better hope that all those salami-claimers also buy a lotta lox. Abe got a real surprise last August when Viola out-dueled Orel Hershiser, 1–0, in Los Angeles, and the next day a guy showed up in New York, claiming a salami with a ticket stub from Dodger Stadium. One can only assume the fan was headed in that direction, anyhow. Otherwise, a pretty expensive salami. Nevertheless, Abe paid off and I wonder if he's ever considered giving away a free salami every time George Steinbrenner changes managers. Maybe a bagel?

I've seen them all now, every ballpark in every city in both leagues, and if I didn't play there, I announced there with the Yankees.

In truth, the basic difference between the National and American Leagues is the cities. Sure, there are more teams in the AL, which dilutes the talent, and there is the designated hitter and longer games and new domed stadiums and more breaking balls, but the basic difference is the cities.

National League cities are much better and if you don't believe me, try taking a few road trips into Oakland, Detroit, Cleveland, Kansas City, or Arlington, Texas. Fortunately, the league also has New York, Chicago, and Boston, all super cities with personalities. Seattle is nice, too, and Toronto is definitely improving. Milwaukee and Minneapolis offer small-town, Midwestern atmosphere (but with some pretty active restaurants and saloons), Baltimore is as old as George Washington (didn't he sleep there?), and although Mickey Mouse is Anaheim's most famous resident, there is nevertheless plenty of sunshine and quick access to L.A. or the beaches.

Ballplayers look at cities differently from most people. Visiting teams want access to the ballpark, decent airports and hotels, and all-night restaurants. You can save the museums and statues for others. But, obviously, opinions differ. Keith Moreland of the Tigers, for example, once played in San Diego and says: "It wasn't much fun trying to play baseball in the middle of the desert with ten thousand fans in tank tops and bikinis just coming in off the beach, not caring whether you won, lost, or tied. They just weren't into baseball there. It was so depressing. Walking into a game there was like walking into a spring training B game."

That may be a first: a guy from Detroit knocking San Diego. Maybe Keith has been reading too much Elmore Leonard.

But ballplayers think differently. Pitcher Bryn Smith of the Montreal Expos, for example, says about playing in Canada: "Two things really get to the players. One, they don't serve catsup with french fries, they serve gravy. And when you order a Coke, they don't put ice in it. They don't even know how to make iced tea. Ice is hard to find and if you ask for it in a restaurant somebody will tell you in French that you're stupid because you get more Coke without the ice."

Maybe the players should do something about ice in their next basic agreement negotiation.

Which reminds me: If you're angry at well-paid professional ballplayers for asking for more and more money as baseball enters the 1990s, don't forget the economics of the game.

Major league baseball made a $100 million profit in 1988 and the final figures from 1989 were headed upward. Baseball also signed a $1.06 billion TV deal. When Peter Ueberroth left his job as commissioner after the 1988 season, he announced that baseball had shown a profit of $209 million over four seasons under his leadership. Ueberroth also suggested in his farewell address to owners that they "freeze ticket prices."

You can imagine how that went over with the owners.

So as we enter this exciting new decade, players and owners are once again in conflict over who should receive how much.

Headgear and Tirack and millions of other baseball fans have nothing to say about it. They just pay the freight.

5

Who Said the Managers Were Sane?

Tom Trebelhorn, manager of the Milwaukee Brewers, once said that running a ballclub was like raising kids who fall out of trees.

Nick Leyva, who celebrated his thirty-sixth birthday last summer managing one of my old teams, the Phillies, said: "I feel ten years older since last August. Maybe they should count managers' years like dog years—multiply them by seven."

I don't know if I could do it.

Admittedly, I've thought about getting back onto the field, maybe even someday managing a major league team. I can't believe there is an ex-player today who sits in an announcing booth who hasn't, at least once, wondered how he would handle the situation below.

But I wonder if I would have the patience.

As a hitter I was a perfectionist. To overcome shortcomings, I worked unbelievably long hours. I changed my swing by hitting tennis balls off a tee during the winter. Sometimes, even during the season, I stayed in the batting cage until my hands bled. I was my own worst critic.

But would I have the patience to manage men with less desire, unwilling to pay the price to make themselves better? I don't know if I could deal with it. I've seen friends such as Jim Bunning and

Lee Elia struggle with it. Certainly they knew the game but, at the time, they didn't have the patience.

Tom Lasorda has it but he paid his dues. He went through all the bullshit of the minor leagues—riding the buses, managing in the winter leagues, coaching, scouting, sacrificing—and only then was he able to enjoy the fruits of victory. I'm afraid that isn't in me and that's why I chose radio and TV to keep me in baseball. I never did like those minor league bus rides.

Lasorda asked me a couple times if I'd be interested in managing in the Dodger farm system but my response was always:

"What, and end up looking like you?"

"Well, it's guys like you and Jerry Reuss and Don Stanhouse and Steve Sax who made me look like this," he would always shout, but he understood my reasoning.

Maybe someday. You should never say never, especially in baseball. But right now I don't think I could sleep nights after a season like Sparky Anderson endured with the Detroit Tigers. Sparky, though, has been on the roller coaster long enough to handle it (though even he had to take time away from the job during the 1989 nightmare). Now he says it's all forgotten: "Amnesia. I just tell people a ball hit me in the head during spring training and I didn't remember a thing after that."

When the Tigers' record reached 36–67 last July, Sparky said: "I doubt even my mother is still reading the box scores."

And when Governor James J. Blanchard proclaimed last September 10 as Sparky Anderson Day in Michigan, Sparky said: "How do you get a day out of a year like this?"

Even Whitey Herzog of St. Louis, one of the best in the business, knows adversity. He looked at his team during a time when five pitchers and four everyday players were disabled and said: "If World War III broke out, I guarantee we'd win the pennant by twenty games. All of our guys would be 4-F."

And when Herzog, fifty-seven, was asked if he wanted to manage until he was eighty (Sparky's avowed goal), Whitey replied: "Why would I want to do that? Sparky's fifty-five now and already looks eighty!"

* * *

I have given managers a few gray hairs. Some I even terrorized.

I guess the worst (or best) thing I ever did, with an assist from Steve Yeager, was tie Lasorda into his room in spring training. The plan was simple: First we "appropriated" a master key, slipped into his private room (number 112) at Dodgertown, and removed the mouthpiece speakers from both telephones. Then, at 4:00 A.M., we slipped across the grass and tied a four-way sailor's knot around a palm tree, thirty feet from Lasorda's front door. The other end was tautly noosed onto the door, which opened inward. Naturally, the next morning when he tried opening the door, the line only got tighter. He couldn't even crawl out the slatted windows (he hadn't discovered Ultra Slim-Fast yet), and even when he telephoned for help, nobody could hear him.

So he was stuck, and he was livid because he missed breakfast. Finally, scout Ralph Avila heard Lasorda screaming and saw him with a chair in his hand, ready to smash the window.

"Don't do it," shouted Avila, untying the rope.

You know how to tell when Tom Lasorda is *really mad*? He won't look at you. When I got onto the team bus that morning, he screamed, "Get to the back of the bus!" and he wouldn't look at me.

I guess he figured I had something to do with his door problem. So, judged guilty without a trial, I was forced to play the entire game (without much sleep) in Orlando that day. Then, finding my street clothes missing, I had to ride back on the bus in my undershorts.

But it was worth it.

You see a lot of younger managers today, but I'm not so sure it's a good idea. Perhaps they're better equipped to handle the physical stress of travel, but are they equipped to handle the players?

I don't think so. I think ballplayers, more today than ever, need a father figure, an authoritarian. When things go wrong, today's player needs to hear some screaming and hollering. My problem with the younger managers in that thirty-five to forty-two age bracket: They're the same age as some of their players, and it's tougher to demand respect. It isn't that they aren't smart enough and certainly they work hard, but the game has changed. As Orioles manager Frank Robinson says: "Managers don't have the leverage they once had. We can't really be the boss. If I say to a veteran player, 'If you don't perform you may be sent back to the minors,' they look at me and say, 'Who are you kidding? I'm not going anyplace. I've already had three years in the major leagues. You can't send me back to the minor leagues without my OK.' "

Coaches receive even less respect. Most coaches are the workhorses of any organization. They work longer hours for less pay than almost anyone, and they take the most crap.

For that, I blame the owners. More than ever, players of today need instruction. Too many kids are rushed into the big leagues without proper fundamentals and *more coaching on the major league level* should be done, not less.

There are some obvious coaches out there who could someday be excellent major league managers, if that's what they want—Bill Robinson, formerly of the Mets, John Vukovich of the Phillies, Bill Russell and Joe Ferguson of the Dodgers, Andy Etchebarren of the Brewers, just to name a few.

But Jay Johnstone? I have a feeling my managing will continue to come from the broadcast booth. Up there, we get one more guess—the second one.

Among the active managers in major league baseball today, I guess I would most like to play under Doug (Rooster) Rader of the California Angels.

He is a closet sicky.

I know he was serious last year but that was a ruse.

After all, Orange County, California, is a very serious place and with the Angels in contention for the AL West all season, Rooster couldn't do anything really crazy.

Like go to the movies, buy an ice cream bar, throw away the ice cream and eat the paper. Or sit in a clubhouse meeting and pretend to eat out of a garbage can. Or advise Little Leaguers to *eat* their bubble gum cards (his theory: that they would digest the information on the cards and grow up to be better players). Or challenge a dozen sportswriters to a fight. Or invite friends over for dinner and greet them at the door wearing nothing.

Maybe he's mellowing some, too. He had some bad experiences the first time around as a major league manager (fired by the Rangers in 1985) and I'm sure there was a conscious effort to change his behavior and image last season.

That's part of what I admire about Rooster. He's a survivor. He paid his dues and knows the game as well as anybody, better than most. As a player, Doug didn't have a lot of talent but played with intensity.

On and off the field.

A typical Rooster escapade, told by Johnny Edwards, his former teammate with the 1969 Houston Astros: Rader was once thrown into jail for slugging a game warden.

"Doug was fishing in the middle of some river without a license and they came after him in one of those airboats," said Edwards, "so he throws his fishing stuff in the bushes and dives under the water, breathing through a reed.

"And he might have made it, but he kept hearing the boat getting closer and closer and he didn't want to be pulverized by the propeller."

That's when Doug surfaced, duked it out with the game warden, and was taken off to jail.

"He came right to training camp from jail," said Edwards. "No shoes. Hadn't changed his clothes in three days."

In Houston, Rader also used the Astros' locker room as a driving range, sending teammates for cover whenever he teed up a golf ball. So why didn't anybody take away Rader's golf clubs, rather than worry about getting hit by a dimpled ball ricocheting off a locker?

"I guess," said teammate Larry Dierker, "because they wanted to live."

Rader carried that same intensity into his first managerial job and the results were disastrous.

"I was really demanding and pushy when I managed the Rangers," said Rader, admitting he often acted like a "jerk," in his dealings with players and the media. "Things got out of hand. I'm much more relaxed now. I'm not out to singlehandedly change the world and it's a much healthier situation."

That doesn't mean the 1989 Angels didn't have some fun. But Rader stayed in the background as pitcher Bert Blyleven (wearing a mop wig) conducted the locker room Kangaroo Court and kept everyone "on their toes" with hotfoots. The Angels also had a team party during the season, passing out gag gifts to each other. Best gift? Relief pitcher Bob McClure gave assistant public relations director John Savanno a live, one-hundred-pound pig. Meanwhile, manager Rader behaved.

No, he did not sit on any birthday cakes in the clubhouse. No, he did not slither across the shower floor on his back ("upside-down seal races"). No, he did not stick bubble gum up his nose and then eat it. After all, such acts—all part of Rader's past—would not be considered becoming in a major league manager. But Rooster didn't fool me. He has always professed to like people and things "off-center" and I can't believe he has really changed, job security or not.

Most impressive was the way he controlled his temper. Nobody got punched out in the Angels' locker room. No members of the media were dismissed from his office in quaking fear. Rooster did get in his licks on some American League umpires, but judging from what I saw on TV replays (they ruled a foul ball by Orioles' Mike Devereaux to be a home run that beat the Angels) they had it coming.

Jerry Reuss tells this story: "It was 1971 and I was pitching for St. Louis against Houston, my first look at the Astrodome, and I couldn't even get out of the first inning. I loaded the bases and gave up a grand slam homer."

The man who hit the grand slam was Rader, and as part of an Astro promotion, he won himself a new car. And, one year later when Reuss was traded to the Astros, Rooster welcomed him into the clubhouse by saying, "Hey, thanks for the car."

* * *

Rocky Bridges, manager of the Salem Buccaneers of the Carolina League, when asked why he doesn't like his players to eat sunflower seeds, answered: "That's for birds to eat. I'm afraid my players will start molting or going to the bathroom on newspapers."

It was also Rocky who said he enjoyed playing exhibition games against Japanese teams because two hours later he felt like playing them again.

And upon rejecting a waiter's suggestion of snails for an appetizer, he said: "I prefer fast food."

Managing in the minors, while having all of the obvious shortcomings, nevertheless offers more latitude for laughs. But you do need some imagination, as was displayed last summer by Mal Fichman, pilot of the Boise (Idaho) Class A team in the Northwest League.

After being ejected from a game against Salem (Oregon), Fichman became team mascot Humphrey the Hawk. He put on the mascot's uniform and stayed on the field ("So I could still have contact with my players") and the umpires never caught on. Mal later confided his action to league president Jack Cain and drew a one-day suspension for "making a mockery of the game."

Fichman isn't the first manager to resort to evasive action after being kicked out of a game. Frank Lucchesi, later to manage the Phillies, Rangers, and Cubs in the big leagues, once scaled a telephone pole outside the ballpark and managed his minor league club from altitude. And Ed Nottle, who managed Class AAA Pawtucket (Rhode Island) of the International League last season, once returned to a game as the Tacoma (Washington) Tigers mascot during a Pacific Coast League game.

Nottle claims the only reason he got caught was that the radio announcer kept saying the Tiger walked like him.

Jack McKeon, manager of the San Diego Padres, has the right attitude—not just because he makes good copy for beat reporters and columnists, but because his teams don't get uptight. Alternating third basemen for the Padres last season, for example, were Tim Flannery and Randy Ready, certainly, by their own description, "no Brooks Robinsons."

"Instead," said McKeon, "they call themselves the Brooks Brothers . . . Foster and Mel."

It was McKeon who said, when juggling San Diego's starting pitching rotation: "Maybe their biorhythms will fall into place."

And, after observing stadium workers as they installed thicker seat pads in dugouts: "I told you we'd improve our bench."

On the name of his newborn granddaughter: "We haven't decided. She's the baby to be named later."

McKeon, who managed Kansas City and Oakland in the American League before moving back onto the field in 1988 as manager of the Padres, is a fifty-nine-year-old New Jersey native (South Amboy) who looks at the world through cigar smoke and a cocked eye.

When observing the hitting success of Chris James during the season, the man also known as Trader Jack observed:

"A lot of guys wanted to cross him off but as Shakespeare said 'How poor are they that have not patience.' "

Surprised at hearing Shakespeare quoted in the dugout, a newsman asked, "From what play was that?"

"Pickoff," answered McKeon.

Othello probably wasn't real popular in South Amboy.

You have to learn to double-talk if you're going to be a successful manager.

Casey Stengel was the best and if I'm not mistaken, he also did a few crazy things, in addition to leading the Yankees to ten pennants and seven World Championships in twelve seasons.

Casey was finishing his career with the New York Mets just as I was breaking in as a rookie with the California Angels in the mid-1960s (you could look it up), but he's another manager with whom I wish I could have played.

Today's master of Caseyspeak is Sparky Anderson, twenty-year managerial veteran, who said about the slow 1989 start by his Detroit Tigers: "If you have a pretty good club there's no sense worrying. If you don't, there's still no sense in worrying because you already know you don't have a good club.''

Huh?

And how important is character, Sparky?

''Character is forty home runs.''

Newcomers to the managerial circus, meanwhile, were finding their own way. Houston's rookie pilot, Art Howe, became so puzzled by his team's poor early season record at home that he told his players, upon return from another successful road trip: ''When we get home, just act like you're on the road. Go meet your wives at a bar.''

Others tried different things. Dom Zimmer of the Cubs banned hotfoots (booooooooooooo), Davey Johnson of the Mets banned off-day golf on road trips, and Jim Leyland of the Pirates banned food in the clubhouse. But after the Bucs played an eighteen-inning game that lasted five hours, forty-two minutes, the starved Leyland said: ''All I've had to eat today was a bowl of Trix at 8:00 A.M. Maybe I made a mistake.''

And when the Montreal Expos were experiencing a slump, my old pal Buck Rodgers, absolutely one of baseball's better managers, resorted to the oldest and best advice: He told his players to loosen up, let their reflexes take over, and ''have some fun.''

Then there was the White Rat of St. Louis, Whitey Herzog. Once again in 1989, he got all that was there *and then some* out of his Cardinals.

By late August he was describing Pedro Guerrero as the ''best player I've ever managed with a hangover,'' and when somebody projected that his not-so-powerful Redbirds might hit only sixty-one home runs all season, he said: ''We'll catch Maris [Roger], sure as hell.''

And when Whitey was ejected from a game by umpires after a two-year stint of good behavior, he said: ''I was going for Lou Gehrig's record.''

After brothers Donell (Giants) and Otis (Expos) Nixon went a combined thirty for eighty-one against the Cardinals: ''If I were managing against our team, I'd go to San Clemente and get President Nixon and put him into the lineup.''

Herzog, though, got off the best of his one-liners after the Cardinals brought in sixty-five-year-old Malcolm (Bunny) Mick as batting instructor to work with speedster Vince Coleman: "What a society we have," said Whitey, "when a rat brings in a bunny to help a rabbit."

Meanwhile, one of Whitey's rivals, Davey Johnson of the Mets, was having trouble solving the mysteries of the team that was supposed to win.

"But at least if something goes wrong," said Davey, "there are at least five million people in New York who think they can fix it better than you."

Hey, fellows, nobody said managing was a luxury cruise. When Nick Leyva of the Phillies returned home after eleven consecutive losses and a hundred-dollar fine for getting thrown out of a game, he discovered that his condo association had also fined him thirty-five dollars for having a birdbath.

"I had a bad week," said Leyva, "eleven losses and a birdbath fine."

Tom Trebelhorn even had his typewriter run over by the Milwaukee team bus after a road trip into Texas. Which makes me ask: When did managers start taking typewriters on road trips? Baltimore manager Frank Robinson even carried a fax machine on the road so he could receive daily advance scouting reports.

Baseball is work but some work harder than others. White Sox manager Jeff Torborg claims he was continually amazed at how much time his coaches, particularly Walt Hriniak, gave to the game.

"For the first time the other day," said Torborg, "I beat Walt to the ballpark. But I couldn't get in because he had the key."

Sometimes, though, when all of the work and strategy and dedication don't get the job done, a manager simply has to resort to instinct. That's what Leyland did when one of his players, Junior Ortiz, kept complaining that he never got a chance to steal. Finally, Leyland told Junior to watch for a "special sign."

"What special sign?"

"When you look into the dugout and I jump into the air and don't come down."

Ever-tenuous is the relationship between the manager and the modern player. Atlanta's Russ Nixon, for example, gave an audience to infrequently used catcher Bruce Benedict and heard this: "Don't think I don't appreciate you not playing me, Skip, but I've gotten 'Yard of the Month' since I've had so much time to work on it."

Ever-changing, too. After Cardinal reliever Todd Worrell gave up five runs in the second half of a rain-delayed doubleheader at Cincinnati at 2:00 A.M., manager Herzog said: "I learned something about managing again. I now know good and well that I should never bring a clean liver into a game after 2:00 A.M., three hours after his bedtime."

Maybe he should have let Guerrero pitch.

In days past, major league managers could say whatever they wanted about their players. No longer. Red Sox manager Joe Morgan discovered that when he did a radio commercial for the New England Jeep-Eagle dealers in which he said: "And you don't have to stroke it like a player."

Sure enough, the Red Sox players took offense and Morgan had to stroke them to make up.

Larry Doughty, Pirates general manager, got in his shots a little differently, saying on his radio show: "Baseball is supposed to be a noncontact sport but our hitters seem to be taking it literally."

When the Chicago Cubs broke training camp in Arizona in 1989, it's a wonder manager Don Zimmer didn't choose to stay behind. That's how badly they played during the spring. Nobody gave them a chance to contend in the National League East.

That's why Zim got so much support for Manager of the Year in the National League. It was no fluke that he did a great job with the Cubs because he's a sound baseball man. As a matter of fact, Pat Corrales, who finished his major league career catching for the San Diego Padres in 1973, said he "learned more about baseball" from Zimmer, then manager of the Padres, than anyone else. That's quite a testimony when you consider that the Padres lost 102 games that season.

Zim has two attributes I admire in a manager—patience and courage. He sat through six- and seven-game losing streaks with the young Cubs last season without reaching for the panic button. And how he endured reliever Mitch Williams's walk-a-guy, fan-a-guy, walk-a-guy routine without having a heart attack I'll never know. But he did it. Also, Zim was never afraid to run. One day I was watching a Cubs game on WGN-TV and saw Zim call the hit-and-run with the bases loaded. That takes balls. When a manager isn't afraid to get second-guessed, he's a better manager.

Zimmer also showed me he cared about people when he said about cutting players in spring training: "It's what I hate most about this job. Monkeying around with people's lives is never fun. On the other hand, when I've picked my team, twenty-four players are monkeying around with my life."

When Andre Dawson was selected to appear in the 1989 All-Star Game, Zimmer waited until Dawson was ready to hit in the third inning of a Cubs game before telling him.

"Get a hit," Zim said as Dawson left the dugout, "and, by the way, get one Tuesday in the All-Star Game."

I still think Zimmer and his boss, Jim Frey, were taking themselves too seriously with their five-hundred-dollar fine mandate against hotfoots, but when departed players Jamie Moyer and Rafael Palmeiro showed up in Texas wearing t-shirts that read "I've been Freyed and Zimmered," I liked the way the Cubs' manager handled it. He just said: "It's a shame I couldn't say what I want to say but I won't. I've got too much class for that."

Players love to laugh at their own managers but have to pick their spots. Giggle at the wrong time and you'll find your buns on the bench.

Catcher Ernie Whitt of Toronto loves to tell this story about former Blue Jays manager Bobby Mattick, who became the major leagues' oldest rookie manager (sixty-four) when he replaced Roy Hartsfield and went onto the field back in 1980: "When Bobby would get mad or excited he'd take off his baseball cap and toss it into the air. Well, one night we're in Baltimore, he's standing on the top step of the dugout, something happened on the field, and he threw his cap into the air.

"But it never came down. The wind caught it and blew it back into the stands. Now it's a tight situation in the game and we're all sitting on the bench trying to keep from laughing out loud. Meanwhile, Bobby is trying to act as if nothing's wrong, but he keeps looking around and you know he's burning. Finally, he just put his head down, went back into the clubhouse, and told the clubbie "Gimme another hat, gimme another hat.""

There has never been a better target for a practical joke than Tom Lasorda. When I played alongside Jerry Reuss, Rick Monday, Steve Yeager, and Don Stanhouse with the Dodgers, we had Lasorda screaming. He didn't have a chance. We put cigar butts into his coffee cups, donned groundskeepers' uniforms to drag the infield during a game, hid his clothes, took down all the Frank Sinatra pictures from his wall and hid them, rigged up an actors' dressing-room mirror in his office, and—most effective of all—we stole his food.

But he survived and he hasn't really changed except that he's older and thinner. I'm just wondering how Tommy survived the off-season banquet circuit. He's the only man I know who gives speeches according to what people feed him. If it's a steak dinner, he gives the steak speech. If it's something less, he doesn't extend himself at the microphone. So what kind of speech do you give for diet milkshakes? Instead of a tuxedo, do you show up wearing a "Please Don't Feed the Manager" t-shirt?

Lasorda likes to see his picture on walls. When he's sitting in a restaurant, he wants to look up and see a picture of himself. That's just the way he is. So he's at Kelly Mondelli's on North Clark Street in Chicago one night and the place has hundreds of sports and celebrity photos all over the walls, and Tommy is miffed because he can't find any of himself. So he's ranting and raving at the owner, Joey Mondelli, and finally gives him a picture of himself.

Well, Joey put Lasorda's mug shot in a prominent position over the jukebox and that made Tommy happy. Except that one night a few weeks later Frank Sinatra was in town and Joey moved Lasorda's picture to make room for Frank. Since he idolizes Sinatra, Lasorda couldn't complain too much, but then his friend Eddie Minasian really got him. He took an eight-by-ten photo of Joe Garagiola and put it over the face of Lasorda, then took Tommy back into Mondelli's for another dinner.

Did I say Lasorda knew how to scream? The neighbors on North Clark still talk about all the noise.

Quickie mind-flashes on other American League managers of 1989—some of whom may not be around for the 1990s:

Tom Trebelhorn, Brewers: The players like him. He lets them go out and play their games. As far as offensive tactics, he may be a little conservative, but on defense, certainly from the dugout he couldn't catch the balls his players kept booting for errors last season. Tom is another of the good, young managers who paid their dues in the minors. I saw him one day hitting golf balls into the center-field seats at County Stadium with a seven-iron, so he obviously knows his priorities, too.

Joe Morgan, Red Sox: He served his apprenticeship within the Red Sox organization and with the younger players that commands respect, or at least, it should. Things don't always work that way in baseball-passionate Beantown. One of Morgan's own passions: raising tomatoes. That I don't understand, unless one day he plans on throwing them at spectators or sportswriters.

Bobby Valentine, Rangers: He is a young man with a lot of talent, and he's well-liked in Texas, even though many still think he may succeed Lasorda one day in Los Angeles.

Bobby not only has a good baseball mind, he's a successful restaurant owner. Digression: More and more players and managers these days are opening restaurants—or, at least, lending their names to restaurants. That can be dangerous, as Lasorda discovered in Pasadena after health officials found rats scurrying around his ribs-pasta joint. Tommy complained that he was "set up" but hey, maybe the little guys just liked Tommy's pasta sauce.

Jim Lefebvre, Mariners: His dad, Benny, taught me as much about hitting as anyone. Jimmy has a lot of good managerial ideas. He's positive, innovative, and took a fine attitude into Seattle, where they haven't had much to cheer about. Jim's big thrust: He keeps progress charts on how to score runs. Now if he can keep his job, I'm predicting the Mariners will show progress.

Tony LaRussa, Athletics: One of his big decisions of 1989 was whether to wear sunglasses for day games in Oakland.

"If I don't, I get a headache from the glare," said Tony, "but if I do, people think I'm being California cool."

Anyone who ever heard Tony throw clubhouse chairs should know he's not always cool. But he's smart (a lawyer, actually), and he's a planner. He charts everything—how many runs his team needs to score, how many pitches his staff should throw, and so forth—and he uses a computer. He also carries eleven pitchers for much of the season, rather than the customary ten, and he doesn't hesitate to go to the bullpen.

Anybody wanting to learn about baseball discipline and preparation could learn from LaRussa.

Sparky Anderson, Tigers: This will tell you something about Sparky. After completing his twentieth season of managing, one in which he had to take a leave of absence because of stress, somebody asked him if he would leave Detroit in search of a winner.

"First, I don't know that I could find a better spot," said Sparky, "and even if I could, it wouldn't be right. The Tigers have given me eleven years, almost twelve. Do you run from them because they're bad? I don't think that's fair."

Sparky's advice to young managers is simple. Know how to motivate and communicate because a manager is only as good as his players.

*   *   *

Cito Gaston, Blue Jays: He was hitting coach in Toronto before succeeding the fired Jimy Williams and the players respect him, as evidenced by their last-half performance. Cito, forty-four, doesn't try to force his will on players. He treats them like professionals and lets them play their game. Also, his team is fundamentally sound.

Frank Robinson, Orioles: Another fundamentalist, F. Robby had his young-and-yessir Orioles surprising all of baseball for most of last season. He emphasizes bunting, the hit-and-run, basic execution of signs, hitting the cut-off man, and so forth—a lot of the things major leaguers let slide once they reach the big show. He credits his coaches, which is important, and he'll be the first to admit he's a better manager now than when he broke the "managerial color line" as field boss of the Cleveland Indians back in 1975.

Jeff Torborg, White Sox: As cross-town peer Zimmer of the Cubs once said about Jeff, "He's a terrific baseball man. He had to be to survive ten years with the New York Yankees. He'll help the Sox get back on track."

A former catcher, Torborg knows how to handle pitchers when he has them. The Chisox, however, gave him the ultimate "team effort" in 1989. The only time they weren't stinko was when they put together that one winning streak to give announcer Tom Paciorek a haircut. By the time the Sox move into their new ballpark, though, Jeff may have them respectable.

John (Duke) Wathan, Royals: What is it with all these ex-catchers becoming managers? Maybe it's because as players they were so heavily entrenched in the game. Baseball execs believe catchers and middle infielders make the best managers: They're always in the game. How many outfielders or pitchers have been successful managers? Guys like Reuss and me are usually off to the side talking to somebody in the first row, or chewing gum, or looking for four-leaf clovers, rather than paying attention to the game.

On the other hand, didn't Herzog play outfield? Didn't Lasorda pitch?

Next theory, please.

Dallas Green, formerly of the Yankees: Dallas, who gets the full treatment in another chapter, went to the mound during a particularly forgettable Dave LaPoint performance last season and asked catcher Don Slaught, "How is he throwing?"

"I don't know," said Slaught. "I haven't caught any yet."

Dallas, though, didn't have much to laugh about in 1989, unless you want to count his bank deposits.

Did I say coaches got little respect in the major leagues? Jimmy Reese is the exception.

Jimmy, age eighty-three and still coaching with the Angels, marked his seventy-second season in professional baseball in 1989. Before throwing the ceremonial first pitch to a nine-year-old at the All-Star Game, Jimmy said: "I just hope I can get it to the kid. After you've hit two million fungoes, your arm tends to go dead."

Reese began his baseball career in 1917 when, at the age of eleven, he was batboy for the Los Angeles Angels of the Pacific Coast League. He later played infield, briefly, with the New York Yankees (1930–1931) and St. Louis Cardinals (1932) and, indeed, once shared a room with Babe Ruth.

"Actually," says Jimmy, smiling, "I roomed with his suitcase."

6

Freak Injuries and Freaky Players

How easily they fall.

The Toronto Blue Jays had a pitcher, David Wells, who cut his thumb last season while sleepwalking.

Brian Fisher, who pitches for Pittsburgh, hurt himself playing miniature golf. No, he didn't get his foot caught in a paddle-wheel. He leaned on his golf club, which snapped and cut his arm (thirteen stitches).

Outfielder Donell Nixon poked himself in the eye with his sunglasses and dislodged his contact lens. As a result he got fined by Giants manager Roger Craig ("because he made me run all the way to the right-field bleachers on my bad knee").

Oakland shortstop Walt Weiss reinjured his ailing knee when he got up to switch TV channels in his Boston hotel room.

Pitcher Jerry Reuss of the Brewers pulled his left hamstring while in the middle of a windup.

Alejandro Peña of the Dodgers didn't even make it to the mound one day. He hurt himself while warming up in the bullpen.

Greg (Moonie) Minton of the Angels did better than that. The Angels reliever pulled a rib cage muscle while putting on his pants.

Taste this one: Kansas City Royals infielder Brad Wellman cracked a tooth while biting into a pizza.

Wally ("Magic") Joyner of the Angels was "just messin' around" on a basketball court, sprained his left ankle, and was welcomed back into spring training camp by the sight of a basketball hoop hanging on his locker.

Then there was former major leaguer Bump Wills, hired last spring to help teach the Texas Rangers how to run bases.

He fractured an ankle. How? He was filming a promotional tape for the Rangers' cable TV network and the soundman needed one more slide into home plate, even though darkness had fallen. So Wills complied and the soundman got the sound of a bone breaking.

Indians reliever Doug Jones hurt his back while lifting his child at Christmas and teammate Tom Candiotti hurt his while taking a shower.

Rob Dibble, reliever for the Reds, explained his mysterious bronchial problem by saying, "I may be allergic to AstroTurf. I only get sick at the ballpark."

It even runs in the family. Rookie Ken Griffey, Jr., was playing catch and caught one with his eye last spring during his first Arizona workout with the Seattle Mariners. At precisely the same moment, 2:15 P.M. EST, in Plant City, Florida, Cincinnati first baseman Ken Griffey, Sr., let a grounder bounce off his chin, opening a seven-inch gash.

My favorite: Ex–major leaguer Chris Brown, who always did spend a lot of time in training rooms, came up with the jewel of 1989. Playing with the Buffalo Bisons (AAA), Brown scratched himself from the lineup by telling manager Terry Collins: "My eyelid is sore. I must have slept on it wrong."

Rash of injuries in baseball? How about epidemic? By the end of last season, more than three hundred players had appeared on the major league disabled list, at least a 13 percent increase over 1987.

Howcum? To a major leaguer twenty years ago, the initials "DL" might have meant Delayed Lunch or Dead Lumber or Doubleheader Lag. But "Disabled" and on a "List" for it? People in automobile accidents got disabled. Ballplayers got linament, tape, and aspirin.

Popular theories about what has happened:

- Today's pampered players, higher paid than any in history, refuse to risk their careers by playing with minor injuries.
- Front-office execs, having invested millions of dollars in player contracts, are fearful of endangering their investments by allowing the players to perform at less than 100 percent health.
- Guaranteed contracts. Why should a player risk further injury or overextend himself when he knows he will be paid for three more years, anyhow?
- Agents. Whenever there is any doubt, it is fashionable (and usually safe) to blame agents.
- Roster moves. Managers use the DL as a tool to maneuver players between the minor and major leagues. (I know about this one, having spent most of my final year with the Dodgers on the DL after stepping on a sprinkler head in the outfield while trying to sidestep Terry Whitfield trying to catch a fly ball.)

Today's players, however, do deserve some scrutiny. I've seen some guys lately who come out of college with degrees in mathematics and don't know how to lace their shoes, let alone keep from getting hurt.

I can remember in 1984, with the Cubs, when I was jogging in the outfield with pitcher Steve (Rainbow) Trout. He caught a spike in the stirrup of his uniform socks and fell face-forward into the ivy-covered brick outfield wall, jamming his shoulder.

"You're not going to believe," I said to manager Jim Frey, "how Rainbow just hurt himself." He was out for two weeks.

I have another theory. I believe today's players, unlike their predecessors, have become such specialists that they put too much strain on their bodies.

Explanation: They're like thoroughbred horses. The only difference is that horses don't have agents or claim to be misquoted.

For years, some of the worst athletes in professional sports could be found wearing baseball uniforms. You could find more bad bodies in a baseball locker room than at a convention of French chefs. No more. Today's player has discovered weights, specialized stretching machines, and year-round training programs.

Then why is he always hurt? This is a layman's theory: When you work so hard to build certain parts of the body, you often don't realize that other parts of your body also have to absorb strain and stress. You see players working on their legs or wrists or forearms to enable them to hit with strength, for example, but they neglect to build around the back or knees.

Digression on this era of specialization: You see it on the field, too. Pitchers don't think about going nine innings. They work toward a solid six. Nowadays they pay middle-inning relievers $1 million a year. You've got starters, long men, set-up men, one-batter men, and closers, the guys who also get paid a million dollars to sit in the bullpen every night waiting to pitch to the last batter.

When Orel Hershiser, Cy Young Award winner from 1988, appeared last summer on the David Letterman show, he was asked, "When you felt that elbow twinge the other night did you think your career was finished?"

"I've got a guaranteed three-year contract," answered Hershiser.

Kal Daniels, coming to the Dodgers after two knee operations in Cincinnati, lasted less than two weeks before going under the knife for a third. Was he worried? Said Kal: "I want to be on the *Bill Cosby Show* and play the oldest son coming back from the Army."

Yeah, sure. Maybe on crutches, from combat.

Dodger manager Tom Lasorda, admittedly an Old Schooler, makes this observation: "I walk into our clubhouse and it's like the Mayo Clinic. We have four doctors, three therapists, and five trainers. Back when I broke in, we had one trainer with a bottle of rubbing alcohol, and by the seventh inning we had drunk it all."

Former manager Dick Williams lays the blame on year-round

training. He says the DL lists are crowded because of improved diagnostic capabilities and management's reluctance to take risks with million-dollar investments.

So whatever happened to rubbing tobacco juice on the sore spot and going back out there? The only guys still doing that are the umpires. They take some hellacious shots from foul balls, bad bounces, and so forth, but seldom do you see them withdrawing from a game. I saw Bruce Froemming, working home plate, take a foul ball to the unprotected ribs in a TV game and he tipped over like a bowling pin. It had to be painful but he walked it off and continued.

Nor did he get any sympathy. In the umpire's room afterward, the phone rang and it was another umpire, John Kibler, calling from another city. He had seen the play on TV, too. Said Kibler to Froemming: "You can tell the Slim-Fast diet isn't working or that pitch would have missed you."

Froemming's reply could be heard down the corridor.

Another theory: Whitey Herzog of the Cardinals says everybody should be eating more red meat.

"In the old days when we traveled by train," said Herzog, "we had beer waiting for us, we had salt tablets in the dugout, and we always had a steak after every game. Nobody ever had a pulled muscle. Nobody eats red meat anymore."

One can understand Whitey's frustration. Last season one of his front-liners, Willie McGee, was out of the lineup for injuries to both hamstrings, his left wrist, and his rib cage, prompting Herzog to say: "Yeah, and if he comes back he'll probably injure his other wrist."

How about toes? Darryl Strawberry of the Mets missed fourteen of fifteen games before the 1989 All-Star Game because of a broken small toe on his left foot. Meanwhile, Ozzie Smith of the Cardinals had a broken third toe on his right foot and didn't miss an inning.

Yes, things are different: George Brett of the Kansas City Royals went on the DL last year after twisting his knee on artificial turf

("My spikes caught when I tried to throw the ball"). And when Cardinal bullpen ace Todd Worrell went down with a strained elbow during the pennant race, teammate Dan Quisenberry described a new game called "bullpen musical chairs."

"When the phone rings," said Quis, "we get everybody up and run in circles until the music stops. Then the guy without a seat has to go into the game."

Before finally losing his job last season, Cincinnati manager Pete Rose also faced an almost-unbelievable rash of injuries. When Scott Madison, an off-season insurance salesman, was called up to replace Paul O'Neill (broken thumb), he looked around the Reds' clubhouse and said: "I ought to make a killing up here, but the problem is that everybody's too high-risk."

Everybody, of course, didn't disappear onto the DL. Some guys beat the medical odds, Giants pitcher Dave Dravecky the most prominent as he came back from cancer before suffering a broken bone. Cubs shortstop Shawon Dunston, too, wears a "Z" on his right hand where it was cut to allow three screws to be inserted. They held together the bone in his middle finger, which was fractured in mid-1987 during a headfirst slide into second base. The "Z" brand remains but when the screws were finally removed, Dunston threw them anyway.

"Those kind of souvenirs I didn't need," said Shawon.

And when catcher Carlton Fisk of the White Sox also performed with a metal plate inserted into his broken hand, Sox manager Jeff Torborg said: "I don't think it will affect his mobility but electrical storms might be a problem."

Dan Gladden of the Twins was also a "gamer." After suffering a broken jaw, he kept playing with a protective shield and said: "I'm going to try to sell some ad space."

Then there was A's shortstop Mike Gallego, who said about his sore wrist during the ALCS media crunch:

"I cracked it three years ago and now I have somebody asking me how it is."

Goose Gossage and Terry Forster, a pair of my ex-teammates with the White Sox of the early seventies, both of whom had highly successful careers as relief pitchers and became close friends, tell this injury story: They were rooming with each other in the minor leagues, watching TV in their hotel room, when they had a "friendly" disagreement over which channel to watch. First Forster changed the channel, then Gossage, then Forster, then all hell broke loose. Goose smacked Terry with a pillow, but when Terry tried to retaliate, he missed with his pillow and slapped Goose with an open hand.

That started it. They began wrestling across the small hotel room and remember, both were in their early twenties, both weighed more than two hundred, and both were strong as horses. Well, Forster ended up banging his ribs when he bounced against a table and Gossage ended up hobbling on a sore toe.

The next day Forster couldn't breathe and Gossage couldn't walk, both had to be flown to Chicago for X-rays, and sure enough, Terry had broken ribs and Goose had a broken toe. That's when the White Sox decided maybe they shouldn't room together anymore.

Forster, also known as Hoss, tells of an injury that occurred on the streets of New York:

"Gossage and I were with the White Sox and when we get off the team bus after a night game at the Sheraton Hotel, Goose says 'Whatta you gonna do?' and I said 'I'm going to the Carnegie Deli' and he said 'I'm not hungry' and headed for Sally's Bar [just off the Sheraton lobby].

"So I start off down the sidewalk with one of the baseball writers, Bob Verdi of the *Chicago Tribune,* and all of a sudden this guy comes around the corner, runs into me, and falls down. So help me, that's what happened. Then he gets up and takes a swing at me.

"Well, that was a mistake. I'm wearing this big, jade ring and I catch him flush with a right hand so hard it dislocated my finger. It's sticking out all crazylike and I thought sure it was broken.

"And just as I hit the guy, who naturally went back down to the sidewalk, a cop comes around the corner and boom, he's out with a gun and got me handcuffed. Still to this day I've got a bone chip in my right wrist from those cuffs. Anyhow, Verdi and I are talking a mile a minute and we finally get the cop to understand what happened.

"But just as the cop is apologizing and taking off the handcuffs, the guy on the sidewalk jumps up and says 'I know who you are and I'm going to blow you away, you baseball son-of-a-bitch.' And the cop is just standing there and lets the guy go.

"Now I've got a temper but I'm not nuts. When a guy says he's going to blow me away that only means one thing to me. So I said to Verdi 'You go eat, I'm going back to the hotel and order room service.'

"So I'm heading through Sally's Bar on the way to my room and as I'm walking through, so help me, this stranger, a different guy, comes tumbling across the room into me.

" 'What the hell is going on?' I yelled, but just then I see Goose.

" 'I just nailed that SOB,' he said.

" 'Why? What did he do?'

" 'I was just standin' there at the bar and he grabbed my balls,' said Goose.

"So I pick up the guy and throw him through the hotel revolving door. Then I turn to Goose and say, 'This may not be our night. Let's get out of here.'

"On the way to the room I tell him about the guy on the sidewalk and we both get scared. So we go inside, move all the furniture up against the door so nobody can come after us, close the blinds, and turn down the TV real low. We thought sure that guy was going to come after us with a gun."

The Dodgers and Expos played twenty-two innings and six hours before Los Angeles finally won at 1:09 A.M., 1–0, on a home run by backup catcher Rick Dempsey.

"I was fresh," said Dempsey, who had played only fourteen innings, having replaced Mike Scioscia in the eighth.

"I was ready again, too," said Scioscia. "I strained my hamstring in the eighth but it was healed by the seventeenth."

Finally, not an awful lot of people can find laughs in a heart attack but Bob Uecker did. After he had chest pains and a burning sensation in his arm, he asked his wife to drive him to the nearest hospital.

"But she had no idea where to find a hospital," said Uecker, later. "Now, if I needed to go to a mall, no problem."

I tried all last summer, while traveling with the Yankees, to lose five to eight pounds. I lifted weights, ran up stadium stairs, and even watched my diet. So what happened? I think some of the weight just turned to muscle because the pounds wouldn't disappear. Anyhow, it really made me mad when one WABC listener wrote: "You're a fathead."

Musclehead I could accept.

Tom Lasorda, meanwhile, went on the most-publicized diet since Oprah Winfrey and lost so many pounds I could hardly recognize him. All the TV cameramen had to refocus with regular lenses (they had always needed wide-angle for Tommy before). By season's end, Lasorda's diet had cost Dodger player Orel Hershiser twenty thousand dollars and Kirk Gibson ten thousand, with the money going to charity and being matched by the liquid diet product that hired Lasorda to endorse and do commercials.

Lasorda started at 218 after a Hershiser-Gibson challenge in spring training but by late season was down to 180 and that tells me two things: (a) when there's money on the table Lasorda will do almost anything; (b) he had a lot of fat to lose. He probably lost the first twenty pounds in two hours.

The nicest part of Tommy's diet was that the Sisters of Mercy in Nashville, Tennessee, received more than fifty thousand dollars for a much-needed home. Lasorda also threw a lavish benefit for the Sisters in late November. Somehow, though, Tommy ended up making more money than anyone from the diet company. On top of that, he was making just as much money selling pasta sauce. How did he pull that one off?

Don Zimmer was a magician, too. He endorsed fried chicken, hardly a slim meal, then went on a weight-loss program, lost twenty pounds, and earned the nickname Slimmer Zimmer. It's no wonder Pirates manager Jim Leyland took one look at Zim and said: "He's the only guy I know who gets paid to eat and diet."

Mets manager Davey Johnson got into the act, too, as did other members of the Mets and club personnel, all aiming to reduce to below two hundred pounds. "Maybe then we'll be hitting our weight," said Johnson, but Lasorda wasn't laughing. When his weight fell below two hundred in early season, five Dodger regulars were hitting below their manager's weight.

Dieting became contagious in major league clubhouses. Dwight (Doc) Gooden even used it as an excuse for shaving his head, saying, "They wanted me to lose weight, so I did."

Some needed to lose more than others. If my buddy Forster had dieted sooner he wouldn't have been ripped by TV's David Letterman, who called him a "fat tub of goo" a few years ago. Some pitchers (why are pitchers always the overweight guys?) still resemble Hoss on the mound. For example, when Rich Reuschel, Don Robinson, and Mike Krukow started for the Giants in Montreal last May, Expos publicist and wit Rich Griffin claimed they established an all-time weight record (680 pounds) for a three-game series.

"How much do you weigh?" somebody asked Reuschel, who hardly ever missed a meal when he was growing up on a farm near Quincy, Illinois.

"What?"

"What's your weight?"

"My weight?" said Reuschel, walking away. "I wait for taxi cabs. I wait for ballgames to start."

Reuschel, forty-one this May, has always been a man of few words. On being taken out of a game after eight innings of a one-hitter last season, he said, "It was past my bedtime."

And when catcher Junior Ortiz once went to the mound to talk with Rick when he pitched for the Pirates, the big fellow looked down and said: "Everything okay, Junior?"

"Oh, sure."

"Then get off the mound."

"Ohhhh, Big Daddy," said Ortiz, departing, "I love it when you talk nasty to me."

One nonpitcher who might consider Lasorda's diet: designated hitter Joey Meyer of the Milwaukee Brewers, who weighs approximately 260. When a group of local art students sketched several Brewers players during pregame workouts, they discreetly bypassed Meyer.

"I guess they didn't have a canvas big enough," said Joey.

In San Diego, before John Kruk was traded away to the Phillies, the Padres were referring to their starting outfield of Kruk, Tony Gwynn, and Carmelo Martinez as "The Three Gorditos." Loosely translated, *gordito* is an endearing Spanish term for a little butterball.

Much farther north in Minneapolis, the Twins have their own little butterball in five-eight, 220-pound Kirby Puckett. When shown a picture of the late Hall of Famer Hack Wilson, who set a National League record for home runs (56) in 1930, Puckett said: "He looks like me. I wonder who his tailor was."

I never had a weight problem as a player but I can understand why some do.

Just look at the junk ballplayers have been eating for years—cheeseburgers, french fries, pizzas, greasy potato chips, and pretzels. Then, just to top off an evening, one of those Whitey Herzog steaks. Or maybe some ribs with plenty of bar-b-que sauce.

And let's not forget the booze. As Mickey Mantle said recently: "If I hadn't drunk so much I could have played another two or three years."

Then again, if he hadn't, he wouldn't have been Mickey Mantle, would he?

I haven't seen any Mickey Mantles around Yankee Stadium lately but I do see ballplayers sticking longer in the big leagues because, finally, they're starting to pay attention to what they eat. I guess they figured out that as you get older you need to be leaner and meaner to survive.

Wade Boggs eats so much chicken I keep expecting him to leave feathers at home plate. He hits too well to ever lay an egg. And there are others. They've learned to store up carbohydrates, not fat and calories. They've hired nutritionists as consultants for the team. And, like Boggs, a lot of them have shied away from so much red meat.

When I played we would finish a night game, release nervous energy by filling our stomachs with the clubhouse "spread," then go out and drink half the night, maybe even eating "dinner" again or stopping for breakfast at the hotel coffee shop. And if we had a bad day we just figured we had a bad day. Nobody ever thought it might have something to do with our stomachs. I guess we all figured that if Babe Ruth could sneak across the street from Comiskey Park and scarf down a few hot dogs and beers at McCuddy's Tavern during a game, then surely we could survive.

Most of us did and we spent a lot less time on that dreaded DL. But most of the guys didn't last as long at the big show, either. Careers were definitely shortened.

Nowadays, when you say "cholesterol count" a player knows you don't mean three and two, bases loaded. Steve Sax of the Yankees, for example, regularly takes niacin and fish oil to relieve high cholesterol. His father died at forty-seven.

There was even the suggestion early last season that Oriole catcher Mickey Tettleton was hitting home runs because he ate Froot Loops, a sugar-coated cereal.

Whatever turns him on. Anything with raisins and nuts always worked for me. Especially nuts.

Pancakes, too. I would always eat pancakes when I was in a hitting streak. Or maybe I should say I always hit well when I ate pancakes. I can remember one streak in Philadelphia when I ate Pigs in a Blanket for six days in a row. I was so hot at the plate I won Player of the Week, four hits one day, then three, then two more, then four more, and all against the Houston Astros. Finally, by the end of the week, I hated Pigs in a Blanket. But I didn't stop eating them until my bat cooled off.

I had other superstitions, too. I would *never* step on a line when running in from the outfield. Other guys you see always stepping on third base as they head for the dugout. I've seen guys miss the bag, turn around, and go back to stomp on it. Others avoid the coaches' boxes like the plague. Then there are the rituals. Almost every player has some kind of ritual—a little sign, a tug on the sleeves, a knock on the cleats with the bat. I've even seen guys kiss their bats, and I'm not talking about the ones who wait in the parking lot.

Don't ask me why ballplayers do the things they do. We're all nuts. For example, I would never adjust my hat with my bare hand, only the gloved hand. If I was chasing down a fly ball and my hat fell off, I'd pick it up, then adjust it with my glove, never touching it with my bare hand. And at the plate, I always put on my right batting glove before the left, then gripped the pine tar.

Hey, nobody said playing baseball was brain surgery. I've seen guys making $1 million salaries wearing underwear you wouldn't give to the Salvation Army. They figure it's their lucky underwear.

Dave LaPoint of the Yankees is a prime example. He's got a pair of undershorts with a hole in them big enough to throw a softball through. But they're his favorite pair and he doesn't let anybody touch them—not that touching underwear is necessarily a normal practice in the Yankee clubhouse. Anyhow, one of these days somebody like Steve Sax is going to slip up and rip those undershorts to shreds. Then if Dave has a bad day he'll blame Saxy.

I couldn't begin to categorize all the superstitions of baseball players. Remember the movie *Bull Durham,* when one player had this ritual of shaking beads over his bat? People around me in the theater were laughing and I'm thinking "Hey, whatever it takes!" Mark Salas, for example, a part Cherokee with the Cleveland Indians, hung an Indian good luck sign above his locker one day and after Joe Carter rubbed his bat on it he got a single and a double.

Pitcher Greg Swindell of Cleveland bites off a piece of his little fingernail and chews it throughout an entire game. Once he lost it in the dugout, went down on his hands and knees, found it, and popped it back into his mouth.

Ben McDonald, the Orioles' number-one draft choice last year, eats sardines with mustard the night before he pitches.

Mets coach Bill Robinson has the lineup card rubbed by the same Shea Stadium security guard before every home game.

Bryn Smith of the Expos has worn the same Rush concert t-shirt every time he pitches. It's at least nine years old.

I told you about my buddy Jerry Reuss and his Sammy Doll. He bought the bobbing-head doll during the All-Star break last year and brought it to the second-half opener against the Brewers, which the White Sox won to begin an 11–1 winning streak. The lucky doll, obviously, was the reason. Reuss named it Sammy after pitching coach Sammy Ellis, whose neck twitches involuntarily when he gets excited. Reuss even had a ritual: Whenever the National Anthem was being played, he'd put the doll on the top step of the dugout.

One day in Boston, however, a batboy knocked Sammy Doll off a railing and broke its neck, necessitating emergency locker-room surgery. But after Sammy returned to the dugout, first baseman Ivan Calderon hit a three-run homer and the Chisox beat Boston, 10–6.

I don't know what Reuss did with Sammy after the Sox traded him to Milwaukee. He probably took him to a brewery and got him drunk.

One of these days, too, Evel Knievel and his son, Robbie, are going to show up at a Minnesota Twins game to claim the tickets being left for them by Dan Gladden, who claims Evel is the only hero he has ever had.

Why not? Maybe Evel will bring Elvis.

Can that be any crazier than the Cubs winning the National League East last year? They won nine games in Arizona during spring training and looked so bad fans had to turn their heads the other way. Yet, somewhere along the way, they got that "winning feeling" and you know what happened.

"Weird things happen," said Cubs' pitcher Paul Kilgus. "Our whole outfield went down with injuries, but here comes a whole new one from Iowa and we go into first place. Then we would be talking on the bench. Someone would say 'Slider down, single to right' and there's a slider down, single to right. It was just joking but it got spooky. You tell me."

One of the spookiest stories I heard about last summer was the

"Jinx Locker" in Baltimore. I can remember lockers that guys didn't want—like nobody with the 1978 Yankees wanted a locker next to Reggie Jackson because he always had so many sportswriters around him—but this was the first haunted locker I'd ever heard about.

It's a spacious, corner locker in the Orioles' clubhouse and for much of last season it was occupied by twenty-nine-year-old rookie pitcher Dave Johnson, who just may have broken the jinx. That, of course, remains to be seen.

Anyhow, my ex-prankster buddy Don Stanhouse once occupied the locker and ended up leaving for Los Angeles, where he hurt his back and flopped. After that, Dan Ford moved into the locker, blew out his knee, and never played again. The year after Steve Stone won the Cy Young Award he became a locker resident and blew out his elbow.

Are you starting to get the picture?

Eddie Murray was next. He moved into the locker after an All-Star career with the Orioles. Next thing you know he was also in L.A., with another locker resident, Rick Dempsey, not far behind.

"I was only in the locker for one year and the Orioles tried to cut my salary 67 percent," said Dempsey. "Then I was gone."

Last spring the first boarder was Jim Traber, a reserve first baseman–pinch-hitter who did not have much of a season, hitting .209 in eighty-six games. By season's end, his future with the Orioles was very much in doubt. In August, though, pitcher Johnson came up from the minors and dealt the "Jinx Locker" a mighty blow, pitching three complete games in his first four starts.

Indeed, the twenty-nine-year-old rookie was one of the Oriole success stories of 1989. But if I were Johnson, I wouldn't send out too much laundry. Jinx lockers don't just roll over and die because some guy won three in a row.

Old ballparks are like old people, their personalities distinct, conjuring up wonderful memories of the past and treating the present with tolerant cynicism.

It will sadden me when the final brick from Comiskey Park, Chicago, hits the sidewalk. I will remember the closeness of the place, which will celebrate its eightieth, and final, birthday this season.

I know it will be better for the fans, members of the media, and players when the spiffy new park opens in 1991 just south of original Comiskey, but here's hoping they built a special wing just for the ghosts of the old joint.

Long before I wandered into the place in the early 1970s, Comiskey Park was a place of charm, too often overlooked because of the reputation of Wrigley Field on Chicago's North Side.

Remember the famous photo of the fan spilling beer onto the head of outfielder Al Smith during the 1959 World Series? How about Jimmy Piersall firing baseballs at Bill Veeck's exploding scoreboard?

This was the place of Shoeless Joe Jackson and the Black Sox. Ed Walsh and Ed Cicotte pitched there, Luis Aparicio and Nellie Fox cavorted around second base. It was the home of Al Simmons and Al Lopez and Dick Allen and Luke Appling and oh, so many names from the past.

It was where the first All-Star Game was held (1933) and where the greatest gathering of baseball old-timers ever congregated (1983), exactly fifty years later to the day. It was where Joe Louis defeated James J. Braddock and where a Chicago disc jockey started a riot by burning disco records.

The football Cardinals played there, Satchel Paige pitched there, and I once hit a home run into the upper deck there with a corked bat.

Oops.

I didn't know it was corked. Honest I didn't. Gene Bossard was the head groundskeeper (his son, Roger, now has the job) and one day, when I was in another of my frequent slumps, he comes to me and says, "I've got something to help your hitting."

So I'm thinking, "Great, here's another amateur who's going to tell me how to swing the bat." But I said, "Okay, how?" and he said, "Give me three or four of your bats."

"Why?"

"Just give them to me and don't ask so many questions. I'm going to cast a spell on them."

So I gave him the bats and three days later, when they came back, the ball was just jumping off them in batting practice. I remember the bat model I used was a K55, back in 1971.

Anyhow, I finally got into a game and jerked a fastball off Mel Stottlemyre of the Yankees onto the upper deck runway. It was the start of a hot streak for me but it wasn't until the following week that I discovered Bossard had corked my bats.

That's when I took all of my bats to him but he refused to cork any more.

"I can't do that," he said. "I just wanted to help you get out of a slump. But I can't do any more because I don't want to get you into trouble."

Trouble? The following season with the White Sox I hit .188 and ended up back in the minor leagues. That was trouble but somehow I survived, returned to the majors, and lasted another thirteen years without corked bats.

How do you cork a bat? You drill out the barrel end, down about twelve to fourteen inches, and fill it with whatever substance you wish—cork, rubber from one of those Super Balls, whatever— then plug it and glue back the end of the bat and sand it down to cover the evidence. A smart umpire, however, can usually spot what has happened by the discoloration on the bat, which has been tempered by flame.

Catchers are always checking bats, so the hitters try to cover any tampering with pine tar or scuff the bat in the dirt so it looks like just another old bat.

The best way to spot a corked bat, of course, is by the hitter. If a guy without power suddenly starts popping the ball against the walls, you know he's been doing something different. Lifting weights? Okay, maybe. But that's why everybody started checking the bats of Howard Johnson of the Mets. He was a guy who lifted weights and changed his batting style, but you can understand why everybody got suspicious. Here's a switch-hitter who had home run production of 12, 11, and 10 for three seasons before 1987. Then he hit 36 (that's a plus-26 jump), came back in 1988 with 24, and added another 36 in 1989.

It all sounds perfectly explainable to me. Somebody probably just cast a spell on HoJo's bats.

Some of the Yankees put nails in their bats. That's a naughty-naughty but they do it, anyhow.

Why? Well, if a player finds a bat he really likes he wants to keep it. Some guys bone them, some sand them, some, like Mel Hall, will put pine tar all the way up to the label. Others will break the bat, literally crack it, then put nails in it and pine tar or tape over the little nails.

Whenever a hitter finds a bat with which he feels comfortable, he'll do almost anything to keep it. This is the primary tool of his trade. That's why I could never understand players who put big gouges in their bats. I might have gouged the handle of a bat to get a better grip, but never the barrel where I strike the ball. I've seen some hitters with bats that look like they've been beaten by a hammer. Then the guy will take the barrel end of the bat and hit his cleats to knock out the dirt. I don't understand it.

Will they ever use aluminum bats in the major leagues? I hope not, because somebody would get killed. But there is a company trying to market a bat that supposedly combines the best characteristics of aluminum and wood, a bat with a chemical coating poured on top of the aluminum, but which still gives the sound of a wooden bat cracking. It never breaks and the only way you cut it in half is with a hacksaw.

I don't think Gene Bossard would like it.

I can understand why Tony Gwynn of the Padres was so upset after his glove was stolen at last year's All-Star Game at Anaheim Stadium. In the first place, there were no fans on the field and the security was terrible, so the glove was probably stolen by someone with a media or VIP pass, although I've never known a sportswriter to steal equipment. Maybe a quotation or a drink, but never a bat or glove.

Players, however, do develop special feelings toward their gloves. A player takes personal pride in choosing the style he wishes and once he gets it, he nurtures it. He breaks it in, cares for it, and oils it. Some guys even put shaving cream or tobacco juice on their gloves. Everybody has his own method of breaking in a glove, and may have a couple on standby.

President George Bush still has the first baseman's mitt ("my McQuinn Trapper") he used for three years at Yale in 1946, '47, and '48, when he was captain. During one interview last summer, he even reached into a drawer at the Oval Office and produced it for reporters.

I once used a glove for ten years and people would laugh at me. I had it restrung three times and once had to put new leather on the pocket. The people from Rawlings were so embarrassed they tried to take their name off it. But it was my glove and I liked it and that was that. If you ever played baseball, no matter at what level, you probably understand. Did you keep your favorite glove? Maybe it's stuck in a closet somewhere or maybe in a cardboard box in the garage, but I'll bet you've still got it. My coauthor, Rick Talley— once a clumsy third baseman who couldn't hit the curveball—still has his original Bill Doak fielder's glove (Rawlings) from forty years ago. Sometimes I think he even types with it.

How important is the "right" glove to a major leaguer, or for that matter, to any baseball player? After right fielder Darryl Strawberry made a sensational, high-leaping (and surprising) catch to rob Nelson Santovenia of the Expos, Mets coach Bill Robinson gave a simple explanation for Darryl's new defensive prowess: "I got him to use a bigger glove. I was tired of seeing balls bounce off the heel."

Ozzie Guillen of the White Sox is one of several major leaguers who coats his natural tan glove with shoe polish to protect the leather. Nobody, though, is *obsessed* with fielders' gloves like Tim Flannery of the Padres. His teammates are fearful of leaving their gloves lying near him on the bench. Not that Timmy would *steal*, but he might find some other way to lay claim. That's why they call him the Great Glove Shark, or as teammate Randy Ready adds: "He's more like a glove snake."

Flannery, who once used a favorite glove for six seasons before it finally fell apart, at last count had at least four—one for practice, a flappy one for hot days, a newer one he has been breaking in, and his game-day glove, which he got one year ago from Angels manager Doug Rader. Flannery covets other men's gloves.

"If your glove feels good to Tim," said teammate Garry Templeton last summer, "he'll find a way to get it."

"I've probably had my hand up thirty gloves over the past few years," admitted Flannery, "but I just keep dealing [trading with others] until I find one I like." Tim even has one glove with the inscription "Anti-Greenhouse Glove" scrawled on the side.

"Because of the greenhouse effect, they've had to give cows steroids," explains Flannery. "That's why the leather on the old gloves is better than the leather on the new ones."

Next thing you know Timmy will also have a "Protect the Rain Forests" glove. Oh, he does?

Many players treat batting gloves with the same reverence. They'll wash the pine tar out of their batting gloves with soap and water and put the gloves in a warm place to dry. Mike Schmidt used to keep his in zip-lock cellophane bags so they wouldn't dry out and harden after use. I always made sure I had four or five pair for hitting, but I never hit in the game with the same batting gloves I used in practice. I had a rotating breaking-in system. Same thing with shoes. Players usually have three or four pair ready for use, others have to change every two or three weeks because of blisters. Today's shoes are so much lighter they don't need the same breaking-in process as the old kangaroo leather ones did.

Smallest shoes in the game? Giants outfielder Brett Butler wears size seven. Joe Morgan wore six and a half. Butler's are so small that he can't even give them away to Little Leaguers. His teammates take the discards home for the toddlers.

Most expensive? Where there's money involved, there's Lasorda again. A Nashville-based shoe company presented Lasorda last season with a pair of handmade, Dodger-blue, anaconda-print dress cleats valued at two thousand dollars, paid for by a fellow Italian and master shoemaker at the company.

I didn't get to see Tommy much during the season so I don't know how many times he wore his blue snakeskins. I hope he didn't spill any diet milkshakes on them.

Ballplayers also get attached to their numbers. When new pitcher Frank Viola reported to the Mets (and became their highest-paid player) during the 1989 season, he found that the number (16) he had worn with the Minnesota Twins was already taken by another pitcher with some ability, Dwight Gooden. Said the good Doctor: "I don't care how much money he makes. He can have my locker. I'll take him to all the best restaurants and show him New York City. He can even have my wife. But he can't have my number. No way."

When Rickey Henderson reported to the Oakland Athletics, he requested number 24, the same number he had worn with the Yankees. Ron Hassey, however, had number 24 and suggested he would part with it only for a price.

So they negotiated and after a few weeks of clubhouse and team bus haggling, this was the deal: Henderson got number 24 and Hassey got twenty-five hundred dollars' worth of equipment from a stereo and appliance company with which Henderson had an endorsement contract. Hassey then took number 27.

Then there was Roger McDowell, the pitcher who left the Mets, joined the Phillies, and requested uniform number 13, which nobody else wanted. He figured it might change his luck.

There was a time, of course, when numbers on the backs of players were more significant. Then ballclubs started printing names on the backs—which I like because it makes sense—and fans identified less with numbers, unless the name was misspelled. That happens. Paul O'Neill of the Reds had four hits in a game last year but later found his name on his jersey was spelled O'Neil. He didn't know whether to complain or change his name.

Nowadays teams are always tinkering with uniform styles and color combinations. Although a few clubs have stuck with tradition (I've been a sucker for pinstripes since Mickey Mantle was my hero), others have gone flashy. Some make their players look like they just won the consolation bracket of a slow-pitch softball tournament. All they need on the uniform back is a bowling lane sponsor.

When Toronto changed from powder-blue to gray for road uniforms last season, the players were happy.

"Anything would look better than what we had," said Lloyd Moseby. "At least now we look like baseball players."

"The only thing I don't like," said teammate Jimmy Key, "is that they show off a good body. The problem is that they show off a bad body, too."

Then there was manager Jimy Williams, who said, when asked what he liked about the new uniforms: "I've got one."

But they made him turn it in when he was fired.

Like pets sometimes match their owners (or is it the other way around?), some teams and their uniforms go together. For example, when the Phillies were outfitted last Saint Patrick's Day in green, manager Nick Leyva said: "We're playing like a circus so we might as well dress like it."

Sports columnist Mike Downey of the *Los Angeles Times* took one look at the White Sox and wrote: "What is that thing on the caps? If you step on it, will you kill it?"

Baltimore Orioles' caps became hot souvenir items after switching from the old cartoonlike Oriole to an ornithologically correct bird. The winning probably didn't hurt, either. Some people do react strongly to caps. When the expansion Montreal Expos unveiled their spiffy red-white-and-blue caps twenty-one years ago, Ron Swoboda of the Mets asked: "Where are their propellers?"

Personally, I've always thought the Expos hit the jackpot with their bright colors. But the Orioles' colors make me think more of Halloween than baseball and the Cincinnati Reds have the worst stockings in sports. I always liked the Phillies' powder-blue road uniforms and pinstripes at home, but I can do without the Giants or Pirates color combinations. On the other hand, I like the Athletics. Their former owner, Charlie Finley, was an innovator. He even suggested orange baseballs for night games and I liked the idea.

The all-time worst uniform was Chicago's when the White Sox

were forced for a few games to wear short pants. The Padres were bad, too, when they wore defecation-brown. Steve Garvey got that changed to a stylish pinstripe after he left the Dodgers to go south.

The Mets wear my favorite color, blue, and I love that Cardinal on St. Louis caps because it always reminds me of Stan Musial. Detroit is traditional and so is Boston. In fact, the Red Sox would look great in pinstripes but maybe it would remind them too much of their hated Yankee rivals.

Atlanta? They should raze the stadium, disband the team, and move to Florida. Dodger uniforms are classy, especially that blue cap with LA on it.

Of course, it's all subjective. But if I were to design a team uniform, it would be red-white-and-blue, with pinstripes, and shoes matching the predominate uniform color. My team logo would be a Smiley Face.

And while designing, I'd like to outfit the umpires in formal wear, either all-white or tuxedo-black. It might give them more of an air of respectability and besides, most of them don't move fast enough anymore to muss up the creases, anyhow.

I wore enough different uniforms over twenty seasons to create quite a montage but in the final analysis, how you "look" is far less important than how you perform, even in this era of market hype.

As former outfielder Curt Flood said while dressing for an old-timers' game:

"The funny thing about these uniforms is that you hang them in the closet and each year they keep getting smaller and smaller."

I'll jog to that.

7

Ballplayers Don't Get Old—They Just Lose Their Marbles

While shaving in the Yankee Stadium clubhouse following an old-timers' game last season, I found myself standing next to Joe DiMaggio, who was combing his hair. Just then Mickey Mantle walked up to my other side and I said, "Hi, Mick."

He looked right past me and said to DiMaggio: "I'm really upset with you."

All of a sudden I get goose pimples. Here I am standing at the bathroom mirror between two of the greatest center fielders of all time and somebody is upset? And me with a razor in my hand instead of a tape-recorder?

"Hey, what's the problem?" I said, playing the role of peacemaker. After all, center field was my position, too.

"I'm really upset," said Mantle, again. "You made me look bad, Joe, in front of all those people."

"What are you talking about?" said DiMaggio.

"Well, goddamnit, Joe," said Mantle, "when they announced your name you ran out there raising your hands like a little kid.

"Then they announced my name and with my knees I could barely walk. You really made me look bad running out there like that."

DiMaggio, seventy-four, smiled. Then fifty-seven-year-old

Mantle started laughing and I returned the razor to my forty-three-year-old face with a steady hand.

The whole world knows it's hell to get old and certainly old ballplayers don't hold any exclusive bitching rights. But when your *very being* has been running, throwing, catching, and hitting, for as long as you can remember, age becomes a relentless enemy. As pitcher Jerry Reuss said: "If I was thirty-eight and working for IBM, I would be considered a junior executive. If I was a doctor, a lot of patients would say, 'Do you have someone with more experience?' But when you're a ballplayer, they look at you like you should be retired."

After Reuss, now forty, was traded in mid-August 1989, from the White Sox to the Brewers, he joined his new team in Cleveland and was sitting alone in a corner of the visiting clubhouse, still in his street clothes, when special assignments scout Sam Suplizio entered.

"Is there a locker where I can put some stuff?" asked Suplizio.

"I don't know," said Reuss.

"What do you mean you don't know? You're the clubhouse man, aren't you?"

"Geez, Sam," yelled Reuss, "don't you recognize me? You scouted me when I came up with St. Louis!"

When the team was packing to head home after the final game in Cleveland, Brewer pitching coach Chuck Hartenstein pointed to Reuss and reminded Suplizio, "Sam, don't forget to tip the clubbie." And from that day, Reuss was known as "Clubbie" to his new buddies in Milwaukee. Jerry, who can make himself look like an albino Scrooge when he hasn't shaved, had played with eight major league teams by the end of 1989, so someday he should receive plenty of invitations to old-timers' games. He tells this one on himself: He was standing in the White Sox outfield with Carlton Fisk, just shagging fly balls and making observations on the state of the nation, when he casually tossed a ball toward the infield, which accidentally struck rookie pitcher Adam Peterson in the leg.

"You asshole," shouted Peterson.

"Can you believe that?" Fisk chided Reuss. "A rookie calling you an asshole? Unbelievable. I guess that just shows how times have changed.''

"You're right," said Reuss. "It's just not right."

"Hey, Patterson," he shouted toward the infield. "You calling *me* an asshole?"

"You got it," came the reply.

"Keeeerist," yells Reuss, "I've got more years in the big leagues than you've been alive. Give me a little respect, will you? How can you call me an asshole? Don't I deserve better than that for being around?"

"All right," Peterson shouted back. *"Mister Asshole."*

Actually, any rookie who takes on Reuss is just asking to get shaving cream in his telephone ear. That man can mess with you. When pitcher Shawn Hillegas, for example, went from the Dodgers to the White Sox he decided to change his uniform number from 45 to 57. Next thing you know there was a press release written on official White Sox stationary circulating in the locker room, announcing that Hillegas had signed a lucrative deal to become a spokesman for Heinz 57 catsup.

"We decided on Shawn being the right guy when we saw him put Heinz 57 on a pizza in Sarasota, Florida," the fake release quoted a Heinz official as saying. "In addition, opposing hitters who do not use our product have hit just .076 against him." Also, as part of the mock agreement, Hillegas was to drive a new car shaped like a king-sized bottle of Heinz 57 catsup.

Was Reuss responsible? He never admitted anything but he sure laughed a lot. You might say he ate it up.

Pitcher Tommy John, when asked by a Yankee teammate early last season what movie he was watching in his Minneapolis hotel room, said: "The movie of my life story, George Burns in *18 Again.*"

Finally, though, at age forty-six, T.J. retired his bionic left arm during his twenty-seventh major league season, and what a remarkable career he enjoyed.

When some well-meaning people decided to honor T.J. at a

luncheon in Fort Lauderdale, Florida, he approached the microphone wearing an old man's white wig, drawing a yuk-yuk from the audience as he demonstrated he wasn't insecure about his "senior citizen" image. But when he was invited to appear on the David Letterman television show, the producer told Tommy to leave the wig behind.

"Only David does the funny stuff," T.J. was told, and I guess that tells us even more about insecurity.

Old ballplayers die hard. Few will admit when it is time to step aside. Besides, where else can they make that kind of money? Therefore, every spring, there are "comebacks" to watch—usually released veterans invited to training camp as nonroster players.

Such was the situation for Pete Vuckovich of the Brewers, who retired after 1986 with arm problems but tried again in the spring of 1987 to "pitch his way onto the club."

His comeback was stalled, however, because he developed a rectal cyst and couldn't get to the mound. Finally, when the pain wouldn't go away, Vuke was forced to retire.

"A lot of people always thought I was a pain in the ass," said Vuckovich, "but I never thought that's what would end my career."

Some of my buddies began their own "comebacks" when they plunged into the Seniors League last winter in Florida.

I took a pass.

Not that I'm saying the Senior Professional Baseball Association was a bad idea. Hey, if I stumble over my microphone enough times I may decide to make a baseball comeback, too. In the meantime, I'm wholeheartedly behind the Seniors League only if they have enough aspirin, splints, and tape. It makes me hurt just to think about it.

But it's got to be a giggle for the participants and the fans. As one of my ex-managers, Dick Williams, said when he signed to manage the Seniors team in West Palm Beach, Florida: "It's going to be a fun league. We won't have any prima donnas making millions and millions of dollars."

With Earl Weaver, Gates Brown, and others joining Williams in the managerial ranks, and with such ex-stars as Steve Yeager, Vida Blue, Al Hrabosky, Graig Nettles, Mark Fidrych, and Tug McGraw on the playing field, the three-month, seventy-two-game league got off to a good start. Curt Flood was serving as commissioner and the maximum salary was to be fifteen thousand dollars a month.

My concern: These guys have been competitive all their lives and just because you're thirty-five or older, you don't quit trying. I'm worried about guys getting hurt. I told them they should take on 600 players rather 160, just to have enough healthy players to last the season.

This suggestion, too: Videotape the games and replay them on your VCRs at fast forward.

Maybe one of the Seniors League's esteemed managers, Bill (Spaceman) Lee, pegged it right when he called the players' new opportunity "a denial of death."

But how do you deny injury?

There is no question, however, that nostalgia sells. Old-timers' games and fantasy camps have never been more popular, so why not a Seniors League? If it works for golf and tennis it can work for baseball. If the fans want it and the players want it, who else matters?

As former utility man Kurt Bevacqua said after participating in a fantasy camp in San Diego: "I experienced a fantasy of my own. I got to play an entire game."

Some classic lines also came from those who participated last summer in the Equitable Old Timers Series.

Joe Garagiola, for example, saw Joe Pepitone at the Yankees game and said:

"You're the only old-timer I've seen whose hair gets thicker as the years go by."

When eighty-three-year-old Doc Cramer was asked to go onto the field for a team photo in Boston, he said:

"I'd like to go out there, but I don't think I can get back."

Hall-of-Fame shortstop Lou Boudreau, on his fielding range:

"I can't go to my left. I can't go to my right. Heck, I'm fortunate to be able to go straight ahead now."

On-field announcer Nick Nickson in Los Angeles told fans while the no-walks rule was in use: "That was Ron Cey hitting a seven–zero pitch into left field."

And in Kansas City, announcer Danny Trease said:

"Here's Ed Baily, who struck out twice his first time up."

Perhaps Carl Erskine, talking about the weekend of activities at an old-timers' game, said it best:

"I like the before and after—it's the 'during' that's scary."

When they held a celebrity softball game at Wrigley Field last summer, Jim Piersall won the "hustle" award. In addition to legging out an infield hit and making a nice catch of a line drive to center field, Piersall, who has had both quadruple- and triple-bypass heart surgery, pushed Mike Keenan out of the way while the Blackhawk (hockey) coach was pursuing one of Jimmy's pop flies.

Ron Santo also played in the game but claimed he had trouble on pop flies because "I couldn't get used to the lights." And when speedskater Bonnie Blair successfully stabbed a line drive off the bat of Don Kessinger, a sexist teammate chirped: "When girls start getting us out, we're in trouble."

I've got news for him. We get deeper into trouble at every birthday. When Houston Astro players Greg Gross, thirty-six, and Larry Andersen, thirty-six, began rooming together last season while Gross was looking for his own place to live, teammate Jim Deshaies said: "If you get Forschie (Bob Forsch, thirty-nine) to move in, it'll be the male version of the Golden Girls."

Let's talk about Andersen.

I call Andersen the Paradox Man and he attributes his warped personality to nineteen years of being traded, loaned, disabled, outrighted, and released—not to mention the thousands of hours spent staring at the clouds from his seat in the bullpen.

Paradoxes? Andersen concocts, collects, nurtures, and disseminates such jewels as: "If Americans throw rice at weddings, do Chinese throw hot dogs?"

"Why is it always raining cats and dogs? Why doesn't it ever rain yaks and wildebeests?"

"How do you explain counterclockwise to a person with a digital watch?"

"How can you tell when you're running out of invisible ink?"

"Why does sour cream have an expiration date?"

"What do they call a coffee break at the Lipton Tea Company?"

"Was Robin Hood's mother known as Mother Hood?"

Are you starting to get the message? And if you are, please relay it to me.

"We have a lot of dead time out there [in the bullpen] and I think up things to keep from becoming a basket case," explains Andersen.

He also pitches quite well—fastball, cut fastball, slider, and certainly has the right "mental attitude" to succeed with middle-inning relief and clubhouse comic relief. He carries a rubber cockroach and conehead mask on road trips and once, when with the Phillies, had forty thousand Larry Andersen masks made up and handed out to fans at Veterans Stadium.

"For the next year or so I was accused of holding up convenience stores all over Philly," said Andersen.

"I'd have to say Larry Andersen is the funniest player in the game today," advised Astro teammate Deshaies. "It's a challenge just to sit next to him every day."

Andersen, for example, also wants to know:

"What did pioneer mothers do about ring-around-the-collar and static cling?"

"What do they package Styrofoam in?"

"Why is a ball fair when it hits the foul pole?"

Larry also sends out messages with his t-shirts. He has one that reads "Roses are Red, Violets are Blue, I'm a Schizophrenic and so am I." Another says "I can't tell if I'm in a groove or a rut," and one reads "All I want is less to do, more time to do it in, and to get paid more for not getting it done."

One of his more mind-boggling bullpen exercises was to determine how a fly could land on the ceiling upside down.

Think about it. Larry did.

"I mean, does it flip over at the last instant?" asked Andersen to anyone who would listen. "Or was it flying upside down all the time?"

"Larry is a left-hander in a right-hander's body," said teammate Jim Pankovits.

"But why do you park on a driveway and drive on a parkway?" asks Andersen.

"Why is it called a shipment if you send it by car and cargo if you send it by ship?"

"Why do they call it freezer burn?"

Andersen was persistent in his search for truth: "I read where a guy was in a dark room and shined a light on the ceiling. He had a camera set up, and he waited for a fly to be attracted by the light. Well, a fly flew into the room and its two front feet touched the ceiling while the rest of him flipped over, kind of like a somersault."

Oh.

"Is it just coincidence that Lincoln and Washington were both born on holidays?" asks Larry.

He also offers some rules by which to live, such as: "If your parents didn't have any children, chances are you won't, either."

"Be alert. The world needs more lerts."

"Money can't buy poverty."

"If at first you don't succeed, failing may be your thing."

And remember, says Larry: "Today may be the first day of the rest of your life, unless you're on the other side of the international dateline in which case yesterday was the first day of the rest of your life."

Andersen is also Houston's team prankster (dollar-bill-on-a-string and so forth), but believe it or not, he does have a serious side.

"I won't sign an autograph for a kid," says Andersen, "unless he says 'please.' "

Okay, I'll say "please."

Please, Larry Andersen, don't change. Baseball needs more like you.

*   *   *

Bert Blyleven is a Crazy of a different ilk.

That's why his California Angels teammates call him The Human Torch. Hotfoots? That's putting it mildly. As announcer Joe Torre said one night on an Angels telecast: "If you say something wrong to Blyleven he's liable to burn your uniform."

Blyleven, the pitcher, also burned up the American League again in 1989 and if there was one person more responsible than any other for the Angels' success, apart from manager Doug Rader, it was Blyleven.

On and off the field.

On a team plane ride to Milwaukee he wore a monster mask and at Boston's Logan International Airport he befriended a live lobster, named it Skippy, plopped it on his shoulder, and appointed it team mascot.

Also in staid Boston, he arrived at Fenway Park early, wearing the same mask and a three-piece suit, and rearranged information on the field-level scoreboard.

He cordoned off the area around rookie Jim Abbott's locker—fashioned a pathway of towels, actually—to give the rookie the "red carpet treatment" after his first major league shutout.

He also torched Abbott's shoes and charred the laces of every other pitcher on the staff.

In truth, Blyleven defrosted the Angels' clubhouse—previously known as one of the coldest in baseball—in more ways than one.

"There are some special people who play this game," said Rader, "and his timing, knowing when to do things, makes Bert one of them. The intangible aspects of Bert Blyleven are some of the greatest attributes that one person could possess."

Even when the pressure was the greatest, with the Angels trailing Oakland by just a few games with less than two weeks left to play, Blyleven was terrorizing his own bench.

"I picked my spots," said Blyleven, "but once we were up in any game by four or five runs, nobody was safe. Hey, when I came here this club was real quiet. There were guys who wouldn't even say 'Good morning' to you. I prefer the atmosphere to be more relaxed."

On the mound, his excellence thrust him to fourth position among baseball's all-time strikeout leaders (3,562), behind only Nolan Ryan (5,076), Steve Carlton (4,131), and Tom Seaver (3,640). But when somebody suggested that Bert should be honored as Comeback Player of the Year, he replied: "Why? I didn't go anywhere."

It was Blyleven, wearing a mop for a wig and a judge's robe, who conducted Kangaroo Court in the Angels' clubhouse. And it was the same pyromaniacal Dutchman, aided by Chili Davis, who inserted a tiny explosive charge into one of Rader's cigarettes.

When the Angels held a promotion that promised vacations for selected fans, Blyleven and Wally Joyner showed up with suitcases, joined the fans' procession, and paraded onto the field.

Isn't that a little silly for a native-born Hollander approaching his thirty-ninth birthday?

"I've embarrassed myself too many times on the field to worry about embarrassing myself elsewhere," said Blyleven. "I'll bet we made somebody smile and if they want to come to the ballpark and laugh at me, that's fine."

Blyleven calculates that during his twenty-year major league career he has taken at least one thousand airplane flights and has spent more than two thousand nights in hotel rooms.

"I guess all of it contributes to your outlook on what you do for a living," said Blyleven. "But I don't know what else I'd rather be doing than playing baseball."

Bert's behavior in Anaheim was infectious. One day the TV cameras caught a classic shot of catcher Bill Schroeder under the Angels bench, literally crawling on his belly from one end of the dugout to the other, trying to "light up" Rader's foot. He failed only because a home run brought the manager to his feet just before Schroeder accomplished his mission.

Blyleven probably wouldn't have failed. As baseball writer Peter Schmuck wrote: "In the land of exploding cigarettes and flammable shoelaces, Bert Blyleven is king and no one is safe."

Blyleven proved it one day in the Seattle Kingdome when he set

Sometimes the game can be a formal affair, but in baseball you either win or lose—no "ties" allowed. (*Author's collection*)

If you need someone to hit in a pinch, you can always call Manny Mota or me. (*Author's collection*)

"That's right, one with mushroom, one with anchovies, and two with extra cheese for Tommy." (*Author's collection*)

New protective rain gear? (*Author's collection*)

When I played, some people accused me of having a big head. And I have the glasses to prove it. (*Author's collection*)

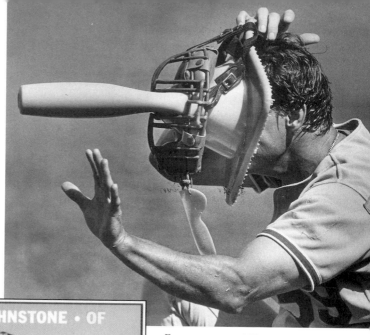

Former teammate Mike Scioscia used to have problems with his nose being broken while he played. That is, until I invented this specially designed catcher's mask for him. (*Patrick Downs, L.A. Times*)

"Don't worry Mike, the Dodgers will never trade you." (*Author's collection*)

JAY JOHNSTONE • OF

ANGELS

Baseball card collectors tell me that this is the one card that is worth less now than when it was first issued. (*Author's collection*)

Most baseball fans don't think Mitch
Williams's bubble has burst. (*Stephen Green*)

Don't forget I played for the Cubs too!
(*Author's collection*)

A couple of candid shots of the Jaybird with two unidentified fans. (*Author's collection*)

When not performing behind the mike, I like to relax by modeling the latest swimwear. (*Author's collection*)

My daughter (Mary Jayne Sarah, on the phone) may be a bit young to be directing radiocasts, but hey, what can I say? She's good. (*Author's collection*)

Most fans don't know that I spent the off-season staying in shape by conducting an air raid in Panama. (*Author's collection*)

Here I am with Norm Crosby. You know, Bing's brother. (*Author's collection*)

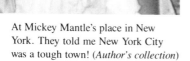

At Mickey Mantle's place in New York. They told me New York City was a tough town! (*Author's collection*)

"So I said to Luis, I don't know, she looks nineteen to me." (*Author's collection*)

afire a pair of Nikes being worn by Mariners manager Jim Lefebvre.

"I never do anything on the days I pitch," said Blyleven, "and I don't get pitchers on the days they pitch. But everyone else is within the limits of lightability."

Last September in Chicago, however, Bert's teammates got some measure of revenge by handcuffing him to a pole in the visiting Comiskey Park dugout while Bert was charting pitches. Blyleven's reaction:

"I screamed. This team is getting kinky."

Another who was able to keep his world in perspective during the pressure-filled days of last September was Joe Magrane, six-five, 230-pound left-handed pitcher with the St. Louis Cardinals. I emphasize *left-handed* because some, particularly manager Whitey Herzog, believe that says it all about Magrane. Joe, articulate and never at a loss for words, disagrees: "Baseball has such a stuffed-shirt mentality that everyone has to have some sort of label," said Magrane in a national magazine interview. "Like, here's your gung-ho guys, here's your flakes, here's your guys who are so stupid it would probably take them an hour and a half to watch *60 Minutes*. Even back in the thirties and forties, everybody had a nickname, like Gabby Hartnett and Dizzy Dean. We, as a society, have created baseball players as being characters."

Hold it. Does that mean that we, as a society, created Joe Magrane? I'm not sure if I'm willing to shoulder that burden.

It was Magrane who said about Cincinnati owner Marge Schott and her faithful dog, Schottzie: "I've heard of the phenomenon of the master taking on the appearance of the dog. But I never knew it went as far as the master taking on the thinking process."

It was Magrane who said, when asked if he would like to play in San Diego: "Naw, I couldn't take it. The place is just too pleasant. I don't feel competitive out there. The weather's so beautiful, the park's so perfect, I think my brain would get a suntan."

It was Magrane who said: "I've pitched in two foreign countries, Canada and Johnston City, Tennessee."

And it was Magrane who described his own manager, Herzog, as "Abraham Lincoln with Dick Clark's agent—very honest and straightforward while being very well-promoted for it."

Magrane can talk. But, as Muhammad Ali once phrased it, "It ain't braggin' if you can do it," and Joe Magrane can do it on the pitching mound. After becoming the National League's ERA leader (2.18) despite a losing record of 5–9 in 1988, erudite Joe came back in 1989 with a record of 18–9 and 2.91 ERA.

Away from the mound, bachelor Joe insists he has been miscast as a flake. After all, he says, being a ballplayer these days isn't that easy. Citing all the publicity from the Wade Boggs–Margo Adams stories, he states: "Nowadays you tell a girl you're a ballplayer and you can see her knuckles whitening around her purse as she gets ready to swing at you."

Joe says he wants to learn to fly because with roster cutbacks the Cardinals may someday need him to pilot the team jet; he orders Killian's Red whenever Michelob Dry isn't available on draft; and he's got his own radio spot on a St. Louis radio station.

Magrane has also labeled spring training "a drag" and suggests that each player should mimeograph a piece of paper with their favorite baseball clichés and just distribute them to every reporter.

His biggest challenge as a major leaguer?

"To keep everything in a state of normalcy, you must have something to bitch about. A ballplayer must have something to complain about, whether it's the lack of hot water in the hotel or the poor bed or the long bus ride . . . I think everybody has to maintain one gripe consistently and keep it going throughout the day."

Joe is on target. It has been my experience that if a ballplayer can't find something to bitch about he'll bitch about not having something to bitch about. Do I make myself clear?

It was quotable Joe who also said, on the possibility of keeping airplanes from flying over Shea Stadium during Mets games: "At least it would keep Keith Hernandez from stepping out of the batter's box. It's like he has this phobia that some plane is doing an emergency landing on the back of his head."

And after Joe beat the Dodgers last July Fourth, even though they pounded the ball, he said: "They hit a lot of rockets but fortunately there was no red glare."

Magrane wore a red glare on his face, however, after teammates victimized him in one of baseball's best practical jokes late during the 1988 season.

I call it the Great *GQ* Scam and it tells you something about the players of today.

Magrane, you see, is one of the growing cadre of major leaguers who enjoys, and can afford, wearing fashionable clothes. That's what made him a perfect target.

It started during a Cardinal road trip to Atlanta when Joe got a phone call from someone in New York claiming to represent *Gentleman's Quarterly (GQ)* magazine. The caller said he was aware that Magrane was a fashionable dresser and could the magazine please set up a photo session with Joe and a female model? And would Joe please bring some fall suits to Busch Stadium for the fashion shoot when the team returned to St. Louis?

Sure, said Joe, who trekked to Busch Stadium in his tailored autumn best, even though it was 110 degrees. The female model didn't make it and neither did *GQ* but Joe ended up modeling his clothes for one photographer from the *Redbird Review*, the team's house newspaper.

Next day, during batting practice, Magrane received a telegram from New York: *GQ* had decided not to run the fashion layout because his pitching record was so poor. Naturally, Joe was suspicious, but after all, he'd already phoned his mother in Kentucky to tell her he would be in *GQ*.

"Everybody on the team seemed just a little too interested in the telegram," said Magrane.

One day later, Joe got another telegram in the clubhouse which read: "ROSES ARE RED, VIOLETS ARE BLUE, YOU'VE BEEN HAD BY YOUR TEAMMATES. THERE IS NO GQ."

"I appreciated the planning, the architecture of it if not the sentiment," said Magrane, later, about the joke, which had been hatched and executed by teammates Tom Brunansky and Ozzie Smith. "It had all the aspects of the Kennedy and Lincoln conspiracies, and was, in fact, a character assassination. It certainly beat the usual: hot stuff in the jock strap, shaving cream in the telephone receiver."

Joe made those comments, incidentally, in the real *GQ* magazine, which had heard about the prank and decided to capitalize on it. Indeed, Magrane's laugh came last and was the best as he modeled clothes and talked about his fashion tastes for the popular magazine. And, at the end of the *GQ* interview, editors ran this note:

> *"Well, Smith and Brunansky, on tobacco you'll chew.*
> *Caps off to Joe M., there really is a* GQ.

Magrane isn't the only baseball player to find himself modeling men's clothing. I picked up a *USA Today* newspaper one day and found a full-color fashion spread featuring San Francisco Giants players Will Clark ("I have thirty-five pairs of snakeskin boots"), Atlee Hammaker ("I have thirty pairs of running shoes"), Donell Nixon ("I collect leather, whole outfits in every color, and Zodiac boots"), Brett Butler ("I have eight or ten fedoras"), and Mike Krukow ("When my world starts moving too fast, I put on my Levi's 501 jeans, a pair of Vans with no socks, and a white t-shirt from Penney's").

All were shown wearing outfits from I. Magnin and Wilkes Bashford, San Francisco clothing institutions.

That's when I decided, with some trepidation, to conduct my own fashion interview with outfielder Mel Hall of the Yankees, a cool man with the threads. Our conversation went something like this: "Mel, I notice you wear a lot of the latest fashions."

"Yeah, I like the leathers, the suede look, European style, you know? Fashionable."

"Why do you think baseball players have gotten so fashionable?"

"Mainly, I think the stature of the game has come from the

older days when all that mattered was to throw in a suit and tie. Nowadays I think there's a certain 'look' that should come with being a baseball player.''

"Has it come because players make more money?''

"Yeah, I think so. Guys can afford to keep up with the fashions and keep themselves looking good. After all, you never know who you might meet.''

"What about those big shoes you're wearing with yellow and blue stripes and no socks and Levi's?''

"Well, Jay, that's part of being fashionable. It's called 'summer attire.' You watch and next week some other players will be wearin' the same shoes with jeans and they'll be rollin', you know?''

"What about your hair style, Mel? Has it got a name?''

"I'm going these days with the 'MC Hammer' look. He's a black rap artist who talks about how times have changed, so I figured I oughta change with them, just a little 'S' curl with the stripes look on the side. I guarantee some other dudes will be following me by next week.''

"Tell me, Mr. Hall, do today's players dress for themselves or for others?''

"For themselves. My wardrobe, for example, is different because I like the weird stuff, the oversized things with bright colors. I'm not saying I'm the best dresser on the Yankees, but I am the most different. You take Steve Sax, now he's right out of *GQ*, with the double-breasted suits and the little hanky coming out of the pocket, the alligator shoes and the hair gelled, so he's traditional. Then you got a guy like Jesse [Barfield], who gets wild once in a while.''

"What about Dave LaPoint?''

"Is he a frigging advertisement for a sailboat, or what? He should be doing an orphan commercial because that's how he dresses; hair never combed, eyes in need of Visine, shirt hanging out in the back, shoes with holes in them. But the thing about LaPoint is that *in his own mind he always looks good*. That's important, Jay, because to be fashionable you must always *think* that you look good.''

Despite Mel Hall's disdain for the traditional, some clubs, including the Yankees, still have coat-and-tie dress codes for team flights. Some things don't change: sports jackets, ties, card games at thirty thousand feet, and rotten airline food, although some players nowadays insist on fruit plates and bring along their own pocket television sets. Rough life, eh?

I get a kick, too, out of the jewelry being worn. Some of the younger players love to weigh down their necks with what I call "Mr. T Starter Kits." The only time it seems to bother them is when they're trying to make a certain weight in spring training. Then they take off the gold and save five pounds. On the playing field, though, they just tuck it in.

One thing does surprise me. When I was coming into baseball, the big thing was a flashy car—Porsches, Corvettes, XKE's, whatever you could score. If you could drive into training camp with a hot car, maybe a Cobra or a Dodge 455, you were on top of the world. Nowadays, they don't seem to go after the flash and speed image. So what does today's player prefer? Mercedes.

Signs of the times, cont'd: Rickey Henderson of the Oakland A's wanted to buy a fur coat in Chicago but didn't want to trek to suburban Elmhurst, where the furrier was located. So how did Henderson handle this hardship? The furrier's president brought coats into the Comiskey Park visiting clubhouse, where Rickey purchased two, a mink and a fox.

Then there was the day when Andy Van Slyke of the Pirates would have been happy with just a clean shirt. Andy, in fact, claims what happened last July in New York was his tip-off that 1989 wasn't going to be his year: "Jeff Robinson and I were walking down the street," Van Slyke told baseball writer Bob Hertzel. "I'd just bought some coffee and it slipped through my hands, hit the pavement and splattered all over this expensive new white shirt I was wearing for the first time. So I bought a new shirt but at lunch I spilled iced tea on the new one. I'd stained two new shirts and I hadn't even gotten to the ballpark."

For the record: Van Slyke is beginning the second year of a three-year, $5.5 million contract, so if he doesn't want to buy any more shirts, he can afford to buy a bib.

8

Did We Forget the Umpires?

During mid-July of the 1989 season, back when the California Angels felt one game might be extremely crucial in the American League West pennant race, they lost one in Baltimore on a disputed home run call.

Indeed, the umpires' ruling was so controversial—an eleventh-inning, game-winning (11–9) home run by Mike Devereaux of the Orioles that appeared on television replays to be foul—that Angels manager Doug Rader was ejected twice, once after the ensuing argument and again the following day.

Our tale begins that next afternoon, Sunday, July 16, when Rader walked purposefully to home plate with the lineup card to greet the same umpiring crew of Jim McKean (crew chief), Ken Kaiser, Jim Joyce (the summer replacement who had made the controversial call from third base), and Larry Young.

Rooster had already made up his mind he was going to be kicked out before the first pitch. The only question: How far could he go? The conversation went like this:

Rader: "You guys [the umpires] been playin' the lottery? Which one is going to screw us today?"

That didn't work so he tried again, this time staring at the Oriole lineup card with mock concern.

"Hey, there are four names missing from the Baltimore lineup."

"Whattaya mean?"

"Your names," said Rader. "They don't have your names in the lineup."

That didn't do it, either, so Rader turned to Kaiser and said: "You were a little late coming out today, Ken. Where were you, back in the Orioles' locker room sitting on Frank Robinson's lap?"

That did it.

"It was just a matter of how long the umpires would let me stay out there," shrugged Rader, afterward. And if he could have been ejected again the same day, that would have happened, too, when he looked at the Baltimore videoboard and saw the controversial play being rerun with this caption: "Close analysis showed that the ball did hit the foul pole."

"What a joke," said Rader. "Enough to make you puke. Forty-seven thousand people left here [the night before] knowing the ball was foul and they're going to try to sell that bill of goods? Give me a bucket.

"But it figures, coming this close to Washington, D.C., where they try selling that kind of stuff all the time."

For the record: I saw the slow-motion TV replay, too, and unless that ball had a baby boomerang inside it and curved back around the pole, I don't see how the umpires could have called it fair.

But they did and that, folks, is baseball.

Walk onto any baseball field in the major leagues, talk to twenty players about umpires, and you'll get twenty diverse reactions. Then walk into the audience and you'll get twenty more opinions.

Jack Clark, for example, National League slugger (Cards, Giants, Padres) who had a cup of free-agent coffee with the Yankees in 1988, returned to the NL with this opinion of American League umpires: "Now I know why Billy Martin threw dirt on them. He tried to cover them up and make them disappear."

That's harsh stuff. I had my disagreements over the years with umps, too, but wish they would disappear under a pile of dirt? Nahhhh. Then who would we rag on?

In fact, after considerable research, I have come to the conclusion that umpires are almost human. Example: When Orioles shortstop Cal Ripken, Jr., played in his 1,198th consecutive game, he almost didn't. He was ejected in the first inning by umpire Drew Coble after a five-minute argument over a called strike.

"He can argue balls and strikes," said umpire Coble, afterward, "but he can't call me what he called me."

Then, however, the umpire showed frailty, indicating that he was *almost* human by saying: "That was the most miserable two-and-a-half hours of my life. It was like throwing God out of Sunday school."

When is the final out of a game not the final out because it's a home run? Have you ever seen a player ejected during an intentional walk? When do you get four outs in a half-inning, with the final score being changed by umpires after the game?

It all happened last summer.

• On May 4 in the Metrodome in Minnesota, the Milwaukee Brewers held a 3–1 lead with two outs, bottom of the ninth, when the Twins' Brian Harper sent a drive deep to center field. Brewers center-fielder Robin Yount raced back, leaped high above the fence, caught the ball just as he smacked into the barrier, and tumbled to the ground as second base umpire Durwood Merrill signaled out and Milwaukee players streamed onto the field to celebrate the victory.

There was only one problem. As Yount lay sprawled on the warning track, he looked into his glove.

The ball wasn't there.

When Yount's wrist hit the top of the wall, the ball had flipped out on the other side for a home run.

"I'm looking at all the guys on the field giving each other high fives," said Robin, "and I thought to myself 'Boy, are they going to be mad!' Then I saw Durwood walking toward me and I knew he was going to want to see the ball, but I didn't have one to show him."

By that time, right-fielder Rob Deer had wandered over to Yount's position.

"Nice catch," said Deer.

"I don't have the ball," whispered Yount.

"You're kidding."

"No, I'm not."

Finally, Yount showed Merrill his empty glove, presenting the umpire with the embarrassing duty of turning the final out into a home run. Harper, who had been standing at second base, now completed his home-run trot, cutting Milwaukee's lead to 3–2.

There was, however, a happy ending for the Brewers. After pinch-hitter Carmen Castillo doubled, Dan Gladden hit a liner back to pitcher Dan Plesac to end the game.

• This silly saga began during a May 31 game in Milwaukee when Terry Francona of the Brewers hit a sinking liner with a runner on second in the eighth inning against California. Left-fielder Dante Bichette of the Angels charged, *trapped the ball on a short hop,* and fired home. The throw was late and the Angels tried to get Francona advancing into second, but were late there, too.

But, wait! Third base umpire Ken Kaiser, not known on the AL circuit as one of your all-time hustlers, had ruled Francona out on Bichette's "catch." Needless to say, Francona and Kaiser had "words" and that set the stage for what happened six weeks later, July 9, when the two met again.

Early in a game at County Stadium, the Orioles' Jim Traber fouled a ball straight back which caught home plate ump Kaiser in the throat. The gasping Kaiser staggered into the Brewers' dugout for a drink of water only to hear Francona say: "See, if you didn't blow so many calls that kind of thing wouldn't happen to you."

That was not a smart thing to say.

"I knew it the second I said it," said Francona, "but it was too late."

Too late, indeed. In the seventh inning when Francona was

sent into the game as a pinch-hitter, the Orioles decided to intentionally walk him. That set up this dialogue between Francona and Kaiser:

"You oughta go to Las Vegas," said the home plate umpire.

Ball one.

"What do you mean?"

Ball two.

"Anybody that's this lucky oughta go to Las Vegas."

"Well, if you'd hustle your fat butt once in a while, you wouldn't blow so many calls."

Ball three.

"You're criticizing me for a play I don't even remember. I make fourteen thousand calls a year!"

"Yeah, and you blow every one of them."

Ball four. Francona never got out of the batter's box. Kaiser ejected him on the spot.

· Only the umpires knew the real score when the Yankees beat the Brewers, 5–1 (or was it 4–1?) one Saturday night last season. I knew I didn't know the score. They should have sent my scorecard to Cooperstown, or maybe the Smithsonian Institution.

What happened: A rare "fourth out" gave the Yankees an extra run but nobody but the umps knew what happened until after the game. So much for communication.

With one out in the eighth inning and New York ahead, 4–1, manager Dallas Green put on a squeeze play with Wayne Tolleson batting, Mike Pagliarulo on third base, and Bob Geren at first. Tolleson's bunt, however, was caught in the air by pitcher Jay Aldrich, who casually tossed to first baseman Greg Brock for an easy double play to end the inning.

Pagliarulo, meanwhile, realizing he had no chance to get back to third, kept running across home plate and toward the dugout to get his glove.

His run counted even though he never tagged up. Why? Umpiring crew chief Larry Barnett, citing Rule 7.10, explained: "Pagliarulo left early but the Brewers never appealed and he crossed home plate before the double play was completed. Milwaukee had to throw the ball to third base for what would have been the fourth out. Then, they could choose to make that one the final out and prevent the run from scoring. But Milwaukee didn't do it and it's not my job to tell them. They have to come up with it."

Barnett claimed he pointed to the plate and motioned to the press box that the run counted, but nobody saw him. I know I didn't. I'd never heard of that play and neither, in fact, had Barnett.

"I haven't seen the play in twenty-six years," admitted the umpire, "I'm just glad I recognized it when I did."

Can you imagine the screaming if the score had been 2–2 instead of 4–1?

Sometimes strict enforcement of the rules, combined with managerial tactics, can produce chaos. Example: In Minnesota, the Twins had two on, one out, in the sixth inning when Boston manager Joe Morgan called on lefty Joe Price to face left-handed hitter Jim Dwyer. So far, so good—except that Dwyer then argued a strike call and was ejected from the game. Now, with Twins manager Tom Kelly calling upon Carmen Castillo to replace Dwyer, Morgan countered with right-handed pitcher Mike Smithson.

But Kelly protested, citing Rule 3.05(b), which states that a pitcher must face one batter or his substitute.

So what to do? After a huddle rivaling NFL zebras trying to decipher an instant replay, the umpires booted Smithson off the mound and recalled Price from the dugout.

"I couldn't keep from laughing," said Price, and I can understand why.

Dave Henderson helped produce a run for the A's by standing still. How? After scoring himself, Henderson blocked the sight of catcher Bill Schroeder of the Angels, who was arguing with an umpire, and waved backhanded to runners Ron Hassey and Tony

Phillips, who advanced bases while Schroeder and the ump were jawing. Hassey later scored on a sacrifice fly, so does Henderson get an assist?

Umpires, believe it or not, also have a sense of humor. After AL ump John Hirschbeck ejected Jose Canseco of the A's, the slugger said about the first such indignity of his career: "Now he [Hirschbeck] can put a feather in his cap and feel good about it."

Ugh. Story not finished. When the A's showed up in Cleveland the next day, with a different umpiring crew, Canseco had to smile when he looked down at third base umpire Drew Coble, who was wearing a feather in his cap.

Entertainer Tom Dreesen, former Chicagoan and longtime fan of the Cubs who loves to wear the uniform and serve as batboy in Wrigley Field, tells this story about big John McSherry, one of the National League's better balls-and-strikes umpires: "I'm retrieving a bat just a few feet away from John and I say 'Bend over, John, and take a better look at those pitches.'

"You be the batboy, I'll be the umpire," replied the unsuspecting McSherry. Then, dusting off home plate, John took one more look at the middle-aged Dreesen and said:

"What are you, some kind of comedian?"

New Hall of Famer Carl Yastrzemski tells this story about ex–American League ump Ron Luciano, who loved to carry on a conversation with each batter: "Listen, Ron," said Yaz, "my kid is batting .300, my wife is fine, I haven't heard any new jokes, and I don't want to know about any new restaurants. I'm oh for fifteen and I want you to keep your mouth shut."

Catcher Gary Carter and I always drove people nuts with our conversations, too. And we were on opposite teams.

We had played and roomed together in winter ball, though, and were friends—so whenever I'd come to the plate we'd have fun.

"I know what you're thinking," Gary would say, and I'd reply, "What is it? Fastball? C'mon, roomie, give me a break." We'd play mind games throughout my entire at-bat. Hey, I was looking for any edge I could get because I always had difficulty hitting in Montreal (maybe because I had trouble seeing straight after just coming from a road trip into New York).

Anyway, we're chirping away one day until umpire Paul Runge had heard enough.

"Listen, you two," said Runge, "if you want to talk why don't you just go out to dinner? Why not get married? Have you picked out the furniture yet?"

Like father, like son. Paul's dad, Ed Runge, was home plate umpire for my first major league at-bat (1966) and when the first pitch went two feet outside, he calmly said "Striiiiiiiiike," just to see my reaction.

Welcome to the big leagues, kid.

I always had fun with umpires, especially Frank Pulli and Doug Harvey, with whom you could joke. I'd yell "Don't forget your seeing-eye dog" and be able to get away with it with Pulli because he knew I was kidding (most of the time).

But these were guys I knew, maybe even played golf with during the off-season. Whatever the friendship, it didn't matter between the white lines, anyhow. Sometimes you get the call, sometimes you don't. I've seen Tom Lasorda and ump Bruce Froemming have some great laughs at the Saint Patrick's Day party at Dodgertown, too, but I've also seen them screaming, nose to nose, during the season.

The main thing for players and fans to remember is that umpires are human, too. Most of them.

I have observed, however, that their tolerance level seems to be dropping. When I first broke in, and as I traveled my journeyman path, if you had a beef with an umpire you could air it, as long as you didn't say anything about his mother. Nowadays you can get tossed at a moment's notice.

Why? I'm afraid the umpires have taken the position that they're an important part of the game, which they are. *But people don't pay to see umpires.* Since the advent of the umpires' union, better pay, vacation time, and so forth—all of which I think are good—I've noticed an attitude shift.

I also saw some colossal mistakes by American League umpires during the 1989 season—everything from foul balls being called home runs to calls on the bases that TV replays plainly revealed to be in error. And I know those things happen. But hey, guys, you've got to show some tolerance at your end, too. Some of those people screaming at you have good reason.

There remains, too, a basic difference between AL and NL umpires. They give you a higher strike zone in the AL but they seem less vigorous in their work ethic. Sometimes we have to make ball-strike calls in the broadcast booth before the slo-mo gentlemen in blue ever get around to it.

Certainly "phantom tags" still exist in both leagues and even though fans are more aware of this mini-cheating nowadays because of all the TV replays, umps are still calling them as they don't see them. Many times the shortstop or second baseman won't touch the base but it doesn't matter if the ball gets there first. The umpire always calls the runner out. And the really good first basemen, such as Keith Hernandez, are masters at cheating by pulling their foot off the bag before the throw arrives. And here's one that really blows my mind: I've seen a first baseman fool the umpire by hitting the glove with his fist just a split second before the ball arrives. He knows the ump is listening for the "sound" to make his call. So what happens when the ball arrives after the sound? The ump has already made his call and isn't about to embarrass himself by changing it.

Which reminds me of one of my favorite "oldie" anecdotes about baserunners and umpires: The runner slides into second base, the shortstop makes the tag, and the umpire signals "out" but yells "safe."

"So what am I?" demands the runner.

"Well," said the ump, "you and I know you're safe and the shortstop knows you're safe, but forty-seven thousand people in the stands saw my hand go up. So you're out!"

If Jack Clark had been that imaginary runner sliding into second, you can imagine his reaction. Jack showed little empathy toward AL umps during his one year in the league.

"They are awful," said Clark, but only after he escaped back into the NL, "they don't have a clue. I don't know if they don't practice or what . . . they've got a lot more lowlifes there."

Clark, however, didn't exactly find utopia when he returned to the NL. During one bad spell last summer when he struck out six times in two games, he was ejected by umpire Terry Tata for arguing balls and strikes, then fined for throwing his bat and helmet after another argument with ump Charlie Reliford. After some reflection, though, Jack the Ripper said: "The way I've been swinging, I shouldn't be complaining about anything. The pitches were probably right down the middle and I didn't even know it."

Lowlife Department: During an argument in the tenth inning of a Baltimore-Cleveland game, Indians hitting coach Charlie Manuel bumped umpire Durwood Merrill.

"If one of your people touches my people again, I'll rip his heart out," umpire Steve Palermo reportedly said to Indians manager Doc Edwards, who replied: "You're not man enough to do it."

More Bumpety-Bump: Some thought umpire Joe West should have been fined or suspended for shoving Cincinnati infielder Ron Oester ("He pushed me not once, but twice") during an argument last summer, especially since former Reds manager Pete Rose had been suspended thirty days and fined ten thousand dollars for bumping umpire Dave Pallone in 1988. There was no action taken, but the whole flap reminded Cubs manager Don Zimmer of his own confrontation with Country Joe five years earlier.

"A guy was coming into third base and I was down telling him to slide," recalled Zimmer, "when all of a sudden I wound up tumbling head over heels. Joe West had grabbed me by the collar and jerked me backward. And I got fined two hundred dollars for the incident."

In contrast, Minnesota's Jim Dwyer was fined for lightly touching umpire Greg Kosc during an argument, bringing this reaction from Twins manager Tom Kelly: "If that's considered bumping, then maybe we ought to be playing in skirts."

Wally Backman, former Met fireball who was traded into the AL last season, also made some comparisons.

"There are only a few good umpires in this league (AL) that bear down. It's not right . . . we're trying to make a living out here and they're just trying to get the game over."

One way to get the game over is to kick everybody out. That wasn't quite the case during a Class AA Texas League game last summer between Midland (Texas) and Wichita, but it was close.

Eight men, including public-address announcer Barry Sykes, were ejected after Midland catcher Otto Gonzalez hauled in a foul pop close to the screen and umpire Brian Owen ruled he had trapped the ball.

Sykes played the Linda Ronstadt tune "When Will I Be Loved?" which begins with "I've been cheated, been mistreated . . ." and Owen promptly ejected the P.A. announcer.

Six other ejections came after a fight later in the game, won by Wichita, 9–1.

Okay, enough Blue-bashing. When do the umpires get their day in court? Indeed, wouldn't it make interesting copy if sportswriters would quote major league umps after every game and relate what they really think about some managers and players? But the umps don't play that way. They usually follow the code of the commissioner's office and button their lips. Richie Phillips, executive director of the Major League Umpires Association, made an interesting tongue-in-cheek suggestion, however, after he learned that players would be "rating" umpires. Obviously, the umps weren't happy to hear that major league players, anonymously, were filling out report-card–like surveys on their competence.

That's when Phillips wondered what would happen if the umps rated the players with this report card:

- Which players swear the most.
- Which players can never hit behind the runner.
- Which pitchers consistently have poor control in critical situations.
- Which players cannot hit the curveball to right field.

- Which players blame most of their deficiencies on the umpires.
- Which players are most respectful of umpires.
- Which players argue calls, then give umpires credit for doing the best they can.
- Which players have the greatest abilities in certain situations.

Actually, Richie could have gone farther. The umps could also vote on:

- Which managers spit on the umpires' chins while arguing.
- Which players know the most four-letter words.
- Which players are most inventive in the use of one particular four-letter word.
- Which players give the best and worst hotfoots.
- Which catchers give off the most unpleasant smell.
- Which players and managers have the biggest "rabbit ears."
- Which players pick their noses in the batter's box.
- Which players take firmer grips on their jock straps than their bats.
- Which players are most aware when a game is nationally televised.

The last umpire's poll I saw in the *Detroit Free Press* listed the NL's Bruce Froemming as the best in the major leagues, and certainly I can't argue—but what makes Brucie better, for example, than his buddy from Wisconsin, Dutch Rennert?

Certainly both rank among the most consistent and entertaining umps. Rennert gives a strike call as distinctively as any umpire in memory, and when roly-poly Froemming gets up a head of steam, he can move across a ballfield like Carl Lewis heading for the tape.

Two little-known, easily forgotten facts about Rennert: (a) his boyhood nickname was Pee Wee but any player who reminds him is venturing into dangerous territory; (b) he was once a driver's education instructor but resigned after one day because his only student ran into a parked car in a school zone.

C'mon, Dutch, are you serious?

"In those days I was in the minors and had to take different jobs during the off-season up in Wisconsin to make a buck. Well, I got this license to teach driver's education, a regular certification.

"So the first day on the job I'm riding along with this girl driver and she panicked and drove right into a parked car in a school zone."

Why, Dutch, didn't you step on the dual-control brake to avert the accident?

"That's what my boss asked," said Rennert. "So I left the job after one day. It wasn't for me."

Beanballs, scuffballs, and oddballs:

One of the damndest places to be on a baseball field is at home plate with a pitcher throwing ninety-mile-per-hour fastballs at you.

High and inside is one thing. Behind your head is something else. Then here comes one into the small of your back and there's nothing to do except scream.

Or fight.

It always amazes me how a pitcher with the control of a fly-casting champion can "let a pitch get away." I always felt like Montreal manager Buck Rodgers, who said last season after Orel Hershiser of the Dodgers shaved a few of the Expo hitters: "That's a Cy Young pitcher who can throw the ball into a teacup so why was it going over heads and into ribs?"

Hitter versus pitcher is endless combat and the umpire is usually caught in the demilitarized zone. Pitchers feel they have to come inside to force hitters off the plate; hitters believe they have a right to dig in without being struck by a guided missile.

Inevitably, when somebody gets hit enough times, either on purpose or by accident, what transpires is loosely described in baseball as a "fight." Mostly, they're pretty funny.

Example: When Red Sox pitcher Mike Smithson hit Texas first baseman Rafael Palmeiro, the left-handed hitter took a few steps toward the mound and the Rangers' dugout emptied. The only player to leave the Red Sox dugout, though, was pitcher Joe Price, who promptly saw he was outnumbered and retreated. Said Bosox outfielder Mike Greenwell after the nonbrawl: "We've got a bunch of wimps on this team. When are we going to act like a team and stop acting like a bunch of sissies?"

Two seasons ago when Andy McGaffigan of the Expos threw a pitch that narrowly missed the helmet of Shawon Dunston, the Cubs' shortstop raced to the mound, launched a haymaker, missed when McGaffigan deftly ducked, and fell embarrassingly on his face. Last season Shawon got smart. After a similar fourth ball came close, he was content to throw his bat twenty feet into the air and slowly walk to first base.

"You don't like pitches at your head," said Dunston, "because it's kind of scary."

Scary? Sometimes downright life-threatening. After Pirates outfielder Gary Redus was struck just below the eye by a pitch from the Dodgers' Tim Crews (and both benches cleared), Andy Van Slyke shouted at Crews: "None of Mike Tyson's victims ever looked like that!"

Pirates pitcher Bob Walk was later ejected for *telling the umpires* that he would retaliate the next inning. There's a twist. Instead of just doing it, he talked about it and got the boot. What kind of retaliation is that?

Walk is the same pitcher who angered the Cardinals' Pedro Guerrero by striking him out on five curveballs when the Bucs held a 5–0 lead. After Pete homered the next at-bat it took him 37.2 seconds from the point of impact until he touched home plate after his five-miles-per-hour tour of the bases (thirteen seconds to get from third to home). Said Guerrero after his "Cadillac" tour: "I didn't like it when he threw five breaking balls to me. Now we're even."

Said a confused Walk: "I apologize for the breaking balls. Next time I'll throw it underhanded."

Poor Pete. He had a marvelous season for the Cardinals but wasn't always in step off the field. After his former team, the Dodgers, honored him when the Cardinals visited Los Angeles, unimpressed Guerrero said: "They gave me a frame with seven pictures in it, which I already had in my house. When I got it, the glass was broken. They just wanted to show me up and embarrass me. I threw it out.''

Then there was the evening in Houston when Pete met two girls at the hotel bar and woke up bare the next morning in an even barer room. Missing was gold jewelry and cash worth thirty thousand dollars. Investigators later revealed that Pete had been drugged by a substance that the girls, perhaps delivering underhanded, had placed in his drink. A similar fate befell Dodgers' announcer Don Drysdale, apparently drugged by the same females at the same bar, who then led him to his room from the parking lot and robbed him.

And who said it wasn't a jungle out there?

One of Guerrero's countrymen from the Dominican Republic, Pascual Perez, continues to pitch to the bizarre beat of his own distant drummer. After being struck by a line drive off the bat of Jerome Walton of the Cubs, Perez then fired a fastball into the Cubs' dugout at Wrigley Field, a version of retaliation that manager Don Zimmer did not find amusing.

"What if he hit someone in the face?" asked Zimmer. "I have no doubt clubs want to beat him more because of the show he puts on out there."

What show? Well, if you haven't seen Pascual's fingerpointing, mock pistol shot from the mound after a strikeout, or his between-the-legs pickoff move, you haven't seen the Master of Mustard.

"You never know what he's going to do," said Walton. "I guess he's just crazy."

"I was just playing," said Perez, who will be playing this season in Yankee Stadium.

Then there was the afternoon last summer when Kirk Gibson, former Michigan State football player, made a bull charge toward Perez after he had nicked the bill of Mike Scioscia's cap with a pitch. Gibby never reached his target, however, because he was tackled by Kevin Gross and held down by four other Expos.

"I was on a mission," said Gibson, who probably moved quicker on that surge than he did at any other time during his entire injury-ridden season. Earlier in that same game, Hubie Brooks had to be restrained from charging Hershiser following a rib-plunker from the man who uses baby shampoo and showers four times a day.

"It was just an alarming run of wildness," explained Hershiser. That's when manager Rodgers labeled manager Tom Lasorda a "prima donna" for his team's actions and defended Perez's antics on the mound.

"Pascual pitches on emotion," said Rodgers. "If I take that away from him, I might as well shoot him. When he came to Montreal I thought he was a hot dog, but he's not. When Kirk Gibson hit that home run in the World Series, he was pumping his fist around the bases. That wasn't hot-dogging. That's emotion. If I take that away from Pascual, I might as well cut his heart out."

Actually, a hitter has only three options when he believes, for whatever reason, that a pitcher is going to throw at him.

- He can turn to the catcher and say "If he hits me I'm going after you."
- He can swing at the first pitch and "accidentally" throw his bat at the pitcher.
- He can complain of a toothache and extract himself from the lineup.

Option number one obviously has drawbacks if the catcher stands six-six and weighs 240. A hitter must carefully scout his opponent. Besides, catchers wear a lot of protective equipment. A guy could break his knuckles just trying to find a soft spot.

I prefer option two. If you release the bat at the right moment, you can nail a pitcher on the shins and it almost always gets across your message.

That's what I did once to Cardinal pitcher Bob Forsch when I was with the Phillies, and here's why.

Forschie knew I hated changeups. I was a fastball hitter and whenever somebody fooled me with a changeup, I'd usually throw my bat at the pitch for a foul tip or even a lucky flare. I probably got four or five hits a season that way, throwing the bat at the pitch rather than swinging and missing. The worst I would get would be a foul ball.

So one night Forsch threw me a changeup and I was dead fooled, so I threw the bat and popped a little fly ball over shortstop for a hit. Well, Forsch was pissed, and although my bat landed about halfway to the mound—not nearly close enough to hit him—he walked over, picked it up, slammed it down a couple of times, then threw it.

I didn't see it because I was running to first base, but when I returned to the dugout, the guys were saying, "Hey, Forschie broke your bat."

"What are you talking about, broke my bat?"

"He slammed down your bat and broke it."

Now I was pissed.

So now I go down into the runway and start practicing the art of bat-throwing. After all, you can't just throw a bat and expect to hit the target without practicing. So I'm down in the runway at St. Louis between innings, swinging and throwing an old bat—just letting it fly but making it look natural.

Next time at bat Forsch threw me a fastball on the first pitch and I fired the bat right into his shins. You should have seen him jump as the bat hit the base of the mound, then caromed up to nail him shin-high.

Naturally, I told him it slipped.

On the field, the Yankees of 1989 had a calm season. Maybe nobody figured they were worth fighting. Most fights are the same, anyhow. Somebody throws a pitch too close to somebody's head and the next thing you know everyone is waltzing.

Players nowadays take it a lot more personally when a pitch comes inside. It never bothered me much because I always accepted it as part of the game. I always figured after two or three hits to expect the brushback. And I think today's successful pitchers are the ones who throw inside, just to remind the hitter of a few territorial rules. Hitters today, however, crowd the plate more than ever before and get very agitated when a pitch comes inside.

A lot of guys get hit by inside pitches, too, but 99 percent of the time pitchers aren't aiming for anyone's head. Hey, if he wants to hit you is there a better target than the ribs? Most of the time, though, when a hitter gets plunked it's unintentional. When somebody gets it in the helmet, though, a brawl usually starts.

I've been in a few fights but the best ones were against the Pirates when I was with Philly in the mid-seventies. We always had problems winning in Pittsburgh and I'll never forget the day we lost a doubleheader, got into a brawl, and half the guys on our team went out and got drunk. Relief pitcher Tug McGraw, who lost both games, got so shit-faced he went to the police station and made them lock him up. The police didn't want to but he screamed and cursed until they finally got tired of the abuse and put him behind bars. The traveling secretary had to go down the next day and bail him out.

That was the day Mike Schmidt broke his thumb in the fight and the Pittsburgh fans came after us when we tried to board the team bus. One big guy stood outside the bus door screaming obscenities, right in front of a woman holding a small child, and just as I got to the first step of the bus he started in on me. So I grabbed the front of his shirt and introduced his face to the side of the bus about three times. Next thing you know his nose is bleeding and our manager, Danny Ozark, is pulling me into the bus and we're out of there.

But that wasn't the end of it. The guy called the police and they came looking for me at the hotel, not knowing they were going to eventually get McGraw, anyhow. They didn't find me because the Phils slipped me into a different hotel and in the meantime, the rest of the guys were getting rowdy in a Pittsburgh saloon. Bob Boone tore a huge sign off the bar and when the big bartender started after him, Greg Luzinski reached out and lifted the guy off the ground. It was a crazy night but we played better the next day. We even made peace with the fan with the bloody nose, too. Our front office invited him and his family to a game and gave him a bunch of Phillies souvenirs.

In another fight when I was with the Phils (we did have a rather combative group), I made the mistake of trying to play peace-maker. I was on the pile of pushers and shovers, trying to pull people away, when somebody started sucker-punching me in the back of the head. Finally, I turned to where I thought the assailant might be, took a giant swing, and punched my former roommate John Stearns, who had just come around the corner of the melee, square on the jaw.

"What are you hitting me for?" he yelled.

I didn't have an answer.

The baseball fight I most enjoyed watching happened in the Yankee clubhouse crapper, which may or may not be significant.

I was strictly a spectator when two of the giants of the 1979 Yankee club, Goose Gossage (six-three, 225) and Cliff Johnson (six-four, 230), began to rumble and tumble. It began like most fights, with Johnson saying something like, "Hey, Goose, I could always hit your fastball," and slapping Gossage on the shoulder so hard his head banged into the wall, and the next thing I knew, from my vantage point in the sauna, my teammates were trying to pound each other and landing half their punches on poor little Brian Doyle, who was trying to break them apart.

In the meantime, Chris Chambliss is sitting on the john with the stall door closed, and as Goose and Cliff are wrestling, they crash into the partition and it collapses on Chris, who has his pants down around his ankles and wonders if Yankee Stadium has been hit by an earthquake.

Somewhere in the scuffle, Goose took a swing, hit the bathroom door, and tore the ligaments on his pitching thumb. He went on the disabled list, the Yankees finished fourth, and Johnson got traded.

But it was a funny fight; I think they should at least put a plaque on the door of the john.

My favorite all-time tantrums: (a) when Pete Rose bumped umpire Dave Pallone and got suspended for thirty days; (b) when George Brett went berserk during the Pine Tar Incident; (c) when Eric Gregg ejected Larry Bowa.

Perhaps you saw taped replays of the first two incidents, but you may not have seen the Bowa brouhaha, which was just a little amazing. I was sitting in the Phillies' dugout next to Ozark and coach Ray Ripplemeyer when Bowa started to charge toward Gregg. Ripplemeyer then came out of the dugout and jumped on Bowa's back, but Larry just flipped him. Then I tackled Bowa and held him long enough for Luzinski to land on top of him.

Later the same season, Bowa slid into home plate in a pile of dust at Wrigley Field, then jumped up screaming with dirt in his eyes. "Am I safe or out?"

"Who's asking me?" said home plate umpire Gregg.

"Larry Bowa!"

"Well, if it's Larry Bowa, you're out," said Gregg.

Somehow, I don't think Bowa and Gregg will ever get along.

Every year the players from at least one team make more headlines fighting among themselves than with opponents.

So let's hear some "attaboys" for the 1989 Boston Red Sox, hands-down winners of the Jaybird Togetherness Award. At the beginning of spring training we had Dennis (Oil Can) Boyd wondering why he had to see a psychiatrist when one teammate, Wade Boggs, was an admitted sex addict. Then outfielder Mike Greenwell called his teammates "wimps" and "sissies" when they wouldn't partake in that Arlington Stadium brawl, and later Greenwell and teammate Roger Clemens exchanged unpleasantries through Boston newspapers.

There were also other Bosox "misunderstandings" during a season of frustration, including pitcher Lee Smith getting fined for not showing up for the Hall of Fame game. Smith said he had a sore back and apparently it was so sore he couldn't even pick up the phone to tell anyone.

Somebody once said "twenty-five men, twenty-five cabs" when describing the not-so-closeness of the Red Sox, and one former Boston player, Bill Buckner, took some of his attitude with him to Kansas City, where he got into a fight in Chicago last season with KC batting coach John Mayberry.

So what were they fighting about? Blood, honor, or money? Nahhh. They were battling over the merits of Chisox hitting coach Walt Hriniak's theories. Buckner, a Hriniak disciple, took exception to Mayberry's disdainful remarks.

But the fight didn't last long because it was broken up by Bo Jackson, and who's going to argue with Bo unless he's wearing a football uniform with a number in the 50s?

Jaybird Crazyman Award goes to Cincinnati Reds relief pitcher Rob Dibble, who said, after throwing an opponent's bat halfway up the wire screen behind Riverfront Stadium home plate: "I'm not as crazy as I appear to be."

Dibble, who grew up idolizing Philadelphia hockey star Bobby Clarke ("I loved that guy because he had no teeth and he was a maniac"), throws fastballs that travel ninety-five to ninety-nine miles per hour and once even gave an intentional walk at eighty-nine miles per hour.

"I can't let up," said the six-four, 235-pound Dibble, who disdains any form of pitching except all-out heat. Of Hungarian heritage and temperament, he once tried to attack an umpire in the minors and body-slammed his own manager, who tried to stop him; he was fined for throwing at Willie Randolph of the Dodgers (and talking freely about it); and he screamed at the Montreal bench last season and once flipped a ball at a Phillies batter after striking him out.

He also got into a late-season argument with Reds interim manager Tommy Helms and said about himself: "I suppose the more money I keep losing (in fines), the more I'll grow up."

Howard Johnson of the Mets had his own description of Dibble's state of maturity after the Reds right-hander hit Tim Teufel in the back with a pitch. Said HoJo: "He's a short reliever and most short relievers are crazy."

Oh, yeah? Tell it to Dibble's dog, Taylor. After Ron picked up his first big league save last April 10, he kept the ball and placed it on a shelf at home for safekeeping.

Taylor, a German shepherd, climbed up and destroyed the memento, and for that he gets my Jaybird Crazydog Award.

*   *   *

Does he or doesn't he? Does Mike Scott of the Houston Astros throw a scuffball? Is that why he became a twenty-game winner or was it just split-fingered jealousy from the rest of the National League?

It's the age-old question. Hitters before me complained about Whitey Ford's spitter, then accused Lew Burdette of loading them up, and we all threatened to wear raincoats to the plate when Gaylord Perry was on the mound.

Scott got publicity again last season when Mr. Clean of the Dodgers, Cy Young Award winner Orel Hershiser, said: "It's not too much fun to sit there and watch him [Scott] cheat. It's unbelievable . . . even the umps say he does it. But they say the league won't back them up on it after Don Sutton tried to sue Doug Harvey for charging him with scuffing."

Example of what usually happens in spitball-scuffball incidents: After manager Jim Leyland of the Pirates accused the Cubs' Calvin Schiraldi of throwing a spitter, Chicago manager Don Zimmer accused Pittsburgh pitcher Bill Landrum of "performing creative surgery" on the baseball's seams.

Response from the umpires: "Play ball."

"I keep sending scuffed baseballs to the National League office," lamented Tom Lasorda of the Dodgers, "but I don't know what they do with them.

"Maybe they have their grandchildren play with them."

9

Checking the Sanity of the Sluggers

As Jeff Ballard of the Orioles went into his windup, the hitter stepped out of the batter's box, signaling for time out. But it was too late, said the umpire. The ball was already on its way to the plate.

So Bo Jackson jumped back into the box and drilled a home run over the right-center-field fence.

There are no small stories about Bo Jackson.

Power and speed. Speed and power. He is the Athlete of the 1990s.

Born on the planet Krypton, where he first learned to leap tall buildings in a single bound, Bo at age twenty-seven appears to be much like any other six-one, 230-pound athlete.

Do not be deceived. He is not like any other.

At McAdory High School in McCalla, Alabama, near the very spot where his parents reportedly found him in a meteor crater, Bo high-jumped six-nine and, as a baseball pitcher in his spare time, achieved a 9–1 record. Representing Auburn University, one year before winning college football's Heisman Trophy (1985), he ran the hundred meters in 10.13 in the Florida Relays.

There was also a day when he walked into the weight room at Auburn, told the strength coach he didn't believe in lifting weights, and proceeded to bench press four hundred pounds without a single grunt.

"He's not human," said Bo's teammate with the Kansas City Royals, Pat Tabler, who calls him Ro-Bo.

"If Bo were with us through the off-season and training camp," said Bo's former coach with the Los Angeles Raiders, Mike Shanahan, "he would become known as the greatest who ever played the game."

Bo, however, is not the greatest running back in the National Football League and he is not the greatest outfielder or home run hitter in the American League.

He is simply the best who ever did both. Some believe he could one day become the first "fifty-fifty man" in baseball history— fifty home runs and fifty stolen bases in the same season. Others believe he could gain two thousand–plus yards in a single NFL season if he would opt to *play an entire season* rather than share his body and soul with baseball. As Mike Downey, *Los Angeles Times* columnist, wrote: "He's a twin-ball wizard . . . in two leagues by himself."

Bo doesn't care what others believe.

"I like to keep 'em guessin'," Bo was saying as he reported to the Raiders again last October, with rumors that the Royals wanted to tie up his abilities (32 HR, 105 RBI) with a long-term, no-football, multimillion-dollar contract.

My opinion and the opinion of most other professional athletes: If Bo can do it, why not? We think it's wonderful.

His knees and troubled thigh muscles, however, may not continue to function so wonderfully, and certainly the risk of a career-ending injury is always present. This has been an ego thing with Bo, however, and I can understand it. He wanted to show everyone he could do both well and he did.

I found it interesting that when Bo hit that giant home run during the 1989 All-Star Game at Anaheim Stadium, the general sports public suddenly *accepted* Bo's status as a baseball superstar, too. Actually, those of us around the ballparks on a daily basis had already been exposed to his obvious talents. I had already decided in my own mind that Bo Jackson would someday become a player in the category of Willie Mays or Mickey Mantle—somebody the paying customer would make a special trip to watch perform.

His peers have helped glamorize the image. Said NL relief pitcher Jay Howell (Dodgers) after Bo's All-Star homer: "On the rare occasions when you see something like this pass overhead, it is usually named Halley."

"The guy is awesome," said AL teammate Kirby Puckett (Twins). "I almost blew out my shoulder giving him a high five."

"I call him Boris," said Angels manager Doug Rader. "Just 'Bo' doesn't sound like enough."

"Bo's like a different breed," said San Diego's Tony Gwynn. "I've seen him do things that are scary. I've got to believe the Nike [TV commercial] people are right. Bo can do it. He can do anything in the world."

"When I become a free agent," said Dodger pitcher Orel Hershiser, "I might sign with his team just to see him play every day."

Bo has hit longer home runs than the All-Star shot. In spring training one year ago at Haines City, Florida, he struck a ball 515 feet that cleared the left-center scoreboard, seventy-one feet tall, short-hopping a fence in the parking lot.

I guess when you hit them that far you can also wear an earring, which Bo does, but not on the field. When asked what he thought about Deion Sanders, another two-sport aspirant (Yanks, Falcons) who also wears an earring, Bo said: "I don't. I have better things to do."

Yes, Bo can be a two-sport pain, too. He sent my head spinning when he said, "There is nothing physical about sports, it's all mental." Following that logic, since Bo didn't play baseball at full speed for much of the 1989 season because of pulled muscles in his left leg, does that mean he was having trouble with the left side of his head?

Fame can be a bitch, I guess. At his home in Kansas City, Bo had a sign on his front door that read: "No autographs—only at the ballpark."

It was too much to resist for Cleveland Indian slugger Joe Carter, who lives in Leawood, Kansas, and decided to visit Bo. "I stopped and asked Bo for his autograph," said Joe, "but he wouldn't give it to me, either."

Bo knows baseball, Bo knows football, and if you believe Nike, Bo even knows hockey and ballet.

But does Bo know how to laugh?

Bo knows.

Example: The Royals were on the field before a game doing their stretching exercises when pitcher Bret Saberhagen started to direct a mock screaming attack at the stretch coach, who had been telling them to "relax."

"I'm tired of relaxing," screamed Saberhagen, "I've been re-laxed," catching the attention of nearby photographers, who thought they had a dissension story on their hands. So they're aiming their cameras at Saberhagen, who continues to rant and rave, and the next thing they know here comes Bo.

He just picked the still-babbling, six-one, 185-pound Saber-hagen off the ground and carried him, like a sack of groceries, across the field to deposit him in the dugout. Even when joking, the man has amazing strength.

Bo got a lot of attention, too, when he broke that bat over his head on national television, but that doesn't make him unique. I once saw Willie Horton swing so hard that he broke his bat on a checked swing. That's power.

I've seen other guys, like Chili Davis of the Angels, break bats over their knees—but the funniest scene comes when a guy tries to break the bat and can't. He'll bang it on his knee a couple of times, then throw it away in disgust.

Anger and adrenaline can cause a player to do strange things. I once saw Billy Buck (Buckner) jump up and down on his batting helmet until it shattered. Another time I saw a batter get so dis-traught that he cracked a helmet between his two hands like an egg.

I don't think I ever got that mad. But if I were a major league farm director who selected Kent Mercker, Paul Williams, Milt Cuyler, Jack Armstrong, Andrew Dziadkowiec, Doug Cinnella, or any of eighty-five other baseball prospects in the 1986 June free agent draft, I think I would be angry.

Why?

Because close to 100 amateur players were chosen ahead of Bo Jackson, who went to the Royals in the fourth round.

Bo does have his critics, though. Wrote columnist Charley Waters of St. Paul, Minnesota, after observing Bo shun a couple of youngsters who sought his autograph at the 1989 All-Star Game: "Bo, you can hit a baseball far, and you can run past and over tacklers with a football. But, Bo, you're also a jerk."

I guess that means Bo isn't perfect.

Kevin Mitchell of the Giants out-distanced all of baseball's sluggers last season with forty-seven home runs, some of them prodigious shots. Said manager Whitey Herzog of the Cardinals during one Mitchell hot streak:

"He's almost forcing me to check his bats. Maybe he saw *Field of Dreams* and thinks he's Shoeless Joe Jackson."

Mitchell's strength was a constant subject of discussion around the Giants' locker room. After Kevin made a bare-handed catch on a drive into the left-field corner by Ozzie Smith, teammate Terry Kennedy said:

"He should have just ripped the cover off with his teeth and thrown the core into the crowd."

Oakland A's strongman Jose Canseco was restricted to only 227 at-bats last summer but still powered 17 home runs and 57 RBI. Project that to 600 at-bats and Jose would have again finished in the mid-40's-to-50 home runs category.

He did hit one during the ALCS which caught some attention— an estimated 485-footer in Toronto's SkyDome that teammates swore had to have gone six hundred feet and was still rising.

"Oh, my God," said teammate Walt Weiss when Canseco's shot soared into the left-field top deck.

"You just saw something you can tell your grandchildren about," said Dave Parker. "You can't hit a home run any farther than that."

Nobody really knows how far the ball went, but it's my opinion that anytime something travels that far it should have food on board. Unfortunately, the A's didn't dispatch anyone to take an accurate measurement of the Dome shot.

As Frank Howard, a colossal dispenser of long balls, once said: "A guy who hits tape-measure homers is only as good as his press agent."

I especially liked the way Kevin Mitchell handled the media crunch. When asked if he was feeling the pressure of their questions, Kevin showed his gold tooth and said: "Pressure is when you're in an alley with nothing in your hands and you're confronted by six tough guys. What do you do? You hit the biggest and run for your life."

Even though today's sluggers aren't hitting as many home runs as I think they should, certainly they're hitting them far enough. Either that or they're building windows too close to the ballparks. One of Fred McGriff's thirty-six homers traveled 450 feet and struck a window of the restaurant that overlooks center field at Toronto's SkyDome. A woman seated near the window was so frightened she walked away from an expensive dinner. Another of his SkyDome homers went more than 400 feet to right field, landing against the window of the Hard Rock Café. The crashing sound caused a victimized Yankee pitcher to later say: "I was wondering where they were going to put that nightclub. Now I know."

McGriff has his backers, one of whom is teammate Lloyd Moseby, who says: "He will be the next man to hit fifty homers. He's more powerful than Jose Canseco, more powerful than Darryl Strawberry."

McGriff, a six-three, 215-pound native of Tampa, Florida, was once in the Yankee organization but went to Toronto after the 1982 season in a trade owner George Steinbrenner would like to forget.

Steinbrenner had wanted Jay's reliever Dale Murray and offered outfielder Dave Collins and pitcher Mike Morgan in trade. Toronto GM Pat Gillick, though, had seen McGriff, a Yankee ninth-round draft pick in 1981, playing in a Florida rookie league and asked that the kid be included in the swap.

Steinbrenner reportedly agreed without checking with Yankee minor league officials.

Another name for the future: Ruben Sierra of the Rangers, the six-one, 175-pounder from Puerto Rico who has already hit sixty-nine home runs at age twenty-four. Only thirteen other major leaguers ever hit that many dingers at such a tender age and nine of those reached the Hall of Fame.

When you're talking about Cooperstown and home runs, though, let us not forget Mickey Mantle, who hit one 565 feet on April 17, 1953, out of Griffith Stadium in Washington, D.C.

According to Arthur E. (Red) Patterson, then publicity man for the Yankees, the ball not only cleared the left-field bleachers but went out of the park about halfway up the scoreboard and was still rising.

"I found a kid with the ball and he showed me where it landed in a lady's backyard," recalls Patterson. "So I stepped off the distance to the outfield fence, then added the home-to-fence distance inside the park. I gave the kid ten dollars for the ball, got Mantle's bat, and convinced the Yankees to put them on display in the Yankee Stadium lobby. We did and somebody stole them. Then announcer Mel Allen made a plea on the radio and some kid returned them, admitting he had stolen them. Today the ball and bat are in the Hall of Fame."

For the record, Bo Jackson's longest HR in 1986 traveled 475 feet. Frank Howard once rocket-launched one in Forbes Field, Pittsburgh, that was stepped off at 565 feet—and the legendary Babe Ruth hit one during spring training in Tampa, Florida, that traveled anywhere from 560 to 656 feet, depending on who was telling the story.

Dave Kingman once hit one with the wind that traveled more than 550 feet out of Wrigley Field and bounced against the walk-up porch of a house three doors down the street. A sportswriter found the kid who retrieved the ball and took him into the Mets' locker room to meet Kingman, who accepted the ball without even saying thanks. Somebody from the Mets' PR department then gave the kid five dollars and another ball and sent him on his way. So much for historical home runs.

Only one player, Willie Stargell, ever hit a fair ball out of Dodger Stadium, and he did it twice—one measuring 506 feet, the other 470. Another epic Mantle homer occurred at Yankee Stadium in 1963, when he hit a ball off Kansas City's Bill Fischer that struck the upper-deck façade, eighteen inches below the roof. It was one of two homers by Mantle that hit the façade, and although there is no record of anyone ever hitting a fair ball out of Yankee Stadium, there have been unsubstantiated stories that Josh Gibson once did it during a Negro League game.

Frankly, I'm beginning to wonder if anyone will ever hit fifty home runs again, let alone sixty. Obviously there are enough strongmen around, but where is the consistency?

Mark McGwire of the Athletics, who hit another thirty-three home runs last year after thirty-two in 1988, believes distraction caused by media crunch is the biggest barrier and I agree. Can you imagine what would happen if someone actually got within four or five of sixty? Even back twenty-nine years ago when the late Roger Maris hit sixty-one homers there was enough pressure to make his hair start falling out. Nowadays there are twenty times more people with minicams, microphones, and talk shows. The demand would be incredible.

McGwire also suggests that to hit sixty, a hitter would need (a) another power hitter next to him in the lineup, (b) the ability to adjust to the changes pitchers would make during the season, (c) an injury-free season, (d) the ability to pull the ball, and (e) the patience to wait for the homers to come without forcing.

Nobody has hit fifty homers in the AL since Maris in 1961. George Foster of the Reds hit fifty-two in 1977. Mitchell fell three shy of the fifty mark last season. Lou Gehrig never hit fifty. Neither did Henry Aaron.

I hit 102 major league homers but it took me twenty years and none of them ever came back with re-entry burns. But I did consider running around the bases backward when I hit my one-hundredth. Then I chickened out.

My favorite home run story of 1989: At Joe O'Brien Field in Elizabethton, Tennessee, just above the fence, 414 feet from home plate, they've got a basketball hoop. Any Appalachian League player hitting a home run through that hoop receives one thousand dollars from Eden's Home Carpet.

Nobody had done it for sixteen years until last season, when first baseman Tom Hargrove of the Martinsville (Virginia) Phillies slugged one high, far, and right through the hoop.

One run, two points, one thou.

When Andy Van Slyke was battling a hitting slump last season, he said: "I have an Alka-Seltzer bat. Plop-plop, fizz-fizz. And when the pitchers see me walking up to the plate they say 'Oh, what a relief it is.' "

John Kruk, when he was still a Padre and slumping, called home one day to talk with his father and got batting advice.

"You know you're in trouble," said Kruk, "when someone tells you what you're doing wrong and they haven't even been watching the games."

Then there was the day Dale Murphy, mired in one of the worst slumps of his career, picked up a stray dog at Atlanta–Fulton County Stadium, took it home, and asked his wife, Nancy, what they should name him.

"Slumper," she said.

For some guys a slump is going an entire week on the road without falling in love. For others, it's torture in the batter's box, and there isn't a hitter alive who hasn't gone through it.

Escaping a slump can test the sanity.

I've seen guys try new batting stances, new bats, new freeways, new diets, new clothes, and new girlfriends in an effort to break out of a slump.

What happens during a slump: A hitter becomes impatient and starts swinging at bad pitches. He pulls off the ball and can't make himself stay back.

That's when you must return to basics: You have to wait and be patient. Look for a pitch you can hit. Try to hit the ball back through the middle.

It's amazing what one base hit can do for a hitter's confidence during a slump. Sometimes even a bunt will do it, or a broken-bat flare over the third baseman's head. Confidence, though, is everything and when fighting a slump, Bo Jackson is absolutely right: hitting becomes a mental game.

That's why you must keep your sense of humor, too. Whenever a teammate was in a slump, I'd take a broken bat and hang it in his locker, smeared with catsup to look like blood. Or I'd take some of his bats, douse them with lighter fluid, and build a bonfire. Anything to crank his head. I've even had managers, the ones with common sense, who would tell an entire slumping team: "I've set curfew tonight for 2:00 A.M. and that means *nobody* comes home until 2:00 A.M. Go have a drink, because with the way you guys have been playing, you need something!"

I had a lot of fun with one of the Yankee outfielders, Mel Hall, last season and may have even helped him some with his hitting.

Mel has a tendency to drop his hands and get too anxious when hitting. So one day after a game in which he'd swung at the first pitch two or three times, I put a note on his locker that said: "Quit swinging at the first damn pitch!—You Know Who."

The next day he took the first pitch, a ball, then stepped out of the batter's box and looked up toward the radio booth with a smile, just to let me know he remembered.

Pretty elementary stuff? Well, nobody said it took a rocket scientist to play this game, but if it did, he'd have to wait for the right pitch, too.

When it comes to hitting, hot is hot.

Kirby Puckett of the Twins, winner of the AL batting title (.339), said during a ten-for-twenty-one streak last summer: "I still don't have my best swing. The police tracked it down in Hawaii somewhere, and they're going to express it to me."

Lonnie Smith of the Braves, who made a major comeback from personal problems by hitting .315, said: "I'm not Superman. I just think I am."

Also, not is not.

Said Pedro Guerrero of the Cards (.311, 117 RBI) after starting two for eighteen against southpaws: "I don't like them. They throw with different hands."

Joey Meyer of the Brewers, after a one-for-twenty-two start while his parents were visiting from Hawaii, went three for three on the day they departed. When asked why they went home, Joey said: "They left after three weeks of me not talking to them."

Pitcher Bruce Hurst of the Padres, after going one for his first thirty-five with twenty-eight strikeouts in his debut as an NL hitter, said: "This is the worst slump of my career. I don't know what it is, maybe a lack of talent."

Hurst, who eventually pitched 244⅔ innings (2.69 ERA) for the Padres, also had a rocky start on the mound. After allowing ten hits and eight runs in his first five innings, he said: "My strike zone was dugout to dugout."

Actually, a manager might as well send his players out for an evening of diversion when they're fighting a slump. There is no magic answer.

"What can you do?" asked Atlanta coach Bobby Wine during a Braves nosedive. "You can't shoot them. You can't release all of them. Sometimes they simply try too hard."

Braves manager Russ Nixon, on the same slump: "We didn't put a crooked number on the scoreboard in weeks."

Billy Doran of the Astros, an excellent all-around second baseman who saw his batting average fall last season from .248 to .219, said about his plight: "Now when anybody else in the league goes into a slump, they say 'I'm in a Bill Doran.' "

One guy who never seems to slump is Wade Boggs, although his batting average did fall from .366 in 1988 to .330 last season. Only Boggsy knows whether the *Affaire Margo Adams* had anything to do with it. All I know is that his much-publicized court battle with Margo, his former traveling companion, produced my favorite baseball statistic, which says everything without saying anything: Boggs hit .221 when accompanied by his wife on road trips but .341 when accompanied by Margo.

It was also reported (by Margo) that he hit better when she wore no underwear to the ballpark but I was never able to get that verified.

I do know that Pete Rose, who was later to have his own tragic summer, showed the single-mindedness of a hitter when he explained why he admired Boggs: "Because he can hit with things on his mind."

Certainly the Rose, Boggs, and Steve Garvey stories produced their share of laughs around baseball, proving once again that nothing is sacred in a major league clubhouse. The most-often-repeated story: Rose was sitting in a bar with Boggs and Garvey when a beautiful blonde walked past. Boggs said, "I slept with her," Garvey said, "But she's carrying my baby," and Rose said, "Wanna bet?"

Margo even bragged that she had also dated Garvey but so what? How many ballplayers didn't she date?

We had fun with Margo on Yankee radio broadcasts, suggesting that George Steinbrenner hire her to help his team break out of its batting slump. I don't think George was listening, though. And she also revived the oldie-but-goodie clubhouse telephone prank. Example: Jay Howell picks up the phone and shouts across the Dodgertown locker room, "Hey, Bulldog, it's for you." Orel Hershiser then breaks away from a circle of reporters, reaches for the phone, and hears his teammate say, "It's Margo somebody."

Another spinoff came when a Kansas City radio station distributed Margo Adams masks to fans as they drove into the Royals Stadium parking lot for a game against the Red Sox. Then there was the organist at Anaheim Stadium who played the theme from *The Addams Family* when Boggs batted.

Yet Boggs kept hitting. The man is amazing. For example, he said he disliked Arlington Stadium because "it's uncomfortable to have people sitting in center field while you're trying to pick up the spin on the ball."

Some players try to pick up the ball, Wade tries to pick up the spin.

Which reminds me of the story Richie Zisk tells about himself: He was in an embrace with his wife when she whispered, "Talk dirty to me, Richie, talk dirty to me," and he said "Uhhhh, oh for four, oh for four."

I think you're starting to better understand the mentality of a hitter.

As for my pal Garvey, he took a lot of heat over one pregnancy that was a setup and another that was an accident. I guess he didn't see me in my movie debut, *Naked Gun,* when we talked about safe sex. Anyhow, Garv took a lot of ridicule ("He's Not My Padre" bumper stickers, "Father of Our Country," and so forth), but any time the public can take potshots at an idol, you know it will happen. America's media seem to enjoy bringing down people and obviously, with his image, Garvey was vulnerable.

But he was also up-front about everything at a time when he was fighting for visitation rights with his two daughters and his ex-wife, Cyndy (who ended up in jail), wouldn't allow them to see him.

Sure, Steve Garvey made some mistakes. So did Pete Rose, so did Wade Boggs. I've made a few myself, haven't you?

But I'm still on Garv's side, the sly devil.

How does it go, ring out the old, bring in the new?

More than one major leaguer of distinction retired during or following the 1989 season. More than one rookie won his place under the sun and lights.

I've chosen to write a little about one of each, the old and new.

Mike Schmidt was truly one of my crazy friends. From 1974, when I joined the Philadelphia Phillies, into 1978, we were team-mates, playing on exciting clubs that won three championships in the NL East.

He wasn't as silly as me but I couldn't hit the ball as far as him so it made us even.

Finally, late last May at the age of thirty-nine, Schmitty retired and I offer this salute to his Hall of Fame career: ten Gold Gloves at third base, 548 home runs, eighteen seasons of dignity, and me as a roommate.

Like everyone else who ever played in Philly, Schmidt heard the boos, especially toward the end. But he knew when to quit and he did it with class, and one day—probably when he steps to the podium at Cooperstown—every one of those Philadelphians who booed him will slap the guy next to him on the back and say, with pride: "Hey, that's Mike Schmidt. He hit more home runs than any third baseman in history and he was our guy!"

Attaboy, Schmitty. Good luck in somebody's broadcasting booth but stay away from mine.

There had been a lot of trade talk around the Seattle Mariners last spring, especially about outfielder Dale Murphy coming over from Atlanta, so it was with some apprehension that nineteen-year-old Ken Griffey, Jr., answered a summons to manager Lefebvre's office in Arizona.

"I hate to tell you this," said Lefebvre, closing the door as Griffey hung his head, "but because of new people coming onto the roster, I'm going to have to send you back down."

Griffey's head hung even lower and Lefebvre could not continue.

"Open the door," he commanded.

And when the kid did, he was greeted by smiling teammates who shouted "April Fool."

It's one of the oldest and, in truth, cruelest pranks of the spring-training rite but one that almost always works, even if the rookie does have a chocolate bar named after him.

The thing that called special attention to Griffey, of course—attention he validated with a rookie season batting average of .329 and sixteen home runs, despite a broken finger that kept him out of thirty-five games—was that his father was also still playing in the major leagues, for the Cincinnati Reds.

Indeed, when Ken Junior walked into the batting cage in Tempe, Arizona, Mariners coach Gene Clines asked him, "What is this, Ken, your second major league camp?"

"My twelfth," Griffey shot back, "Two here and ten with my dad."

When Ken Senior heard that his son had stood up and applauded during a visit to Riverfront Stadium when his father delivered a double, the elder said: "He'd better or he'd be grounded."

About that chocolate bar: A Washington State candy company produced the Ken Griffey, Jr., Chocolate Bar (even though the youngster is allergic to chocolate) and Ken Junior was paid five thousand dollars to sign the contract and receives a five-cent royalty on each bar sold. At last report, sales were approaching a half-million—how come nobody ever wanted to make a Crazy Jay Bar?

Players reacted differently to Ken Junior's presence. Rick Sutcliffe, after getting shelled by the kid in an exhibition game, said: "That's not unusual. I couldn't get his dad out, either."

Harold Reynolds, a teammate in Seattle, said: "A couple of years ago I was playing against his dad when he was with the Yankees, now I'm in the locker next to Junior. It's hard to figure."

You can imagine what it was like for Ken Junior growing up. But Ken Senior, who played his twentieth big league season in 1989, always made sure his son didn't get too cocky. One day after missing a fly ball in the sun, Ken Junior came home to find his dad wearing sunglasses and his brother wearing a blindfold.

Somewhere along the line, however, something wore off and it appears there will be a "Griffey" in somebody's major league box score for years to come.

Meanwhile, I think it's time to talk to my only child, Mary Jayne Sarah, about her batting stroke. She's been spending entirely too much time with dolls.

10

Baseball's Wacky Memorabilia and Movies

It bugged me that Hollywood had Shoeless Joe Jackson batting right-handed in the movie *Field of Dreams*. Here's a man who was obviously one of the greatest left-handed hitters in the history of baseball (.356 over thirteen major league seasons), was banned for life because of the Black Sox Scandal of 1919, and was the inspiration for a movie that sent people away from the theater feeling terrific.

So why couldn't he have batted left-handed?

I didn't mind the fantasy. In fact, I love it. You can fade ball-players away into a cornfield all day long and I'll buy it. But a lefty hitting from the right side? Would you make a movie with Sandy Koufax throwing *right-handed?*

When you grow up in Los Angeles you pay attention to what happens on the movie screen. It's the only city I know where the audience remains seated after a film until all of the credits have rolled. After all, you might see the name of a grip or makeup artist who lives on your street.

It has also been said that in El Lay (that's New York magazine slang for L.A.), everybody has a movie script in his desk drawer. But mine is in my head. Someday I want to write the ultimate baseball novel/movie screenplay and make enough money to buy the Yankees from George Steinbrenner.

The storyline: This billionaire recluse from Chicago (a little punchy after a lifetime of rooting for the Cubs) wearies of all the problems in baseball (drugs, strikes, sushi in concession stands, and so forth) and wills his fortune to a group of evangelists, with the proviso that they use the money to purchase a baseball team to play for God.

The evangelists then hire a hardball manager, who in turn signs all of baseball's rejects for his twenty-four man roster—sort of a Dirty Dozen Times Two, all guys you wouldn't leave alone in a room with your wife, daughter, or dog.

Somewhere along the way the manager also drafts one Goody Two-Shoes, physical fitness fanatic named Garrett Smith (Steve Garvey's initials, backward) who falls in love with an aerobics teacher while his teammates are out carousing. They begin dating but G.S. doesn't know that his true love, on the side, is running a group of women known as the Happy Housewives, women not satisfied at home who earn spending money as hookers. Example: They go to the Kentucky Derby every year, come home with purses full of money, and tell their husbands they won the daily double.

G.S. eventually learns about the housewife-hookers and also discovers that some of them are married to his teammates, leaving him in a moral quandary. Meanwhile, one player catches the evangelist with his hand in the till and the crook plots to have his discoverer killed. He plots an accident but the victim doesn't die, ending up in a coma.

Our Goody Two-Shoes hero, meanwhile, becomes the rallying leader on the team. All of the misfits are playing for him but he still can't figure out a way to tell them their wives are part-time prostitutes. They also rally around the player in the hospital and battle from the cellar into first place.

I will not reveal the finish of this epic because there is a lot of thievery in the world and some reader/movie producer might try to steal the story.

What part would I play in the movie? One of the misfits, naturally, and I would probably have green hair and be responsible for all of the clubhouse pranks. Actually, I wish I could have played the Joker in *Batman* instead of Jack Nicholson. I got a kick out of the movie but they played it too seriously. I preferred the old Batman stuff on TV with Bang and Pow and Zowie.

Back to *Field of Dreams*. I really did like it, especially the expressions of love and gratitude between father and son. I left the movie with the same feeling I got one day last summer during an old-timers' game ceremony at Yankee Stadium. It had been ten years since the death of Thurman Munson in a plane crash at Canton, Ohio, and his son, who was just four years old at the time, was in Yankee Stadium with the entire family for the ceremony. And here was this fourteen-year-old boy watching his father play baseball in a film presentation on the Stadium screen. It was very touching as this boy looked at his father, who was only thirty-seven when he died.

Anyhow, I walked away from *Field of Dreams* feeling happy and that's how you should leave a movie, even if the director was stupid enough to have one of the greatest left-handed hitters of all time batting right-handed.

They could have done what director Sam Wood did with Gary Cooper when he filmed *Pride of the Yankees,* the story of Lou Gehrig. Actor Cooper, who was chosen for the role over Spencer Tracy, Brian Donlevy, and Eddie Albert, was a natural right-hander who just couldn't hit left-handed. Gehrig, of course, was a southpaw.

Director Wood also had another problem. He had to find some way to duplicate Yankee Stadium's famous three o'clock shadows at old Wrigley Field in Los Angeles, where they were filming. Finally, he came up with some ingenious cinema to solve both problems: He had Cooper bat right-handed, run toward third base, and beat the throw to a right-handed third baseman wearing a first baseman's glove.

Then he reversed the film and viewers saw a left-handed Cooper running toward first in afternoon shadows. To avoid the giveaway backward uniform numerals, Wood used the numbers 1, 8, and 11.

Aren't movies great? I even liked Ronald Reagan playing pitcher

Grover Cleveland Alexander in the 1952 movie *The Winning Team*, even if he did throw like a girl, and Jimmy Stewart in the 1949 *The Stratton Story*, in which Stewart had his leg taped from ankle to waist so he could hobble like White Sox pitcher Monty Stratton, who had lost a leg in a hunting accident.

Robert Redford was really convincing as a hitter in *The Natural,* and so was Michael Moriarty as a pitcher in *Bang the Drum Slowly.*

Actors take their baseball roles seriously, especially those like Redford and Kevin Costner who obviously have athletic ability. Redford told Ron Fimrite of *Sports Illustrated* that he believes everyone wants his "at-bat" sometime in life and when he hit one 310 feet while filming *The Natural* in Buffalo's War Memorial Stadium, in front of thousands of movie hands and extras, it was a thrill he'll never forget.

Another of my all-time favorite baseball movies was *It Happens Every Spring,* starring Ray Milland as a professor-turned-pitcher who concocted a secret tonic that he applied to the baseball to make it allergic to wood and "hop" over bats (another valid argument against the use of aluminum bats).

I thought *Bull Durham* was a little far-fetched because I never had that many beautiful girls chasing me in the minor leagues, and *Major League* was stupid in that it had the players sleeping in dormitory bunkbeds in spring training. It was fun seeing Steve Yeager on film, but since when do ballplayers sleep in bunk beds?

My semistarring role helped make *Naked Gun* a standout film (Leslie Nielsen didn't do badly, either) and I didn't even have any lines! I was in a scene that took almost nine hours to film from every possible angle and they kept moving the crowd of extras to make it look like the stadium was full. Nielsen, of course, was amazing and watching Reggie Jackson was hilarious. He had only five words to speak but he kept blowing his line, "I must kill the queen."

Reggie got so involved in his robotic walk that he kept saying "I must kill . . ." or "I gotta kill . . ." or whatever, and we were all over him.

It has been said that life imitates art (or is it the other way around?) so perhaps our next hit baseball movie will be about Pete Rose or Steve Garvey or Wade Boggs.

Or maybe some enterprising producer will hire all three, throw in Jimmy and Tammy Bakker, and incorporate them into my screenplay idea.

We'll call it *Hook Slide for God* and remember, I'll be the one with the green hair, batting *left-handed*.

Confessions of a baseball collector:

I've got old uniforms, cracked bats, ragged batting gloves, autographed balls signed by Joe DiMaggio, Ted Williams, Stan Musial, and Mickey Mantle, and believe it or not, I even *paid cash* for authentic autographs of Ty Cobb and Babe Ruth.

My own 1967 Topps rookie card is worth ninety cents and my lifelong ambition is to reach one dollar. According to Mimi Alongi, collector extraordinaire from Mimi's Dugout, DuQuoin, Illinois, my 1968 card is valued at forty-five cents, my 1969 and 1970 cards are worth thirty-five cents each, the 1971 card worth thirty cents, and the 1972 card worth twenty cents.

It's a humbling experience to know your autograph on a bubble gum card isn't worth one American dollar, but who can argue with fair market value? Just think about it: twenty major league seasons with 4,703 at-bats with eight different teams and top price for a Jay Johnstone card is ninety cents.

Nevertheless, I believe in baseball collectibles. One man's trash really can be another man's treasure and nowhere is that more evident than at a baseball card show.

I did a baseball show with Cable News Network (CNN) last summer with a professor from Marquette University who said that the "collectibles" market had increased in recent years by 36 percent, far ahead of any stock market gains. He also indicated that many small investors are pulling out of the stock market to invest in baseball memorabilia.

I'm one of them, but more for my own personal satisfaction than for monetary gain. At one card show in Connecticut last year I bought the autographs of Cobb and Ruth. Now I'm looking for one from Lou Gehrig to go with them.

Over the years, I've collected souvenirs from men I played with and against—I've even got one ball with the autographs of Joe, Vince, and Dominic DiMaggio on it. I've also got complete sets of baseball cards at home and whenever I attend an old-timers' game, I'm always grabbing baseballs and getting them autographed. I've got one bat at home that's really nothing more than a shattered handle. It was the one I broke in the hallway of one of my clubhouses—just a personal reminder to myself that I wasn't always laughing. I've also got the batting gloves I wore in the 1978 World Series, and uniforms from the Dodgers, Yankees, Phillies, and Cubs.

If you're a baseball fan and have never been to a major collectors' show, you've missed a unique and exhilarating experience. As John Leptich of the *Chicago Tribune* wrote about sports memorabilia, "P. T. Barnum must have had some sports collectors in mind . . ."

In other words, not everything is worth collecting. Some of the stuff being offered at these shows, and through advertisements in collectors' publications, is downright bizarre. Some examples:

- The dental records of 1919 Black Sox pitcher Ed Cicotte can be purchased for five hundred dollars.
- For sixty dollars, you can buy a plaster mold of Bob Feller's pitching hand. Autographed, of course.
- One central Illinois company auctioned doors from former Peoria Chiefs players' lockers. If you admire Mark Grace of the Cubs, how can you live without his locker door?
- One Minneapolis sports store offers Metropolitan Stadium ushers' caps for auction; one from Pennsylvania will sell you a complete Tiger Stadium usher's outfit from the 1950s. You supply the shoes.
- A Ty Cobb brand cigar, in original 1916 wrapper, can be purchased from a company in Havana, Cuba.

• One New Jersey company is even offering a ten-by-twenty-one Natural Light advertisement with autographed Mickey Mantle. And that's ten-by-twenty-one *feet,* not inches. The damned thing was a billboard.

Yet, there is some wonderfully valuable real stuff out there, too. More than four hundred dealers from forty-five states gathered last summer at the Tenth National Sports Collectors Convention in Chicago and it was a veritable World Series of sports memorabilia. Ex-players were there, too, signing autographs (fifteen dollars for Sandy Koufax, not personalized, and so forth) and people stood in lines to pay their money. It has all become part of the baseball economy and I see nothing wrong with it, as long as everybody remembers the Internal Revenue Service, which has been keeping a close eye on the booming, cash-out-of-pocket business.

Personally, when I attend a card show, I prefer to sign autographs for free after people have paid their money to attend. In other words, I might take up-front appearance money from the show sponsor, but I've never felt comfortable charging some kid four dollars for my signature.

Autographs are a phenomenon.

When Joe DiMaggio, seventy-five, appears to sign autographs at a major show the rules are as follows:

• Price thirty dollars, limit of two.
• No bats signed; no duplicate items signed.
• One oversized item only; items must be flat.
• Persons ejected if caught in line twice.

I had a girl once ask me to sign her breast. Another wanted my name on her buttocks. One lady actually had her husband get me to sign her Modess wrapper.

"Couldn't you have found another kind of napkin?" I asked.

"Sorry," he said, and they took the autograph.

I've signed dollar bills, hundred-dollar bills, and even fifty-cent pieces. Bras, panties, and shoe bottoms. Once a girl wanted me to sign her tight denim jeans so I started inside and above the knee with a large "J" and started working upward. She got a little nervous until she realized I was writing the rest of my name in small letters inside the "J."

Billy Martin once signed a lady's rear end on the team bus. But that didn't compare to the day in spring training when two girls drove past the Dodgers' team bus and mooned us. Then nine of us yelled for the driver to catch the car so we could return the greeting and Tom Lasorda was going nuts.

Somewhere, too, there is a baseball card of me wearing an umbrella hat. C'mon, collectors, that's got to be worth something, doesn't it? Maybe one dollar?

Mistakes by card companies can cause freak values. Best recent example was the Bill Ripken card that showed Ripken holding a bat with an obscenity written on the butt of the bat handle. They even used the situation on *The People's Court* television show, with a case involving two ten-year-old boys haggling over the value of a card.

Then there was the kid in West Pittsburg, California, who claimed another kid stole his 1909 Honus Wagner card worth seventy-five thousand dollars. It seems he opened his screen door to show another fourteen-year-old, who grabbed the card and ran.

Ol' Honus, incidentally, once appeared on a card produced by a tobacco company, but the card was recalled when Wagner, who did not smoke, objected to his picture being used. It reminds me of Glenn Davis of the Houston Astros, who last year objected to his inclusion in a beer promotion involving Astros home runs.

Mickey Mantle remains the biggest name in baseball memorabilia. One collector peddled a framed, glass-enclosed display of Mantle cards last summer for approximately $25,000 at the National Show, and there was a three-by-five-inch Mantle painting—the original artwork for the 1953 Topps card—that sold for $103,000. That 1953 card still sells for approximately $8,500, depending on condition, and people keep asking why.

I think I know the answer, because he and Duke Snider were my idols. Mickey and Duke were the American dream and there are a lot of middle-aged, successful men with money who still look back on the 1950s and think about Mickey and Duke. Remember actor Jack Lemmon standing at the window in a scene from the movie *Save the Tiger,* looking out over the L.A. smog and traffic while reciting the names of Pee Wee Reese, Jackie Robinson, and others from the old Brooklyn Dodgers? It was a simpler time, I guess, as evidenced by the fact that nostalgia now has a price tag.

Mantle, incidentally, says he can remember when he lived in New York and Topps would send boxes and boxes of bubble gum to his kids.

"My kids would chew the gum and throw away the cards," recalls Mickey.

And you thought your mother was the only one who did it.

It's too bad they didn't make baseball cards of Yale University players. Can you imagine how valuable a George Bush card would be these days? He was no Will Clark or Mark Grace at first base but he did make it into the Oval Office and that would have made his card at least as valuable as mine with the umbrella hat.

There have been other presidents who were baseball fans but we've never had one as dedicated and knowledgeable as President Bush. *He played the game,* which gives him an edge on former President Richard Nixon, who talks the game. Bush has also been a close friend of new commissioner Fay Vincent for years, and the President's son, George W. Bush, has become majority owner of the Texas Rangers.

And if that isn't enough, the younger Bush's daughter, Barbara, has a dog named "Spot Fletcher" in honor of Rangers shortstop Scott Fletcher, her favorite player.

Talk about job security. As long as Spot lives a long and healthy life, how can manager Bobby Valentine release or trade the namesake of the owner's daughter's dog?

The Yankees were in Texas when First Lady Barbara Bush threw out the first ball for the Rangers' home opener last summer. That was the night my announcing partner John Sterling couldn't get to the press box because the Secret Service wouldn't let him into the elevator. John tried the usual "Hey, I'm the Yankee announcer'' routine but it didn't wash. We finally had to send somebody down to identify him.

That kind of stuff happens all the time around sports stadiums when presidents attend, but hey, what's a little inconvenience compared to the importance of his attendance? I would like to see President Bush attend some games in Yankee Stadium this summer because it would mean (a) that he's got spare time on his hands and the world isn't on the edge of crisis and (b) the Bronx still belongs to the United States.

Which reminds me that former President Ronald Reagan did a network announcing stint at last summer's All-Star Game in Anaheim and I am almost sure I heard him identify the shortstop from St. Louis as Ollie instead of Ozzie.

How could he have done that?

I could understand if Herbie Swift made that kind of identification mistake. Herbie is the father of fifteen children, one of whom is Seattle Mariners pitcher Billy Swift. Said Herbie: "I threw a baseball into the crib with all the kids and only Billy threw it back.''

Mark Guthrie, who was a twenty-three-year-old rookie pitcher last summer with the Minnesota Twins, has a brother, Mike, who is fifteen years older.

"My dad saw me pitch one game and I threw a ball to the backstop,'' said older brother Mike. "That's when he decided to have another son.''

Then there was the day outfielder Glenn Wilson's son, Glenn Junior, was playing his first baseball game.

"Now, son,'' said father Glenn, calling home to offer encouragement, "I want you to lay off the curveball and sit on the fastball.''

"But dad,'' said six-year-old Glenn Junior, "this is T-ball.''

Peter Gent, who played football with the Dallas Cowboys and wrote the book *North Dallas Forty,* once said "Baseball players are the weirdest of all athletes. I think it's all that music.''

All what music?

Maybe Pete was talking about stadium organists who try to outdo one another by playing songs that fit the names of batters. Vince Lascheid, organist at Three Rivers Stadium in Pittsburgh, plays "The Gambler" when Greg Booker comes to the plate and "A Small Hotel" when it's Howard Johnson's turn. John Tudor gets to hear "Teach Me Tonight" and Vance Law gets "Dragnet." It happens elsewhere, too. In Seattle they play "School's Out" when relief pitcher Mike Schooler comes to the mound and by now everybody in baseball knows that "Wild Thing" was the early-season choice of reliever Mitch Williams of the Cubs.

Some players have their own musical talents. Dwight Smith of the Cubs sang the national anthem at Wrigley Field last summer (the first such player rendition since third baseman Carmen Fanzone trumpeted the anthem in 1972), and another group of Cubs from the bullpen cut a record called "It's a Bullpen Tradition," sung to the tune of Hank Williams Jr.'s "It's a Family Tradition." I have nothing against the talents of Mitch Williams, Pat Perry, Calvin Schiraldi, Jeff Pico, and Les Lancaster but I am glad I didn't hear it.

Eric Show of the Padres produced and recorded a jazz album and was planning a Christmas record; Mets manager Davey Johnson took voice lessons from Julius LaRosa (Davey said he wanted his voice to carry better in arguments with umpires); and Steve Sax was all set to play drums with the Beach Boys at Yankee Stadium but there was a mixup and he blew them off. And after San Diego's Tim Flannery sang with Jimmy Buffett at a club in Chicago, he said to his wife: "I can die and go to heaven now. I've been in the playoffs, played in the World Series, and now I've sung with Jimmy Buffett. What else is there?"

I once sang the National Anthem with the Mormon Tabernacle Choir.

Well, not exactly.

I was playing with the Dodgers at the time. We were in Philly for an NBC Game of the Week, and the Tabernacle Choir was out behind home plate performing. So all I did was stand in the back row with them and lip synch the song. The only way people knew I wasn't part of the regular group was the uniform I was wearing.

That was probably the highlight of my musical career, outside of singing in the shower. But if I could play an instrument I'd like to play piano like Jerry Lee Lewis in *Great Balls of Fire.* That's one of my later-in-life ambitions: learn to play the piano and speak Spanish. Then I could communicate with more players in baseball and mingle with Elton John instead of Tommy.

The Dodgers have a pitcher, John Wetteland, who is multitalented. His father, Ed, is a professional pianist in San Francisco and John plays both clarinet and saxophone. He also entertained teammates last summer by reading poetry he wrote, prompting manager Tom Lasorda to say: "I'm not sure our guys understood it but it sounded great."

Lasorda wasn't sure about a lot of things last season except his weight. One day he was sitting in his office at Dodger Stadium when a youthful player entered and introduced himself.

"At first I thought he was the batboy," said Lasorda. "Then I said, 'Are you here for a workout? Are you in high school or college?' "

The newcomer was twenty-five-year-old outfielder Bill Bean, who had been acquired in a trade from Detroit.

Trading and traveling. Ballplayers keep hearing that "it's part of the game" but nobody ever really gets used to it.

In chronological order, I played baseball in San Jose, El Paso, San Jose, El Paso, Seattle, Anaheim, Seattle, Anaheim, Seattle, Anaheim, Chicago, Oakland, Tucson, Toldeo, Philadelphia, New York, San Diego, Los Angeles, Chicago, and Los Angeles, with a few winter league stops in Puerto Rico for good behavior.

And that doesn't set any records, although playing for eight different major league clubs is above the norm.

Some players accept the inevitability of a trade, others fight it through contractual clauses if they have the leverage.

Pitcher Mike Morgan, when traded from the Orioles to the Dodgers in 1989, said: "I'm so tired of moving. I've got a house in Baltimore, one in Seattle, one in Las Vegas, and a cabin in Utah. In L.A., I'm renting Tim Leary's condo and he's a great landlord. Part of the deal is that he drives me to the park every day."

Then Leary got traded.

When Toronto pitcher Mike Flanagan heard a rumor he might be traded back to his old team in Baltimore, he said: "I guess I could be had if the price was right—maybe a bar of soap and a couple of dozen balls. But I really don't know anyone with the Orioles, anymore. Maybe a couple of ushers."

Sometimes it's easier to find the silver lining. Pitcher Randy Johnson said the best part of being traded from Montreal to Seattle was getting rid of his passport, work permit, and Canadian money. When pitcher Walt Terrell was swapped from the Padres to the Yankees after spending only four months in San Diego, he said: "My family just got there and we'd only been to Sea World. My kids are pretty upset. We never had a chance to go anywhere else, like the San Diego Zoo. Maybe now we can go to the Bronx Zoo."

I'm sure the kids loved that.

When pitcher Ken Howell was traded from the Dodgers to Baltimore he got so excited he drove to the nearest sporting goods store and bought himself a $9.50 Orioles cap. Four days later he was dealt from Baltimore to Philadelphia and the Orioles, with apology, sent him a check for $9.50 to pay for the cap.

Kevin Mitchell, despite hitting forty-seven home runs and helping the Giants into the World Series, remained leary about his future in San Francisco. He was still wearing a gold chain with the number "7" interlocking "NY" of the New York Mets, his former team. Said Mitchell: "Some players told me to get it replaced with 'SF' but I told them I wasn't sure how long I'd be around with the Giants."

When the Reno Silver Sox swapped pitcher Tom Fortugno to the Milwaukee Brewers organization, negotiations began with Reno co-owner and GM Jack Patton asking for four thousand dollars. He settled for twenty-five hundred dollars and 144 baseballs. That reminded California League statistician Bill Weiss of some other strange minor league deals.

In the 1920s, the owner of the Omaha club traded a pitcher to St. Joseph's for an airplane. The deal was subsequently canceled because the plane, not the pitcher, was defective.

Oyster Joe Martina, who won 355 games in a twenty-two-year pro career, got his nickname because he was traded for a barrel of oysters.

An infielder named Leonard Dondero was once swapped for a dozen doughnuts.

Glazed.

Trades are made for the damndest reasons, too. I once got traded, indirectly, because Reggie Jackson wasn't hitting. The whole domino tumble started during spring training, 1979, when I hit above .300 with the Yankees and literally won the starting left-field job. Lou Piniella was in right field, Mickey Rivers was in center, and Reggie was the designated hitter.

But after about thirty games at DH, Reggie was slumping and went to owner George Steinbrenner and said something like, "I don't feel right playing DH. I need to get back into the outfield and then I'll start hitting again." So owner George sent Reggie to manager Bob Lemon, who put Reggie in right field, moving Piniella over to left.

"Okay," I said, "I'll be the DH."

Wrong. Jim Spencer, also a left-handed hitter, had a clause in his contract that said he had to DH in so many games if Reggie didn't. How Spencer's agent got that past the Yankee front office I'll never know, but it was fact.

Anyhow, Spencer became the DH. He was a close friend, too, and a former roomie, but I was leading the club in hitting at the time and suddenly found myself on the bench.

So I went to Al Rosen, then the GM, and said, "Al, this is a ridiculous situation and I want to be traded. This is my option year and I've got to produce some numbers so I can get a good contract."

"My hands are tied," said Rosen.

Now we go into Anaheim to face four straight right-handers and I figure I'll at least get a chance to hit in front of my family and friends. Nada. I don't play and I'm screaming for a trade.

Finally, on June 13, just beating the trade deadline, the Yankees traded me to San Diego for a no-name pitcher (Dave Wehrmeister) with a losing record (2–7) who never pitched for the Yankees until 1981 (0–0, 5.14 ERA) and never won a game for them.

I ended up hitting .295 for the Padres that year and missed .300 by one hit. But I had beaten the Dodgers in two games with key hits late in the season and that's how I ended up signing a free agent contract with Los Angeles. Two years later I hit a home run against the Yankees in the World Series, which the Dodgers won.

I've often wondered what would have happened if Reggie had gotten off to a hot start in 1979 and remained at DH.

Nowadays, players only room with their own suitcases, but they still have to endure the travel—plane instead of train, night instead of day—with a few thousand bus rides (airport to hotel to ballpark to hotel to airport, and so forth) along the way.

Twice last season when the Cincinnati Reds traveled into Los Angeles they felt earthquakes. During the first shaker, pitcher Scott Scudder was just leaving a meeting with GM Murray Cook after being told he was being sent down to Nashville.

"Does this always happen when you send someone down?" Scudder asked Cook.

Scudder returned to the majors, however, and was sleeping during the next trip into L.A. when another earthquake hit.

"My hotel bed started shaking and I thought 'This must be a sign that I'm going down,' " Scudder said. "So I woke up and took the phone off the hook."

Strange things happen on the road. When Frank Howard was coaching with the Milwaukee Brewers back in 1986, he returned to the team hotel in Baltimore one morning about two o'clock and lit up a very large cigar as he boarded the elevator. Hondo, of course, is also very large (six-seven) and as he fired up his stogie, he also triggered the elevator's smoke detector.

Fire alarms emptied the hotel full of sleepy, angry, pajama-clad patrons—including members of the Milwaukee baseball team, who encountered a sheepish Howard in the hotel lobby.

"Gee," said Hondo, "I wonder what happened."

Word got back, however, that Howard was responsible and the next day he was visited in the Brewers' clubhouse by a uniformed Baltimore policeman.

"Mr. Howard," said the cop, "I understand you know something about a false alarm at your hotel last night. You're not under arrest, but we'd like you to come downtown to answer some questions."

Howard, mortified, then asked the policeman if he could change out of his uniform into his street clothes because he didn't want to "disgrace the organization."

That's when everyone started laughing and Howard, realizing he'd been had, said sheepishly, "Aw, I knew it was a joke all the time."

Aerophobic I am not. Fear of anything except maybe spiders, snakes, or slumps isn't compatible with being a major league baseball player or announcer, but fear of flying is as troublesome as fear of the curveball.

Not that I haven't had a few anxious moments at thirty thousand feet. Mostly, I'm just glad I don't know what's going on in the cockpit.

Consider the wild ride the San Diego Padres had into New York's LaGuardia Airport last summer during a violent thunderstorm.

"One plane went right under us," said Padre hitting star Tony Gwynn, "then another went right over us and one was on our tail like a Russian MIG. I thought we were in *Top Gun.*"

Stories abound. There isn't a ballplayer alive who hasn't experienced a few "incidents" in the air—his food tray becoming weightless, his stomach diving five thousand feet and leaving his heart behind, and so forth. Usually I just reach for the nearest stewardess but you have to be quick or she'll be taken.

John Madden fears flying but he's able to meet his network football and TV commercial commitments by riding in a superbus. Baseball players and announcers don't have that time luxury. Muhammad Ali was always afraid of flying. So was hockey superstar Wayne Gretzky (he went from sedation to hypnosis to sitting in the cockpit), and Hall of Famer Carl Yastrzemski never flies without white knuckles. Unfortunately for Yaz, one of his Boston Red Sox teammates, Luis Tiant, was also afraid and would let out a screech whenever a plane made a bumpy landing. Said Yaz: "I never liked shaky landings but once Luis let out his howl, I liked them even less."

Pro bowler Johnny Petraglia stopped flying after experiencing a near-fatal crash over Lake Michigan in 1981 and now drives forty thousand miles a year to tournaments. Pro basketball coach Doug Moe hates flying (he even scours the weather reports) and so did NBA star Sam Lacey and NFL quarterback Billy Kilmer. A friend of mine, former Dodger pitching great Don Newcombe, claims aerophobia nearly ruined his career and life.

"In 1951," says Newcombe, "there were so many crashes near Elizabeth, New Jersey, that they closed down Newark airport. Out of curiosity, I visited some of the crash scenes with my friends on the police force. Something triggered and after that I got scared every time I boarded a plane."

Newk says the fear contributed to a drinking problem, until finally he had to seek help. He learned self-hypnosis and even today, as a spokesman in the community relations office of the L.A. Dodgers who travels more than 350,000 miles a year, speaking to groups about the dangers of alcoholism, Newcombe has to tell himself to "relax, relax, relax" before boarding a plane.

Most ballplayers live by statistics, but the numbers don't faze aerophobics. Tell them there are fifty times more fatal accidents on highways than on scheduled flights and they'll just look at you with a blank stare and say "I don't care, I want *off!*"

The late Jackie Jensen's story was the saddest. Before the term superstar was fashionable, Jensen was one at the University of Southern California, where he was All-American in both football and baseball in the late 1940s. As a major leaguer, Jackie hit thirty-five home runs, drove in 122 runs, and was named MVP of the American League in 1958 with the Boston Red Sox.

One year later he had twenty-eight home runs and 112 runs

batted in at the age of thirty-two, but quit because of his fear of flying. He came back in 1961 for one more try, but nothing worked, and he retired.

Max Patkin was another story. Mad Max, the Clown Prince of Baseball, once flew from Philadelphia to Alaska to Vancouver to Portland to Honolulu to Nashville in five days. Even last summer, at age sixty-nine and suffering from bad knees, bone spurs, and herniated discs, slapstick entertainer Patkin was barnstorming in his forty-fourth year.

You may have seen him in the movie *Bull Durham,* but your father or grandfather may have seen him along the third-base line of some obscure minor league park, doing chicken imitations or spewing water into the air as part of his Old Faithful routine. Max was a ballpark entertainer long before San Diego ever had a major league team, let alone a feathered mascot.

"I even made Connie Mack laugh," said Max, who started his career as a righthanded pitcher for Wilkes-Barre, Pennsylvania, in the Eastern League. A sore arm sent him from the mound into the comedian's costume, however, and he's been at it since.

And, as ballplayers know, some nights are better than others.

"On the night we landed our first man on the moon (in 1969) I was booked into Great Falls, Montana. I counted four fans in the audience. There were more people in my bed that night than in the ballpark."

Worst town he ever played?

"Monroe, Louisiana. The mosquitoes were so big they thought my nose was a landing field."

Max, who celebrated his seventieth birthday in January, was expected back at it this spring, putting him into his sixth decade—forties through the nineties—as a ballpark entertainer. Even though he has reduced his workload to seventy-five performances a year, he still travels about 150,000 miles each season and receives twelve to fifteen hundred dollars per show.

"Compared to what that Chicken makes, the newsboy cashes my checks," said salty Max last summer in a magazine interview, "but that cheap little bleep doesn't even leave anything for the clubhouse boys. I always leave the kids five or ten dollars. The only thing I ever heard of the Chicken leaving was one of his dolls and he makes $1 million a year."

Max probably wishes his exposure from *Bull Durham* had come along earlier in his career, and did you know there really is a very successful minor league team named the Durham Bulls? The movie was shot at the Bulls' Class-A park and helped drive attendance in 1988 up to 270,000, more than 50,000 above a record 1987.

The owner of the Durham Bulls, Miles Wolff, also publishes *Baseball America*, a weekly newspaper that has become the bible of minor league baseball with a circulation in excess of 50,000.

Wolff knows about scuffling in the minor leagues. Back in 1971 at age twenty-six he was general manager of the Savannah Braves, one of the worst teams in the minors.

"We were so bad we once went a whole month without winning a game at home," recalls Wolff. But that didn't keep him from promoting his product.

Savannah once held a Pray-for-Pitching Night and anybody who brought a church bulletin got in for half-price. Wolff said he assumed that if they'd been to church they had also prayed for his team.

He also held Free Deodorant Night, which drew a good crowd, especially kids who began lighting the spray from the aerosol cans and turning them into blowtorches.

The one I'm really glad I missed, though, was Free Hot Dog night, when the fans got tired of eating hot dogs and started throwing them at the players.

Is there a word for fear of riding a bus? Maybe Fumophobia? Surely there can't be an athlete alive who hasn't been subjected to some memorable, if not horrifying, bus rides in his career.

Phil Itzoe, as traveling secretary for the Baltimore Orioles for twenty-six years, loves telling about one such incident when the Orioles were in Seattle for a night game at the Kingdome.

"Our assistant PR director was making his first regular-season trip with the club and after the game, he asked me when the bus would leave for the hotel. I told him 10:35 P.M. and that was that."

What Itzoe didn't know what that O's manager Frank Robinson had called a team meeting after the game. Therefore the departure time was moved to 11:00 P.M. The only problem was that nobody told the assistant PR man, who showed up shortly before 10:35 P.M., waited patiently for about ten minutes, then told the bus driver to leave.

"The bus left with just him and the driver," said Itzoe. "Now the team comes out of the clubhouse and there's no bus. It was unbelievable. We had to call the hotel to send back the bus."

That is a mild experience compared to some that have occurred, and still do occur, in the minor leagues. As Hall of Fame pitcher Bob Lemon recalls about riding the team bus in the lower minors: "You'd sit for seven or eight hours, arrive at dawn, try in vain to get some sleep, then make it to the game just in time to put on your uniform. My goal was to make the Southern Association because they took the railroad."

"Every athlete should spend a few years taking all-day bus trips," says Larry Andersen of the Houston Astros. "It makes you more appreciative. Buses put a permanent note in your head that you've been through some rough times."

Hub Kittle, seventy-four, who only made it to the majors as a coach, told *Sports Illustrated* about "Pat House, the best bus-riding pitcher I ever had."

What makes a good bus-riding pitcher?

"He never slept before a start. Had a system," said Kittle. "He wanted to pitch the opening game of every road series. He figured that after seven hours in a bus, the guys are loose and ready to hit the hell out of the ball. And he was right. They did score a lot of runs for him. Of course, the game after that, bus lag would set in and they couldn't hit worth anything."

Kittle claims he almost drowned in a bus when managing the Hermosillo Naranjeros in Mexico. Seems his team was busing home after a game in Mazatlan when they reached a river with no bridges. The ferry wasn't around, either, so the bus driver drove into the river and started following a parade of trucks and horse-drawn wagons. Everything was fine, too, until the bus hit quick-sand, started to sink, and muddy water started coming into the bus and down the aisles.

So everybody jumped out and waded to shore, where they built a mesquite fire to dry off and drank beer and tequila, and Kittle sang his rendition of ''The Bullpen Pitcher's Lament,'' which he claimed was written by a deaf knuckleballer, Tin Ear Medigini, in the back of a bus when Kittle was managing Bremerton in the Western International League. The lyrics:

> *I've been working in the bullpen,*
> *All the livelong day.*
> *I've been working in the bullpen,*
> *Just throwin' my arm away.*
> *Can't you hear Hub Kittle shouting*
> *Hey, come here on this mound.*
> *And try to stop these sons of bitches*
> *From knockin' the ball around.*

Remember Phil Linz, Yogi Berra, and the infamous harmonica on the Yankee bus?

As legend has it, the incident occurred in 1964 aboard the Yankees' airport shuttle, after the team had just dropped four straight to the White Sox in Comiskey Park. Needless to say, it was not a happy group en route to O'Hare Airport.

That's when, from the back of the bus, came the screeching sounds of ''Mary Had a Little Lamb'' from the new harmonica of utility infielder Linz. But in the first row, manager Berra's face was not as white as snow.

''Hey, Linz,'' he shouted, ''go stick that harmonica in your ear.''

Or something like that.

''What did Yogi say?'' Linz asked, leaning forward to Mickey Mantle.

''He said to play it louder,'' said Mantle.

Linz complied, only to look up and see a livid Berra headed for

182 *Some of My Best Friends Are Crazy*

him. Linz, as quick as a utility infielder should be, tossed the harmonica to his manager, who angrily flung it back, hitting Joe Pepitone on the knee. Pepi immediately fell to the floor screaming, "Oh, my god, he broke my knee!"

The next day Berra fined Linz two hundred dollars and one day later Phil was offered a five-thousand-dollar contract to endorse harmonicas. The Yankees won thirty of their next forty-three games and the pennant and when Linz signed a new contract the following winter, GM Ralph Houk tossed in a two-hundred-dollar bonus.

"For harmonica lessons," said Houk.

Pat House, that "bus-riding pitcher" of Hub Kittle's memory, perhaps would have scoffed at some of the logistical problems that got attention last summer in the major leagues.

Rick Sutcliffe of the Cubs, who pitched the third inning of the All-Star Game but was nicked for two runs on four hits, was excused by some observers because of his hasty preparation. Rick, you see, didn't learn of his selection until he had played thirty holes of golf (stopping only because of darkness) in suburban Kansas City the day before the game. As a last-minute replacement for injured Mike Scott of the Astros, Sutcliffe flew early the next day but didn't arrive at his Anaheim hotel until 1:15 P.M., thirty minutes before the National League team was to leave for the stadium.

Meanwhile, Ned Colletti, the Cubs' media relations director, was trying to get Sutcliffe's uniform and glove flown from Chicago. The uniform arrived at Anaheim Stadium at 3:05 P.M., less than two and a half hours before game time.

Then there was the nightmarish debut of Giants rookie pitcher Russ Swan.

Recalled from Phoenix, Swan was trying to catch a morning flight to Los Angeles when he was pulled over by an Arizona policeman and handed a speeding ticket for driving fifty-seven miles an hour in a forty-five-mile-an-hour zone. By the time he reached his plane, his seat had been taken. So he caught the next flight and arrived at Dodger Stadium at 5:10 P.M., where he was met in the dugout by manager Roger Craig, who said, "Hurry up, you're starting."

"What?" said Swan, who hadn't even been told whether he was being called up as a starter or reliever.

"I was in shock," said Swan, but there was more shock to come. Despite being staked to a 3–0 lead on Kevin Mitchell's thirty-fourth home run, the Dodgers nailed Swan, 6–3, to ruin his major league debut.

I have to figure, under those conditions, that bus-riding Pat House would have thrown a shutout.

11

And Now, a Word from the Sportswriters . . .

Baseball players say the strangest things.

Pedro Guerrero of the Cardinals, for example, says about sports-writers, "Sometimes they write what I say and not what I mean."

Pirates outfielder Glenn Wilson, who owns a service station in Texas, said after being told during batting practice that he needed to improve his mechanics: "I can't afford it. I just gave them a raise."

Catcher Benito Santiago of the Padres, responding to manager Jack McKeon's urging that he "grow up," said: "If I grow up any more, I'll be like Big Bird."

Then there was Atlanta outfielder-turned-pitcher Terry Blocker, who told writers: "My pitching coach [Bruce Del Canton] says my fastball has good movement and philosophy."

And considering some of the utterances coming from second baseman Jim Gantner of the Milwaukee Brewers, he could be headed for a successful career in announcing.

Gantner, also known to friends as "Gumby," or "Dog," is the current baseball version of Norm Crosby. He may fracture the English language but he always knows what he means, so what's the problem? Some Gantnerisms:

When reporting to training camp one spring, Jim was asked

what he did over the winter. "I went hunting in one of those Canadian proverbs."

When he complained to an umpire about a runner bumping into him while he tried to field a ball: "That's construction, that's construction!"

Another time, Gumby was recalling a round of golf he played on a course under construction. "They made us play on the contemporary greens."

During batting practice once, Gantner cracked a ball to the right-field wall and yelled, "I hit one into the garner."

"What's the garner?" asked teammate Robin Yount.

"That's when you hit it into the gap and the corner at the same time," said Gantner.

And when he was asked the proper way to be prepared on defense when the pitcher releases the ball: "You've got to stay on the palms of your feet."

Read my lips: Baseball is not rocket science. When somebody made a comment about the intelligence level of the World Champion Oakland A's to outfielder Dave Henderson, he replied: "I don't see any Stanford guys running around here. Look at Terry Steinbach. He thinks hockey is a sport."

I like Henderson's attitude. After he robbed the Angels' Brian Downing of a hit with a sensational catch, he watched as Downing threw his batting helmet.

"Nice, wasn't it?" said Henderson, afterward. "It's an outfielder's dream, making somebody break their helmet."

When reliever Steve Bedrosian was traded to the National League Champion San Francisco Giants, he tried to get around a team rule against beards.

"I tried to pull the I-was-in-Vietnam routine but that didn't work. They didn't buy Korea, either. So I guess I'll try to fit in here. I don't want to be revolting."

Just "being there" is important enough for most players. There are few enough jobs for all those men who dream of playing in the major leagues. When pitcher Don Aase returned to the "bigs" last year with the Mets, he said: "I'm like a whale. Every once in a while I resurface."

White Sox pitcher Jack Hardy, finally reaching the "show" after eight years in the minor leagues, was asked by a reporter if he preferred to start or relieve.

"I'll do anything," said Hardy, "even carry the water if they want."

Pirate rookie Morris Madden, before pitching a winning game against the Cardinals in St. Louis, described his apprehension: "It was tough getting to sleep. I'd look out the window of the hotel [Marriott Pavilion] and see that big ballpark across the street and know there would be forty thousand people out there. I got so nervous I decided to imagine I was just playing against Pawtucket, and it worked."

After Toronto rookie pitcher Alex Sanchez walked the leadoff hitter in his first major league game, he looked up to see catcher Bob Brenly walking toward the mound.

"Well, kid," said Brenly, handing him the ball, "look at it this way. You've got your first big league hitter out of the way and you've still got your no-hitter."

Remember that scene in the movie *Bull Durham* when the catcher (played by Kevin Costner), irritated that his pitcher wouldn't follow instructions, tipped the hitter on the next pitch, which was belted for a home run?

It reminded me of the story told by Hall of Famer Johnny Bench about a game in 1969 when the Reds sent Jerry Arrigo to the mound against the Dodgers. Arrigo was fond of his fastball. Bench wasn't.

"He was pitching against hitters I knew he couldn't possibly throw it by," said Bench. "I called for a curve and he shook it off. I called a curve one more time and he shook it off. He finally threw a fastball outside."

Bench caught the ball bare-handed. Arrigo got the point.

More rocket science: When Steve Lyons of the White Sox plays first base he always draws a Tic-Tac-Toe board in the dirt near the bag and competes against other first basemen in the American League.

"They all played me except Fred McGriff and Randy Milligan," said Lyons. "I don't think they know how."

Lyons is the same hustler who feels he needs to bunt to remain in the big leagues. He figures he's a .240 hitter who can hit .260 or .270 with ten bunt hits a year (in 1989 he hit .264). I guess that's why Steve was considered so different when he played back in 1985 for the Red Sox in Boston.

"We had an older team of guys who waited to hit the ball into the street. They didn't want to get their uniforms dirty. I'd bunt and slide into first base and it got the fans' attention."

Lyons probably felt a lot like talented shortstop Alan Trammell felt last season, playing with the Detroit Tigers, who lost 103 games. As somebody said, "Poor Alan. He's like a kid who's lost in a mall, all alone."

Most of the rest of Sparky Anderson's Tigers played like scout Ellis Clary once described his own playing abilities: "My coordination was so bad I had to pull my car off to the side of the road to blow the horn."

Nobody ever said hitting a baseball was easy, Ellis. Four members of the Pittsburgh Penguins hockey team discovered that last summer when they took batting practice at Three Rivers Stadium against Pirates coach Rich Donnelly.

"They were all low-ball hitters," said Donnelly about Mario Lemieux, Dan Quinn, Paul Coffey, and Kevin Stevens. "If you rolled it up there, they'd knock the hell out of it."

Randy Bush of the Minnesota Twins has hit fourteen home runs during President George Bush's administration in the White House, leaving him 88 short of the 102 dingers Gary Carter hit during the Carter administration.

Deron Johnson led the Johnsons with 98 during the LBJ era, Danny Ford belted 35 during the Gerald Ford years, John E. Kennedy hit one during the JFK era, and Art Wilson clouted 30 during the Woodrow Wilson administration.

Somehow, Russ, Otis, and Donnell Nixon went homerless during the You Know Who administration, and the country never had a president named Ruth, Maris, Aaron, or Oh.

For that information, I present a Jaybird Award in Wacko Stats Competition to sportswriter Jayson Stark.

Where would baseball be without them, those numbers upon numbers upon numbers compiled by men who probably spent their childhoods playing Cadaco's All-Star Baseball Game and saving the box scores?

Surely baseball historians would record more *significant* statistics in recent seasons than the ones to follow, but these are other JWS (Jaybird Wacko Stats) recipients, all worthy honorees:

- Right-fielder Scott Lusader of the Tigers for committing three errors in the first inning against the White Sox. On three separate plays, he dropped a fly ball, made a throw to the wall behind home plate, and allowed a single to get past him.

   Said Lusader: "No excuses. I just butchered it."

- The Cincinnati Reds, who scored fourteen runs on sixteen hits in the first inning against Houston.

   "I played for one run and got fourteen," said Reds manager Pete Rose.

   "The last time I saw anything like that," added Astros reliever Dave Smith, "I was playing for Tastee Freeze in Little League."

- Jimmy Qualls, now a farmer outside Quincy, Illinois, for breaking up Tom Seaver's no-hitter with one out in the ninth inning twenty-one years ago in Shea Stadium. Seaver had retired the first twenty-five members of the 1969 Cubs before Qualls's clean single.

   So what? That was the closest any pitcher from the New York Mets ever got to throwing a no-hitter. The N.Y. pitching staff has played 4,505 games since entrance into the National League in 1962 without throwing a single no-no.

- Benny Distefano, Pittsburgh, who on May 14 against Atlanta became only the sixth left-handed catcher in the majors since the turn of the century. Distefano entered the game in the ninth inning, recorded a putout on a strikeout, and said afterward: "I'll do anything to get a chance to play."

• Jerome Walton of the Cubs, Rookie of the Year in the NL, who hit safely in thirty consecutive games.

• Jose Canseco of Oakland, who was roasted by a San Francisco police chief for being a member of the forty-forty-forty club: "Forty home runs, forty steals, forty moving violations."

• Gregg Jefferies of the Mets, who has 107 career hits, for telling a minor league roomie that his goal was Pete Rose's career record of 4,265 hits.

Responded Mets manager Davey Johnson: "Why not aim high? Should he have said he was aiming for Rod Gaspar's hit record?"

Gaspar had fifty-four career hits.

• Dick Allen, Reggie Jackson, Mike Schmidt, and Nelson Liriano—all men who have broken up Nolan Ryan no-hitters in the ninth inning.

• The Chicago White Sox, who would have to sweep every series from now until 2008 to draw even in career standings with the New York Yankees.

• Ron Kittle of the Chisox, who after going oh-for-fourteen and striking out ten times against Roger Clemens of the Red Sox, took his bats into the training room and dumped them into the whirlpool.

"They went around and around," said Kittle, "but they still didn't hit anything."

• Atlanta catcher Bruce Benedict, for being involved in three triple plays—a catcher in one, runner in another, and hit into a third.

• Rick Sutcliffe, Jerry Reuss, Tommy John, Charlie Hough, Brian Holton, Dave Stewart, Bob Welch, and Ken Howell— all eight former L.A. Dodger pitchers who won games for other teams during the first three days of the 1989 season.

• Finally, this Jaybird Mr. Moto (Master of the Obvious) Award to rookie catcher Rick Wrona of the Cubs, who said, excitedly, after hitting his first major league home run:
"You don't get your first home run too often."

I'll tell you something else you don't get too often: a well-dressed sportswriter.

There are exceptions. I've never seen Joe Durso of *The New York Times,* for example, without a coat and tie. Most of his peers, however, dress as if they just came back from watching the Grateful Dead in the rain. They apparently believe appropriate work dress is a Batman or Rolling Stones t-shirt with jeans and dirty Nikes.

But I like the Scruffs from the BBWAA (Baseball Writers Association of America) because they talk straight. They all have those built-in bullshit detectors and whenever some GM or player starts with the excuses or tilted rationale, you can almost hear the "beep-beeps" going off in their brains.

More and more I find myself hanging out around the press boxes during rain delays. Not much around a baseball operation slips past them, except how to dress.

Maybe their choice of clothing is dictated by poor salaries paid by newspapers, or by the late hours they're forced to spend in press boxes, taxicabs, and saloons. All I know is that some clubs have made reference to appearances of the BBWAA Scruffs in recent seasons.

The Yankees actually sent out a memo last year stating that writers who ride team charters should dress better (clean t-shirts, pants without holes, and so forth). After all, reasoned the Yankees, when a plane full of players wearing coats and ties unloads, why should another dozen guys traipse through the airport looking as if they just got out of the soup line?

Typical BBWAA response: "You guys do your jobs, we'll do ours, and don't worrry about how we dress."

And, based on 1989, I'd say the writers did their jobs a little better than the Yankees.

One club executive who took a shot at the Scruffs was Don

Grenesko, president of the Chicago Cubs. It all started with the unfortunate heart attack death of a writer (Bud Saidt, *Trenton (N.J.) Times*), within a few days after he had covered a Phillies-Cubs series in Wrigley Field, where a new press box had been built in the upper deck.

There is no elevator at Wrigley Field, however, and some of Saidt's peers felt the stress of trekking up the ramps may have contributed to his heart attack. Phil Pepe, national head of the BBWAA, wrote a letter to Grenesko protesting the lack of an elevator for the working press.

Grenesko, mixing his apples and oranges, reacted by saying: "This is a workplace. People should dress accordingly. It offends me to see grown men with t-shirts hanging out and short pants or cutoffs."

Writers responded that (a) not all press boxes are kept clean, (b) many have exposed seats and wall nails that tear decent clothing, (c) coats and ties are uncomfortable in summer heat, (d) three-piece suits are out of their price range, and (e) what in hell does it have to do with no elevator in Wrigley Field, anyhow?

Nobody won. There is still no elevator in Wrigley Field (although there are sixty-seven new skyboxes at an average rental cost of fifty-five thousand dollars each) and the Scruffs are still the Scruffs.

Grenesko of the Cubs, incidentally, was the same club president who banned beer in the home, visitors', and umpires' clubhouses at Wrigley Field.

"I don't think that it's appropriate to have beer in, in essence, a workplace," said Grenesko.

Needless to say, the Cardinals, owned by the Busch family, brought their own.

And one wonders how Grenesko would have handled one former Cubs pitcher, Dick Radatz, a huge, fun-loving reliever who wound up his career in 1969 with the expansion Montreal Expos. On a particularly steamy afternoon in Atlanta, a member of the grounds crew dumped a wheelbarrow stocked with crushed ice on the steps of the visiting clubhouse. Asked what had happened, Expos manager Gene Mauch barely blinked and said: "Nothing. Radatz just spilled one of his cocktails."

Darryl Strawberry of the Mets once said about baseball writers: "They're my buddies. Check 'em out. Can't live with 'em, can't live without 'em."

Mickey Hatcher of the Dodgers, always a favorite with the Scruffs because of his sense of humor and cooperation, said during a road trip rainout: "I'm working on a new ark with a cage for writers."

Unquestionably, a more adversarial relationship has developed between players and writers in recent years, perhaps because the players are so well-paid they believe they no longer need to be cooperative.

Bill Buckner, formerly of the Red Sox, for example, blames the media because people keep reminding him of the ball that dribbled past him in game six of the 1986 World Series.

"The media keep harping, harping, and harping on it," said Buckner. "It's not offensive to me but the media think it is. People keep asking me if I'm going to shoot myself."

Tom Lasorda has had his highs and lows with writers, including a low in 1989 when he challenged a young reporter in Pittsburgh. No blows were struck, however, and Lasorda later claimed he was kidding.

Writers as official scorers is another issue. There was a time when almost all scoring was done by writers, but many newspapers no longer allow it because they figure the writer puts himself into a conflict-of-interest situation by accepting the sixty-dollar-per-game stipend paid by major league baseball. Also, newspaper editors and managing editors—many of whom have never been out of the office—can't comprehend how a baseball writer can remain objective while scoring and then interviewing a player who may have been involved in the scoring decision.

There can be problems. Example: When Mike Schmidt of the Phillies ended his career last summer, he went oh-for-three with two walks in his final game in San Francisco. Schmidt's slow roller in the seventh inning, booted by shortstop Jose Uribe, was first ruled a hit, then changed to an error by official scorer Mike Lefkow of the *Contra Costa Times*.

The next day, as Schmidt was preparing to announce his retirement, Lefkow received a call at Candlestick Park from Vince Nauss, Phillies publicity director, who said it would be nice if Schmidt could end his career with a hit and couldn't Lefkow reverse his call? Nauss also said he was calling at the direction of Bill Giles, president of the Phillies.

Lefkow, however, said he had solicited a number of opinions, reviewed the replay, and decided the play should stand as an error on Uribe.

"After this year I'm not going to do it anymore," said Lefkow, later. "I'm a reporter. I shouldn't be making the news. They should have a fifth umpire traveling and they should take turns as official scorer."

Sports writing can be perilous, as anyone can attest who was in Candlestick Park last October for game three of the Earthquake World Series.

There are also the Killer Pigeons of Anaheim to worry about.

When sportswriter Jon Heyman of the *South Bay Daily Breeze* was making a call from a telephone booth outside Anaheim Stadium last year, a pigeon walked up to him—that's right, *walked up to him*—looked him over, then flew up and hit him in the chest.

Heyman warded off the attacker with his arm and headed for his car, but the pigeon, either angry or enamored, gave chase, flying in close pursuit as Heyman dashed for the parking lot, where he finally got into his car and slammed the door.

Give that pigeon a Jaybird Award and let's move on to fish and dogs.

A number of visiting writers gathered on a research-and-destroy mission in a saloon called Jukebox Saturday Night a few years ago when the All-Star Game was played in Minneapolis. One late arrival was Steve Wulf of *Sports Illustrated,* who immediately became a celebrity because of his date, a northern pike, deceased.

Wulf, earlier attending a lavish party thrown by major league baseball at a nearby hotel ballroom, had noticed the lonely northern pike resting on a block of carved ice as he prepared to depart. And, inasmuch as he was going to meet friends, why not bring along a new one?

The writers, once introduced to the fish, soon found themselves posing for a "team picture" in the saloon, and somebody climaxed the festivities by slam-dunking their new, semifrozen friend through a barroom basketball hoop.

The next day as well-dressed Wulf was walking across the field in the Metrodome during pre–All-Star-Game ceremonies, the tuba player from one of the marching bands pointed toward him and shouted, "Hey, that's the guy with the fish!"

"It was most embarrassing," said Wulf.

One of the fringe benefits of being a baseball writer or broadcaster is spring training. As Gordon Verrell of the *Long Beach Press-Telegram* said following a particularly productive March with the Dodgers in Vero Beach, Florida: "I knew it had been a good spring when I discovered that most of my notes were written on cocktail napkins."

Strange things happen during spring training, such as the evening during 1989 when a group of L.A. writers met the Dog Lady of Vero Beach.

She had appeared as a vision, wearing shorts and an attention-getting halter, out of nowhere on a warm, spring evening, leading her expensive dog along the beach (which was forbidden) and drinking Long Island Iced Teas (which was not) as if they were free (which they were, once she fell into the company of the L.A. writers).

Reports are that she eventually was pulled into the surf after her legs got tangled in the dog's leash, and that one brave scribe, ever gallant, staggered to the rescue and took her home to dry. Details get a little hazy after that. Except that the Dodgertown press room conversation the next day went something like this:

"Where did the dog sleep?"

"In the other bed."

"You know you may be the only guy to catch AIDS and fleas in the same evening."

"Oh, no, everything is okay."

"Really? What did you use, a condom or a flea collar? You may have given new meaning to safe sex."

I miss spring training at Dodgertown. Not that Fort Lauderdale, where the Yankees train, isn't nice. Where else can you find topless bakeries and handicapped parking at all-night strip joints? But that's not my style, anyhow, and I miss the "family" atmosphere of Dodgertown, where owner Peter O'Malley also lives during the spring. He throws a Saint Patrick's Day party every year, a holdover from his father, the late Walter O'Malley, and last spring the party was dedicated to recent Hall of Fame inductee Bob Hunter, aka The Chopper, a writer who has covered the Dodgers since they came West from Brooklyn.

It's a party I'm sorry I missed because nobody was more deserving. Chopper was never a Scruff, either. He always knew how to dress, drink, and write, so over a half-century of sports writing, I don't guess he missed much.

When Tracy Jones of the Giants banged into the Candlestick Park fence early last year, right where Hall of Famer Christy Mathewson's name was inscribed, somebody in the press box said: "That's the first pitcher he's hit this year."

When it was reported that the Expos had signed a pitcher in the Dominican Republic who had six fingers on each hand, a Scruff said: "I guess that means he'll be twice as good as Mordecai (Three Finger) Brown."

I know one baseball writer, Tom (Blumpy) Keegan, who covers the Chicago Cubs, who admits he once aspired to be a "human experiment."

What does that mean, Blump?

"To just go in and let them use me for tests."

Not only are baseball writers interested in advancing science, they are literate, as evidenced by Peter Schmuck's favorite Latin saying "Temperis Fuckit," which means: "Time flies whether you're having fun or not."

Temperis Fuckit, however, has yet to stand the test of time as has Koppett's Law, the creed by which the BBWAA exists. Former *New York Times* baseball writer Leonard Koppett once said: "Whatever will cause the greatest inconvenience to the most people is what will happen," and baseball-writing colleagues live by his truth, figuring that by following that logic they will never be disappointed. What happened last October before game three of the World Series, however, may have pushed Koppett's Law to the limit.

Two more Jaybird Awards:

- Bill Jauss of the *Chicago Tribune* receives the 1990 Jaybird On-Camera Scruff Award for his appearance on *The Sports Writers on TV* show in Chicago, where his red suspenders broke, with the rear strap flipping over his head to land in a cup of coffee two feet in front of him.
- Rich Griffin, publicist for the Montreal Expos, receives the Jaybird Attitude Award for his continuing ability to find humor in his job. Poring over Griffin's daily publicity notes can be a journey of joy for writers. Example: Griffin reacted to a rain delay at domed Olympic Stadium last season by listing his five favorite reasons for delays or postponements at the "Big O."
  1. Explosion and fire in the stadium tower (which holds up the roof) in 1977.
  2. Roof up, rain down. The retractable roof was stuck open by rainy, windy conditions.
  3. An eighteen-wheeler truck hit the outfield fence and destroyed a section of it in a pregame parade in 1987.
  4. Seals loose on the field from a pregame circus in 1985.
  5. (Tie.) Five hundred marching bands take the field and can't get off in time for a 1987 game; squirrel loose on the field and couldn't be caught in 1983.

And to complete this press section, did you know the San Diego Chicken celebrates his sixteenth birthday this year and now prints his own newsletter with the slogan "All the News That's Fit to Peck"?

Price of the paper is "cheep, cheep."

If this announcing career doesn't work out, perhaps I could stay in baseball by becoming a mascot. I couldn't compete with the Chicken or the Phillie Phanatic, because they're the best—but I could do better than that awful parrot they had in Pittsburgh or the crab in Baltimore or the Redbird in St. Louis. Those fellows should look for some other line of work, because they're just not funny.

One club that doesn't have a mascot is the Cubs (maybe they figure they've got enough in the bleachers) but they had an unofficial one in spring training for eight seasons before he got the ax.

The guy, James Kopf, called himself "Cubby" and there was such a stir when he was banned from HoHoKam park in Mesa, Arizona, last spring that other mascots demonstrated in his behalf.

When fans showed up for an exhibition game, they were greeted by a devil, a gorilla, a couple of birds, and a dog wearing a trench coat, all picketing for "mascot rights."

It didn't work. Even the presence of McGruff, the crime-fighting dog, didn't help. He would have been more help bringing Colin McLaughlin down from the mountain.

It was just another spring-training story: McGothlin, a pitcher trying to make it with the Seattle Mariners, decided one day to climb the butte above their Tempe, Arizona, training site to contemplate his future. While he was on the mountain, however, his future was being decided down below. He was cut from the squad.

The Mariners didn't want to release the news, though, until they told McGothlin, so everybody sat around all day waiting for him to come down.

Why didn't they send someone up to tell him?

Would you like to climb a mountain to tell a guy he had just been sent to the minors? They should have sent McGruff.

12

The Pride
of the Yankees?

Sometimes there aren't an awful lot of laughs around the Yankees.

Last summer, for example, was an on-field snore. Oh, sure, George Steinbrenner fired his manager, Dallas Green; some guy jumped out of the upper deck at Yankee Stadium; and one of the players, Luis Polonia, got arrested on a sex charge—but what's so unusual about that in New York?

It got so dull around the never-in-contention Yanks (74–87, fifth place) that I started riding the subway home from the Bronx *late at night* just to keep on my toes.

Anybody can ride the subway *to Yankee Stadium.* Getting home intact is the challenge. I get on board about midnight with my box score and briefcase and make believe I'm Charles Bronson in the movie *Death Wish,* but even there, nothing exciting seems to happen, at least to me.

Maybe this year.

Maybe Bucky Dent won't get fired.

Maybe the Yankees will once again be contenders.

Maybe Pascual Perez won't get lost in the Bronx.

Maybe I'll have that second cup of coffee with Steinbrenner.

Last year as Yankee radio announcer for WABC I played the

role of Ensign Pulver (Jack Lemmon), the stay-anonymous, frog-in-the-pocket Laundry and Morale Officer from the 1955 Warner Bros. movie *Mister Roberts*. Steinbrenner, of course, was the Captain (James Cagney) who had more serious problems on his mind—such as who (Henry Fonda) threw the plant overboard or who (Dallas Green) nicknamed him Manager George.

George and I talked only once all season so I can't be blamed for anything that happened on the field.

It's not like I was really ducking the owner of the ballclub. It's just that we never crossed paths. We had one cup of coffee in the press lounge when he happened to sit at my table, but that was it, which was okay, because owners shouldn't be soliciting radio announcers for their opinions, anyhow.

I was sort of the see-nothing, hear-nothing Teflon Man caught in a running battle between the Yankees' front office and WABC radio. First there was the tiff over whether we should wear neckties in the radio booth—that was Steinbrenner's idea after my partner, John Sterling, showed up for a spring-training game in shorts. Then WABC President Fred Weinhaus told the Yankees we certainly didn't need a "dress code" since nobody could see us on the radio, and one day he even peeked under my sweater to check for a tie and said, "If you wear one you're fired."

That's when I started wearing Hawaiian shirts.

There was also some Yankee-WABC hassle over the use of hospitality suites at Yankee Stadium, and that's one of the things I didn't enjoy about broadcasting Yankee games: The announcers were considered "outsiders" and not really part of the club. One day I'll probably consider that a blessing but being a rookie, I was accustomed to the "team" relationship and it didn't apply to broadcasters. We weren't invited to team social functions (meet the fans at Gallagher's, and so forth) and often we had to make our own travel arrangements because the Yankees neglected to reserve a hotel room for us.

During the final month of the 1989 season we were even told not to walk through the Yankee executive offices. Knowing my reputation, maybe somebody thought I was making free long-distance calls on Yankee phones. Actually, I just liked to cut through the offices because (a) it was a shorter route than going through the media gate, and (b) I could pick up the press notes early and prepare for work.

No big deal. This is a new season and the more important question is not whether I can short-cut through the Yankee offices—it's whether the Yankees under their young manager will be contenders.

Unless they get some new pitching talent it's going to be difficult.

You know those little transparent miniglobes you see in souvenir gift shops—the ones you shake upside down to make the fake snowflakes settle to the bottom? The Yankees last summer were like all those snow flurries, floating every which direction without any magnet to draw them together.

There was little unity and little leadership, other than from newcomer Steve Sax, who had a tremendous season and earned such respect from his teammates that he emerged during the last half as the team leader.

My opinion of George Steinbrenner as owner of the Yankees?

He's a powerful man with a toy but it's his toy. The franchise is worth more than any in baseball ($200 million, estimated) and no matter how much heat George takes from Yankee fans, and it got pretty bad last season, it's his team and he can do with it as he chooses.

Ironically, George had few problems during 1989 with his players, only his manager and coaches. The differences between Steinbrenner and the Dave Winfield Foundation were settled and, at least from my vantage point, I detected little anger from the clubhouse aimed toward the front office.

That wasn't the case when I played briefly with the Yankees twelve years ago (1978). That's when half of the clubhouse hated George and actually banded together with a ''we'll win in spite of him'' mentality, and we did win the World Championship. There was no such animosity or unity last season.

Every owner in baseball has a different style, but can you imag-

ine Peter O'Malley of the Dodgers, for example, making sugges-
tions about who should hit where in the batting order? But that's
the way Steinbrenner runs his team and the numbers are there to
prove it: In seventeen seasons as Yankees' owner, Steinbrenner
has had eighteen managers, twenty-seven pitching coaches, ten
publicity directors, and TMC (too many to count) other front-
office personnel.

It was a decade of frustration for Steinbrenner because it was the
first since the 19-teens that the Yankees didn't win at least one
World Series. They were champions of baseball during the Ruthian
1920s ('23, '27, '28) and 1930s ('32, '36, '37, '38, '39), the
1940s ('41, '43, '47, '49), the glorious 1950s ('50, '51, '52, '53,
'56, '58), the 1960s ('61, '62), and even the 1970s ('77, '78), but
all of George's managers and all of George's men could not bring
home a World Championship during the 1980s.

They did, however, make some delightful headlines.

Consider the case of Polonia, the talented twenty-five-year-old
outfielder from the Dominican Republic who came into New York
in early 1989 in a trade with the eventual World Champion Oakland A's for Rickey Henderson and said: "I'm going to make
people forget about Rickey Henderson."

Responded Henderson, who went on to become MVP in the
American League Championship Series: "Tell him I'm a legend."

Polonia, however, became somewhat of a legend himself by
being convicted in Milwaukee for having sexual intercourse with a
fifteen-year-old girl during a Yankee road trip.

"YANKEE PANKY," screamed the headline of the *New York
Post* (where else?) when Luis was arrested last August.

Polonia claimed it was just a misunderstanding—that the girl
said she was nineteen (age of consent in Wisconsin is sixteen).
Sorry, said the Milwaukee judge, and Polonia ended up being
sentenced to sixty days, plus community service in Wisconsin,
plus paying a fine of eleven thousand dollars.

He also rewrote the Yankee dictionary.

Girls who hang around the ballparks and hotels hoping to

meet players are no longer called Groupies. They are now Polonias.

Luis's Yankee teammates were merciless.

"She said she was eighteen when I nailed her," offered one sympathetic teammate.

"But Luis should have known better," counseled Steve Sax, "when she broke out her birth control pills and they were shaped in the form of Freddy Flintstone."

"Just look at it this way, Luis," said another, "you're now Rob Lowe's favorite player."

Moral of the immoral story: Kids from small cities like New York should be careful in big towns such as Milwaukee.

And, at this writing, good-hit (.300), shaky-field Luis was still a member of the Yankee roster and expected to report for spring training, 1990, even though at one time he was listed by newsmen as being on Steinbrenner's "hit list."

But then, wasn't almost everybody?

Henderson, incidentally, didn't endear himself to the Yankees by calling his ex-teammates "Bronx Boozers" because of their drinking habits during 1988.

"I saw people stumbling off planes, stumbling to their hotel rooms," said Henderson, last spring.

"Those who live in glass houses shouldn't throw stones," responded pitcher Dave Righetti. "Rickey drinks as much as anyone else."

When somebody said he had observed Henderson taking miniature gin bottles off Yankee charter flights, Rickey responded: "I collect the little bottles."

Whether Rickey's accusations about 1988 were valid is a moot point. There was no booze on Yankee charters last season because Dallas Green had a rule against it. As for Henderson, plain-talking Dallas simply said: "If the players are upset with what Rickey said, they should go kick the shit out of him. It's between them."

As a Yankee newcomer and observer, I found myself in the

camp of ex–Yankee captain Ron Guidry, who said: "I've never known alcohol to be the reason a team didn't win."

Guidry finally retired last July after thirteen seasons with the Yankees and said: "Anyone who plays here ten years does a couple of extra years service."

And how did he adjust to life in his hometown of Lafayette, Louisiana, after a career in the Big Apple?

"There's not as much night life here as in New York, and there's not as much day life, either."

It was the night of August 23, during the eighth inning of a game against the Red Sox, that John Sterling said "Jesus" into the WABC microphone as a body dropped from the upper deck at Yankee Stadium.

Steve Krisztin, age twenty-four, from Old Bethpage, Long Island, allegedly a Yankee fan, later told security people he leaped onto the screen behind home plate because he was "bored" with proceedings on the field.

The young man, a skier who bounced off the screen unharmed, was taken to the Forty-fourth Precinct and booked for reckless endangerment or some such charge, and probably paid his fine by collecting money from friends in the upper deck.

He should have been fined for lack of motive. Being bored by the Yankees is hardly reason enough to jump. Considering the quality of play by the team last season, I could have jumped at least thirty or forty times. If things don't improve in 1990, maybe Sterling and I should request parachutes as part of the WABC dress code.

After they were all but eliminated late last season, the Yankees played their best baseball. That is not an unusual occurrence. Once there is no pressure, major league teams often perform better and have more fun.

Or do they have more fun and perform better? It's the classic chicken-egg question of baseball. My contention remains that players who know how to laugh and relax also find it easier to win.

The Yanks started doing both last September under new manager Bucky Dent, and perhaps the most enjoyable evening of the season came during a chartered flight from New York to Seattle.

It was the night catcher Bob Geren had his head shaved bald and got paid two thousand dollars for the misery.

It all started during the All-Star break when Yankee trainer Gene Monahan said, "If the Yanks win five in a row this year I'll shave my head." Well, on September 3 the Yanks swept the Angels for their fifth straight, 2–1, and after the game Mel Hall and Alvaro Espinoza led an invasion party into the training room, where Monahan received a closed-door scalping.

From there it was fun and games on the bus to the airport and the long, cross-country flight to Seattle. And, on the flight, Hall and Jesse Barfield continued the War Party by walking up and down the aisle trying to bribe others into getting their heads shaved.

Geren, who has one of the bigger heads in the league, was the prime target. At first they offered him five hundred dollars. Then the ante went to one thousand and he still refused. When the pot reached two thousand dollars, however, with even the pilots and stewardesses contributing, Geren relented. He said he could use the money to buy a new washer and dryer for his wife.

"But when she sees this head," said Hall, "she'll leave you and take the washer and dryer with her."

As I watched the scalping of Geren, with Hall, Espinoza, Lance McCullers, Lee Guetterman, and Steve Sax leading the entire team in screaming and laughing, I couldn't help but say to myself that the Yanks could have used a dose of this earlier in the season. It's the kind of craziness that bonds a group of men.

Up front, new manager Dent wondered if he should go back and settle things down but coach Champ Summers implored him to "let it go." So Bucky stayed away and by the time we landed in Minneapolis for refueling, the entire plane was in uproarious laughter and Geren was nearly bald. When he looked into the pocket mirror produced by Hall, Bob almost threw up. But it was too late.

Meanwhile, the players were led in chorus by Don Mattingly as they hummed the theme to *The Addams Family* (I guess they figured Geren looked like Uncle Fester).

For the record, the Yankees went on to win four more games before their longest winning streak of the season (nine) ended on September 8.

Mattingly, incidentally, for all of his quiet demeanor and intense dedication to the craft of hitting (.303, 23 HR, 113 RBI again last season), is not a man without humor.

Once as we walked across the grass at Yankee Stadium before a game he put his arm over my shoulder and said, confidentially: "Jay, I want you to do me a favor."

"Sure, Don, what do you need?"

"I want you to announce today on the radio that I'm retiring."

"What? You're only twenty-eight years old. How can you retire?"

"I've had it, Jay. The game is no fun for me anymore and I want to leave while I'm on top."

"Okay, whatever you say. When do you want me to announce it?"

"Just kidding, Jay . . . just kidding."

When somebody asked Mattingly if he ever came in from first base to calm down Guidry, he replied: "He never needed that. He'd step behind the mound and put a dip in his mouth and he'd be all together. Besides, what was I going to tell him?"

Many players, perhaps more than you imagine, get involved in charity and community service. Mattingly does his share. One touching moment came last summer when my boss, Fred Weinhaus, affiliated with the Make-A-Wish Foundation, asked Mattingly to visit with an eleven-year-old boy, Joe Mauceri, who was suffering from leukemia. The youngster and his brother were brought into the Yankee dugout where Mattingly and many other players signed baseballs and visited with them. Young Joe's hero was Mattingly and just to see the two of them, sitting there together, quietly talking, gave me one of the season's special moments.

*   *   *

Team "togetherness" can be difficult to achieve when a player frequently has to be introduced to the man occupying the next locker. Because of player movement caused by free agency, it's a problem throughout baseball. Example: When the Yankees gave out plastic mugs to mark Fan Appreciation Day last season, the team photo was so outdated that five players, four coaches, and even the manager, Dallas Green, were no longer with the team. And even though the Yanks acquired Ken Phelps last season, by the end of the year he was already tenth on the roster in seniority.

It made me wonder about the Yankees' marketing theme last year: "It's a Whole New Ballgame."

Boy, they weren't kidding. When the first team picture was taken, only eight guys from the 1988 photo were still around. After that, Henderson, Richard Dotson, and Mike Pagliarulo departed, leaving only five. When Dallas Green was asked why he held so many team meetings, he answered: "Hey, you got any kids? Well, I've got four and you gotta keep tellin' 'em the same things over and over. It's the same here."

It could have been that Dallas was also trying to learn all their names.

The Yanks even tried to lighten up things early last season with a Kangaroo Court with forty-five-year-old Tommy John presiding ("He's the only one who looked like Judge Wapner," said Dave LaPoint) but then T.J. disappeared from the locker room, too.

One acquisition from Cleveland, outfielder Hall, when asked if he had ever imagined himself in pinstripes, said: "In prison."

Let's face it, Yankee fans. Your franchise has a reputation. After former Yankee catcher Rick Cerone became a member of the Red Sox, his teammate Mike Smithson said: "He doesn't like the Three Stooges as much as I do. I guess he spent so much time in New York with real stooges, he doesn't appreciate them."

After Pagliarulo, who never did get untracked last summer with the Yankees, was finally traded to San Diego, an unidentified former Yankee coach said: "The key to the trade for the Padres will be getting Pags to relax. He's a hypertense person by nature and the Yankee-Steinbrenner business ate away at him until he wasn't the same player.''

''Everybody blames me when we lose,'' says Steinbrenner, ''but how many games have I played or managed?''

LaPoint, one of twenty pitchers who labored in pinstripes last season, was disabled much of the season and enjoyed little success (6–9, 5.62). That's unfortunate because I'm sure Dave's troubles inhibited his behavior. He's a soft-throwing left-hander who played with seven other teams before landing in New York. Said Dave: ''I definitely lead the league in teammates.''

He did not lead the league in innings pitched (113 2/3), however, and I'm sure it kept his sense of humor under wraps.

LaPoint is the guy who once said to then–Vice-President George Bush, ''Hey, I like your beer,'' and has turned spitting tobacco on teammates' shoes into an art.

''The only time I ever got in trouble doing that,'' said LaPoint, ''was in San Diego when I got Steve Garvey. His face turned red, the veins in his neck stuck out, and he grabbed me and applied a bear hug that nearly made me pass out. Here was the All-American boy strangling me as he very quietly said, 'I don't like that.' ''

When Dave was a senior at Glens Falls, New York, High School in 1977, it was his duty to come up with a graduation prank. He came up with two hundred marbles, and whenever a student shook hands with the principal, he or she dropped a marble in his pants' pocket.

''By the end of the ceremony,'' said LaPoint, ''his pants were halfway down.''

LaPoint also collects hats and claims to have three hundred.

''My favorite is one that fell off the head of a drunk in a greasy spoon in Clinton, Iowa. I just kicked it up with my foot and kept on walking.''

I hope Dave will be back in his junk-throwing groove in 1990. His fastball could never be arrested for speeding but he's got changeups for his changeup and, if healthy, could pitch two-hundred–plus innings and provide at least that many laughs.

Something else the Yanks could use this spring: calendars and alarm clocks.

Infielder Wayne Tolleson, enraged, showed up in the Yanks' clubhouse one day last season with his suitcase and clothes-carrier.

"Where's the luggage, damnit," he yelled. "I left my stuff in the lobby and the goddamned bellman didn't take it. Where's the luggage?"

He was then informed that the team had one more game to play on the road trip and wouldn't be departing until the next day.

Then there was the day pitcher Chuck Cary rushed into the Yankee clubhouse, saw pitching coach Billy Connors, and said, "Billy, Billy, hold the game, I'll be right out, honest."

"Well, you can go out now if you want," said Connors to his scheduled starting pitcher, "but I'm not going out for another twenty minutes."

"Whatta you mean," said the obviously confused Cary. "I just heard them singing the national anthem and I'm not even warmed up!"

What he had heard was "The Star Spangled Banner" being played before an old-timers' game to precede the regular Yankees game. Cary hadn't pitched in almost a month, though, and was afraid he'd blown his start. Then along came Whitey Ford and Joe DiMaggio walking through the clubhouse and he got even more nervous.

And remember, fans, these are *big-leaguers*.

The pitching was so bad when the 1989 Yankees got off to their worst start in fourteen years that Jesse Barfield suggested the grounds crew should start dragging the warning track at midgame instead of the infield. That's how many line drives were banging off the wall.

"I could see only a few cleat marks on the infield but the warning track was dug up everywhere," said Barfield, after watching teammate Roberto Kelly crash into the wall and take a ball off his head.

This about Jesse, who came from Toronto and hit only .234: He has the best outfield arm I've seen since Reggie Smith and before that, Rocky Colavito.

Another who helped, defensively, and surprised a lot of people with a .282 batting average, was shortstop Alvaro Espinoza, who was earning a minimum annual salary of sixty-eight thousand dollars. He and Steve Sax led the league in double plays for much of the season. It's always hazardous to guess who will be playing anywhere with the Yankees, at any time, but you have to like Espinoza and Sax, both at the plate and around second base.

I expected Sax, a former teammate with the Dodgers, to become a superstar in the American League and he did, hitting .315 with forty-three stolen bases, 205 hits, twenty-six doubles, five home runs, and sixty-three runs batted in. He also struck out only forty-four times in 651 plate appearances and scored eighty-eight runs. That's superstar stuff, especially with a fifth-place team, and that's why owner Steinbrenner said: "I wish I had twenty-four Steve Saxes. I rate him with Goose Gossage, Reggie Jackson, and Catfish Hunter."

Sax was accepted as a leader within the Yankee clubhouse and that isn't easy for a first-year man.

He's also funny—not in the sense of "Hey, Steve, say something funny," but he's an accomplished mimic (he can recite, almost word for word, every line from the movie *Caddyshack*) and he and LaPoint were often seen turning pregame stretching exercises into impromptu song-and-dance routines. With Saxy, humor is spontaneous and that's the best kind (he may go into a *Rain Man* routine while playing catch).

When L.A. baseball writer Matt McHale asked me about Saxy's transition to pinstripes, I remember saying: "Someday when he looks back at this place [New York] he can say 'This is where I became a man.' The Dodgers never let him do that. He was always the little kid. He has grown up here."

When Sax arrived for spring training with the Yanks he immediately attracted attention by asking for Babe Ruth's number.

The truth is that he didn't know Babe Ruth's number. Saxy simply asked if he could wear number 3, the number he had worn with the Dodgers.

"So after they told me I couldn't have it," said Sax, "I asked for Lou Gehrig's number (4). Hey, it's not like the Babe needs the number anymore."

In Los Angeles, Sax and manager Tom Lasorda had a running routine, each using the other for fodder. Said Sax last spring: "I saw Tommy last Thanksgiving. He was a blimp in the Macy's Parade," then "He was sunning on the beach and Greenpeace tried to roll him back into the water."

Lasorda, in kind, recalls the first time he took Sax to a horse track.

"After five races, we never cashed in a ticket," said Lasorda, "but there were two guys who came back after each race and they were dividing up stacks of twenty-dollar bills. So, before the sixth race, these two guys get up and I give Sax ten dollars and say to him, 'Stay on these guys like a new suit. When you get in line, take the same thing they do.' Fifteen minutes later, Sax comes back with three roast beef sandwiches."

One of my favorites about Sax: With the Dodgers, he became such buddies with David Raymond, the Phillie Phanatic (mascot) at Veterans Stadium that Steve started calling him by his first name.

"Steve would come up to me and say 'Hey, Dave, what's going on? How's the family?' said Raymond. "Then one time I came up to him in street clothes and he didn't know who the hell I was."

Neon Deion (Prime Time) Sanders didn't know, either. When the former Florida State football and baseball star showed up with the Yankees he said to clubhouse assistant Nick Priore, "Look, I'll take any low uniform number you've got."

"Well, that should be no problem," said Nick, who has been Pete Sheehy's assistant for more than twenty years, "there's a bus over there, so get on it, go to Cooperstown, and pick out any number you want. They're all retired!"

Sanders, who ended up with number 44, then proceeded to make his own historic mark. He became the first man in history to hit a major league home run and score an NFL touchdown in the same week.

Think about it, Bo Jackson.

Sanders hit his second career home run for the Yankees on a Tuesday, signed with the Atlanta Falcons on Thursday, and three days later returned a punt sixty-eight yards for a touchdown against the Los Angeles Rams.

His first major league home run was almost as memorable but for a different reason. Deion, twenty-two, claiming he was so sick of media attention that he refused to talk with reporters, went into a slow trot after his first homer in Milwaukee and even stopped at home plate to fix a shoelace.

Humility, where art thou? Actually, he learned a little with the Yankees in spring training. He showed up, of course, wearing as much gold as Mr. T and carrying his own telephone and Gucci luggage.

But when he trotted onto the field with that gold earring he was met by a giant, who said: "Hello, Deion, my name is Frank Howard, and I'm the batting instructor for this team. I also played major league baseball and hit 382 home runs. Now take that fucking ring out of your ear!"

Deion, no small man at six-one, 195, looked up at Howard, who stands six-seven and weighs 255, and decided to take the ring out of his ear.

Actually, Deion has a chance to become a pretty good baseball player if he makes it his priority. He won't have the impact of Bo Jackson because he doesn't hit that many home runs, but he's fast and made some tremendous defensive plays in the outfield.

What I really like about Deion is that he hits down on the ball, and with his speed, that's a considerable asset. Also, he doesn't have that earring to slow him down anymore.

There is no news like old news and George Steinbrenner firing a manager is hardly news at all.

As deposed Dallas Green said last August 18 when Steinbrenner made his seventeenth managerial change (eleven different men) in his seventeen seasons as owner of the Yankees: "Anybody can manage [the Yankees], but for how long?

"Bucky [Dent] will be fired. You could book it."

There isn't a bookmaker alive who wouldn't take that action.

Before discussing Bucky, however, let's take one final, brief glimpse at the 1989 de-Greening of the Yankees.

Consider, first, New York City, media capital of the world and home of both the Yankees and Mets. You have the *New York Post, Newsday,* and *Daily News* battling for the portion of circulation that *The New York Times* doesn't possess, plus all major television networks and publishing houses are headquartered in Manhattan.

Some call it war, others call it a circus. Sportswriters and producers are told to get stories that make the back pages or 11:00 o'clock news.

Also, the New York baseball fan is fickle, smart, tough, and demanding. Bragging rights in New York are no small goal. Yankee Stadium may be the House That Ruth Built and there may be awesome tradition associated with those monuments in the outfield, but the Mets have also had spectacular success and when it comes to baseball, just as it was when the Giants and Dodgers were still in the East, New York is a city divided.

Steinbrenner is aware of all of this. He knows that if the Yanks and Mets ever met in a World Series, the Planet Earth would shake with a different kind of rumble.

He acts accordingly. When he says "We stink," he knows "We Stink!" will be tomorrow's headline. He doesn't have to say it to a reporter, either. He just has to whisper it in the men's room. That's how many "news leaks" there are around Yankee Stadium.

Therefore, when the 1989 Yanks got off to their worst start since 1975 and Green said, "I've never quit a job in my life . . . I'm not about to quit," the ball had already started to roll.

Then, as a team without adequate weapons continued to stagger through the summer and Green and Steinbrenner began picking at each other in the press, the inevitable became reality. Obviously, Dallas wasn't going to quit and walk away from the second year of a two-year contract paying him $350,000 to $400,000 per year.

So he helped Steinbrenner make the decision. Dallas helped with the firing by coining the phrase "Manager George," and keeping the owner in the dark about clubhouse activities.

Let's face it. Steinbrenner has given new meaning to "hands-on" ownership, but when Dallas assembled his own veteran coaching staff, he left George without private access to the clubhouse.

There were incidents, too, such as the time Steinbrenner tried to reach Green by phone, eventually found him in a bar, and asked, "What are you doing there?" only to hear the reply, "Well, I'm sure as hell not holding a prayer meeting."

Small digression: When Clyde King, sixty-four, special adviser to Steinbrenner, was building an elevated playhouse last summer for his six grandchildren, he fell and broke five ribs and his collarbone. When asked for Steinbrenner's reaction to the accident, King said: "He wanted to know what I was doing in a treehouse."

Green and Steinbrenner, meanwhile, two strong-willed men with a losing team on their hands, were on a collision course.

If the Yankees had won, everything *might* have been different. But the 1989 Yankees never had the look of winners. Green was appalled in spring training at the lack of fundamentals and he drilled his players hard, causing some dissension. He was also confronted with the loss of Jack Clark, Dave Winfield, and Claudell Washington and a pitching staff that, for various reasons, became the worst in the American League.

How soon did it start? When the Yanks lost seven of their first nine games, a radio station in Geneva, New York, started a contest to guess the date when Green would be fired. Steinbrenner responded by saying: "If you want to go out and make a bet, Dallas Green will be sitting in that dugout this year all the way."

By mid-May, however, Steinbrenner was saying, "These guys are a bunch of little babies . . . I've watched them night after night play like Little Leaguers."

By early August I had the distinct impression that Green didn't care whether he got fired or not and, indeed, would help precipitate it, which he did.

"There are times," said Dallas, "I wonder if I should go nuts and beat the hell out of them [his team], but I'm not sure this team could take that kind of beating."

Dallas had his clubhouse explosions. Nobody ever accused him of being a diplomat. He has always been a manager who took no prisoners. But winning is everything in New York and when it became apparent the Yankees weren't going to win, everybody from the mayor to the shoeshine guys at Madison Square Garden knew what was going to happen.

Then it did happen and there were the usual, acrimonious words—Dallas suggesting that George had surrounded himself with "yes men." Green was especially supportive of his own dismissed coaches (Frank Howard, Pat Corrales, Lee Elia, Charlie Fox), saying to Steinbrenner: "George, it's a shame you're so good to those people [Billy Martin, Lou Piniella, Clyde King, Syd Thrift], give them so much money, and get no return. And then, you get a group like we brought here and you fire them. It's a disgrace. You surround yourself with people who steal from you."

The "steal" remark obviously angered Steinbrenner and brought responses from both Piniella and Martin.

"That was the real trigger," said Steinbrenner. "Those people mean an awful lot to me."

So Steinbrenner hired Dent after Piniella, who had been offered the job again, said, "No thanks." And how did the local press react?

"So Bugs Bunny lives," wrote Jerry Izenberg of the *Newark Star-Ledger*. "Take a good look at this organization. . . . It has become the French Foreign Legion in pinstripes."

"What a pity," wrote Bill Madden of the *Daily News*. "Across nearly five decades, the Yankees epitomized stability. Steinbrenner always loves to talk about that great Yankee tradition, but what he has done is turn this once-great franchise into the laughingstock of baseball. Welcome back, Bucky."

"The Yankees managing job is the Devils Island of baseball," wrote George Vecsey of the *Times*. "Inmates are to be pitied rather than admired."

It wasn't long after the dismissal of Green that Steinbrenner also dumped his recently hired "general manager," the veteran Syd Thrift. Why Thrift, sixty, was ever hired remains a mystery to me. When Steinbrenner decided to "cut expenses" by restricting travel for Syd and his scouts, that relationship quickly deteriorated. Example: When Thrift showed up one night at Shea Stadium to watch the Mets and Reds, he said to reporters, ''I wanted to see the National League and it took me only two tokens.''

And when Green was asked if he had any interest in signing free-agent pitcher Goose Gossage (which he eventually did), he said, ''Somebody would have to tell me first if he could pitch and we don't have any scouts on the road so I don't know.''

I guess it rankled both Dallas and Syd that there was little budget for scouting personnel when the Yanks already had at least $58 million in the bank before they even opened Yankee Stadium doors, all from radio and television rights.

The cost-cutting was felt elsewhere, too. On one road trip the Yanks couldn't get a hotel room in downtown Cleveland and ended up in the Westlake Holiday Inn, twelve miles from the stadium. Explained Dave LaPoint: ''One of the guys got into a cab and said, 'Take me to the ballpark,' and the cabbie said, 'Which one? Pittsburgh, Detroit, or Cleveland? They're all the same distance.' ''

Interestingly, it was a remark by Green about the scouting situation that became, in Steinbrenner's mind, ''the straw that broke the camel's back.'' After the Yanks were beaten, 5–4, on August 14 by Milwaukee pitcher Jeff Peterek in his major league debut, Green made an off-the-cuff remark that the team didn't know what to expect from the rookie because it no longer had scouts on the road.

''We had reams of material on that guy [Peterek],'' responded Steinbrenner. ''He blamed me for the loss in Milwaukee and it was a blatant lie.''

Conclusion: At last count the Yankees had eleven former managers on their payroll and you never know when one will be rehired to replace Dent, who will make it twelve. Not that I want to see Bucky fired, but older and wiser men than Bucky have failed to survive the Yankee blast furnace. It reminds me of the exchange between Piniella and White Sox manager Jeff Torborg, who coached under Lou when he managed the Yanks: ''I remember that when you managed you lost weight,'' said Torborg. ''But look at me. I'm putting it on since becoming a manager.''

"You don't have George calling you," replied Piniella, now the Reds' manager. "That sort of deters your appetite."

Nevertheless, the thought of managing the Yankees under Steinbrenner must be some kind of narcotic that stable-minded men simply can't resist. Bill Virdon couldn't resist and neither could Billy Martin (five times), Dick Howser (twice), Bob Lemon (twice), Gene Michael (twice), Piniella (twice), Clyde King, Yogi Berra, Green, and now Dent.

What would you do if Steinbrenner asked you to manage the Yankees?

I know what I'd do. I'd say "You gotta be shitting me," and go ride the subway.

Russell Earl (Bucky) Dent, thirty-eight, managed five years in the Yankees' minor league system, the last three in Columbus, Ohio, before succeeding Dallas Green. He was also the Yankee shortstop for five entire seasons, 1977 through 1981, and part of 1982.

We were teammates with the 1978 World Champion Yankees and almost became teammates five years earlier with the Chicago White Sox, missing by just one season. I left Chicago after the 1972 season and Bucky, the handsome, fresh-faced rookie from Savannah, Georgia, came up in 1973.

It was Bucky's dramatic 1978 home run against the Red Sox at Fenway Park in Boston that forever emblazoned his name in Yankee lore—the home run that beat the Red Sox, 5–4, in the one-game playoff for the American League.

How well I remember it: With Boston leading, 2–0, in the top of the seventh inning, Dent, who had hit only four home runs all season, drove a Mike Torrez pitch over the left-field wall for a three-run homer. The Bosox never recovered.

I was sitting on the steps in the Yankee dugout when the ball went over the wall and I remember looking immediately toward the Red Sox dugout, where manager Don Zimmer looked as if he had just swallowed his chewing tobacco, as maybe he had.

Now Bucky is back wearing pinstripes and it's good to be with him again. We're friends and have many of the same friends. Example: Bucky and Goose Gossage, the pitcher who returned to the Yankees last season to record a save in Bucky's first major league victory.

You can go back twenty years with Goose and Bucky, when they were both babies breaking in with the White Sox' Class A team in Appleton, Wisconsin. Pitcher Terry Forster, now retired after seventeen productive and well-fed seasons in the big leagues, tells this story about those early days: "We were just three kids but I was the veteran. I got to Appleton three weeks before Bucky and Goose, so I asked them to be my roommates. We went out and bought a beat-up, 1955 Chevy for seventy-five dollars and named it the Green Monster. Then we went to Goodwill Industries to buy pots and pans. Goose and I slept on the mattress on the apartment floor in front of the air conditioner and shared a blanket. Bucky got the bed but slept on the springs because we had the mattress. None of us came from families with much money.

"Remember, though, we were teenagers. We thought we had it made and who needed a car more expensive than seventy-five dollars, anyhow? I didn't even know they had roads in Wisconsin from one end to the other.

"I especially remember one crazy, rainy, muddy day in Appleton. Ira Hutchinson, our manager, had told us 'If it rains a lot, don't even bother coming to the ballpark' and on this day it had rained and rained, so I said, 'Hey, if we're not going to hit or anything, let's have some fun.'

"So we took these cardboard boxes, flattened them, and made sleds. Our apartment was located on a big hill next to the cemetery so we had a natural 'run.'

"Whoooosh. You should have seen us sliding down that hill, at least three hundred to four hundred yards, whooping and hollering and jumping over gravestones in the mud. Then we'd climb up the hill and do it again.

"But all of a sudden somebody looked up and saw the ballpark lights. They were on!

" 'Oh, shit,' said Goose, 'we're going to have a game tonight.' So we all ran up the hill, changed into our clothes, and jumped into the Green Monster and raced to the park. But we were already forty-five minutes late and the manager was waiting. He fined us each twenty-five dollars and those were our first fines in professional baseball.

"I know it doesn't sound like much but with that seventy-five dollars we could have bought another car."

Bucky Dent, twenty years later, probably wishes he could get away from the pressure of being Yankee manager and slide down a few cemetery hills. It was rough when he first came up last August and the Yanks went into the tank, losing eleven of his first thirteen games. Bucky knew he couldn't scream and yell because he hadn't been there long enough to earn the players' respect, and I know it worried him. In truth, he did a good job during that early slump, managing the team to the brink of victory on several occasions, only to see players not come through in the clutch.

Bucky's goal this year: to instill a feeling of team togetherness into the Yankees. There wasn't a lot there last year.

Now it's 1990 and the new manager enters a new season with a somewhat new cast. I mentioned this to one of my cynical newspaper friends over the winter and he quickly responded, "Yeah, but the owner is the same."

New York is the same, too. I travel across town on a bus just for the fun of it. Sure it's crazy but you should try it. If you can't entertain yourself observing people in New York City, you can't be entertained.

I'll get on the bus at York Avenue and ride all the way to Eighty-Sixth Street on the West Side. Then I come back, or hop into a cab and go downtown.

In fact, if you see me on a New York bus or subway, make sure you come up to say hello. We'll talk baseball. You tell me what's wrong with the Yankees and I'll give you George Steinbrenner's phone number.

Just tell him you got it from some goofball on the subway wearing a Hawaiian shirt.

13

A Few Final Thoughts . . .

Bruce McCampbell, a man who lives in the remote mountains of Santa Cruz County in California, is recipient of my first annual Jaybird A&P (attitude and perspective) Award.

When the 7.1 earthquake of last October 17 tore a huge gash through his yard at 5:04 P.M. PST, McCampbell turned to the woman he was divorcing, pointed toward the ravine, and declared: "This is your half."

I was standing with a friend, Jerry Callahan of Anheuser-Busch, in section three, lower deck of Candlestick Park, behind home plate, when the World Series shaker hit and everybody started cheering.

At first I thought the noise and vibration was coming from a plane passing overhead. It sounded and felt like Bat Day at Yankee Stadium with everybody pounding their bats on the floor. Then I saw the concrete walkway rolling and light standards swaying and I knew it was an earthquake.

I wasn't scared and neither was anybody around me. In fact, the fans thought it was terrific for a pregame show that lasted only fifteen seconds.

Five minutes later, however, when news of damage to the Bay

Bridge and Nimitz Freeway began to reach us via portable radios and TVs in the audience, we quit smiling.

I'd been through earthquakes before in Southern California—one so large, in fact, that while I was talking on the phone in my home in San Marino, about six miles from the Rose Bowl, I looked up to see a huge crack open in my kitchen ceiling. That one scared me because it dropped plaster in my coffee.

The Series quake, however, will be part of baseball lore forever. Not only did it take lives and cause billions of dollars in damage, it was nationally televised.

Flash recollections: Candlestick Park seats moving up and down like a roller coaster . . . and the Giants' players rushing onto the field to look up into the stands for their families with me wondering "Where are the A's?" Then I realized they had probably gone out the back door from the visiting locker room into the fenced-in parking lot.

In retrospect, I'm still amazed Candlestick didn't suffer more serious damage, because we were right in line with the quake as it rolled up the peninsula from the epicenter near Santa Cruz. My first thought was that the Marina district in San Francisco, where the legendary Joe DiMaggio makes his home, was hit hardest, because the quake snapped like a whip at the end. It was only later that I realized the Marina suffered most because of the soft landfill on which so many older structures had been built.

It took the players about three days to start thinking again about baseball but I knew their minds were back when Steve Bedrosian walked into the Giants' clubhouse wearing a bright yellow plastic hard hat. Then, a few days later, Giants manager Roger Craig said: "I'm not afraid to play again in Candlestick but I'm going to manage from second base."

And you knew the shaker had affected some thinking when Giants' pitcher Don Robinson, who lives in Florida, said, "I wouldn't live here if they paid me $10 million and gave me a free home."

Athletics pitcher Dave Stewart, eventual MVP of the interrupted, four-game Series sweep and a native of Oakland, was perhaps the most articulate of all players during the difficult rescue and recovery period before play resumed ten days after the quake.

"There is a shadow over this Series that will never go away," said Stewart, who was active in organizing a players' relief fund. "Baseball goes on, it always will be played. But human life is precious and when it is lost, you feel it."

Indeed, everyone in sports "felt" the World Series earthquake, no matter where he lived, and when the ballplaying was eventually finished, it was fitting that the A's celebrated without champagne in their locker room.

Unfortunately, the new World Champions were also robbed of the adulation they deserved. I'm not much on comparing teams of different eras, but certainly a strong argument could be made on behalf of the 1989 A's being one of baseball's better teams of the half-century.

Tony LaRussa, manager of the A's, perhaps said it best: "The 1975 Reds or the 1927 Yankees weren't any better than the 1989 A's."

The Reds and Yanks also had the benefit of playing on solid ground.

Was new commissioner Fay Vincent right and proper in continuing the Series? Certainly he was, and he handled the delay with good taste and sound judgment. Baseball didn't *cause* the earthquake and, indeed, lives were saved because of the Series, as many Bay Area people were home watching TV and off the freeways and bridges.

There were those in baseball, however, who viewed the World Series earthquake as final proof that 1989 was a season scarred, but I don't view it that way.

Not that it wasn't rough. Pete Rose was banned for gambling; Wade Boggs and Steve Garvey saw their names in lawsuits and tabloid headlines; a former player and one of the game's good people, Donnie Moore, committed suicide; and there was the shocking death of Commissioner A. Bartlett Giamatti.

But there was a flip side. The Cubs made Chicagoans delirious again (25 million phone calls to buy eighty-four thousand playoff tickets). The Blue Jays brought joy to the SkyDome in Toronto. The Giants reappeared in a World Series for the first time in twenty-seven years and gave us two young power hitters for the future, Kevin Mitchell and Will Clark.

Attendance once again went off the charts, with 55 million in attendance.

And there were the human stories.

Consider pitcher Jim Abbott of the Angels. Born without a right hand, he proved naysayers wrong by holding down a spot in the California starting rotation all season (12–12, 3.92 in 181 1/3 innings) and proved an inspiration to scores of handicapped youngsters who turned toward his achievements with pride. He received hundreds of letters from handicapped kids and he not only answered them all, he probably met more than fifty of the writers personally.

After a while, observers and hitters simply forgot that Jim Abbott pitched and caught baseballs with the same hand and that's the way he likes it. He knew he was accepted when opposing players started calling him "Slots."

Slots?

"As in slot machine, as in one-armed bandit," said one enemy coach. "Hey, it's part of the game."

Also consider pitcher Dave Dravecky of the Giants. He beat cancer (tumor removed from the deltoid muscle in his upper left arm), made a miraculous recovery to win two games on the comeback trail, then broke the same left arm while pitching.

Still not ready to step away, Dravecky stayed in uniform with his arm in a cast and broke the darned thing again during the Giants' National League pennant celebration.

Finally, after the season, courageous Dave announced his retirement upon medical advice.

Consider, too, Nolan Ryan. Better yet, marvel at Nolan Ryan. At age forty-two, he went 16–10 and struck out 301 batters with the Texas Rangers, five times flirting with no-hitters, and winning the All-Star Game.

"When he's through," said Tommy Lasorda of the Dodgers, "they better send his arm to the Smithsonian. I've never seen anything like it."

Oh, I almost forgot. He also punched out his five-thousandth victim, finishing the season with 5,076, and nobody in the history of baseball has that many K's beside his name.

For the record, I struck out twice against Ryan in fifty-seven at-bats, which is acceptable when you realize he has struck out 117 Hall of Famers, 42 MVP's, 6 father-son combinations, 10 brother sets, and all 3 Alous.

Many believe The Express pitched better during 1989 than at any time in his career, still throwing the ball ninety-five miles per hour and breaking off hellacious curves. Stories abound about Ryan's "heat," but one of my favorites is told by the right-hander, on himself, when he pitched in high school in Alvin, Texas, twenty-seven years ago.

"I hit the leadoff batter in the helmet and broke it," admitted Ryan, "then I hit the number-two hitter and broke his arm. The third guy begged not to hit."

White Sox manager Jeff Torborg, who caught no-hitters by both Ryan and Sandy Koufax says, "When you talk about velocity, Ryan threw the hardest—harder than any human being I ever saw. In 1973 against the Boston Red Sox, Nolan threw a pitch a little up and over my left shoulder. I reached up for it and the ball tore a hole in the webbing of my glove and hit the backstop at Fenway Park."

Ryan, with 289 career victories, needs just 11 victories to reach the 300 plateau this season. Then he can make a lot of guys happy by quitting and waiting for his day at Cooperstown.

Now consider two other men who retired during 1989 and left baseball a little poorer.

Tommy John, born two and a half years *before I was, for Chrissakes,* finally retired from pitching last summer at age forty-six. T.J. began his major league career with Cleveland in 1963, the same summer I began in organized ball with San Jose. His best season was 1977 with the Dodgers (20–7), but after signing with the Yanks as a free agent, he went 21–9 and 22–9.

John is the only player this century to play in twenty-six major league seasons and I tip my hat. The crazy thing, too, was that he actually could have won some games last summer for the Yankees if they'd gotten him any runs. I've never seen a more experienced ground-ball pitcher in my life than Tommy and although he finished 12 victories shy of 300, surely he's another who will one day reach the Hall of Fame.

If not Tommy, they should at least induct his left arm.

Another who finally took off the uniform, at age sixty-four, was Houston Astro coach and Yankee Hall of Famer Yogi Berra.

There isn't a thing I could write about Yogi that Yankee fans don't already know. Indeed, he became a legend in his own time ("Nobody ever goes to that restaurant anymore. It's too crowded."), and even during his final season, Yogi was dazzling interpreters with his tongue. For example, he was asked these questions late during the season:

Reporter: "Do the Astros still have a chance?"
Yogi: "What do you think?"
Reporter: "Is it too late to catch the Giants?"
Yogi: "What do you think?"
Reporter: "Is the season basically finished?"
Yogi: "What do you think?"
Reporter: "Do you believe the pennant race is all over?"
Yogi: "I gotta catch the bus."

One of the enduring quotations in American literature has been attributed to Berra, who is said to have said, "It ain't over 'till it's over," ranking Yogi right there with the legendary verbal exchange at thirty thousand feet between Muhammad Ali and an airline flight attendant who told the heavyweight champion to fasten his seat belt.

"Superman don't need no seatbelt," said Ali.
"Superman don't need no airplane, either," said the stew.

If ever a man needed a sense of humor, it was Pete Rose last summer. It was amazing how he endured the media coverage and seemingly interminable investigation of his case, which was eventually resolved with his lifetime suspension from baseball.

"There were six or seven network people just standing around looking at me," said Rose, during one period of his ordeal. "It was crazy. If Dan Rather were being investigated, do you think he'd let a bunch of people stand around in his office for hours, just staring at him?"

My feelings about Rose: I played with him, admire him, and feel confident he will one day be inducted into the Hall of Fame. I'm also hopeful he will be reinstated and return to baseball.

I also felt very sad about what happened, but I'm glad to see he's coming to grips with his affliction.

I want to see him back in baseball. Let's face it, the term "permanently ineligible" simply doesn't fit alongside the name of Pete Rose.

Speaking of names, what about Fay? Is one of the qualifications for being commissioner of baseball that you have a name nobody else has or would want?

Think about it. We've called commissioners by the names of Kenesaw Mountain (Landis), Happy (Chandler), Ford (Frick), General (William Eckert), A. Bartlett (Giamatti), and now Fay (Vincent), which makes about as much sense as Jay. Only Peter Ueberroth had a normal first name, but we paid for it trying to pronounce his last.

If I were commissioner I'd be more concerned about substance abuse than any other problems with the business we still call sport.

We called them Greenies. The pharmacist called them amphetamines, and they were, by medical definition, "nervous system stimulants."

There was a time when ballplayers could find those little pills by the water cooler and could grab one on the way out the door. That's how prevalent they were when I played with the Angels in the late 1960s and Phillies in the mid-1970s. Hey, the trainers on ballclubs would even monitor the distribution. But that was way back when—before cocaine took its addictive hold on so many within professional sports.

The term "Greenies" was used because the Dexamyl tablet was

green. It was that simple. Hey, I remember one day during the 1976 pennant race with the Phillies when it was 130 degrees on the field at Busch Stadium in St. Louis and I took a Greenie. First, understand: There were two kinds—one was five milligrams, about a two-hour, quick, speed-up-the-heart rush. The other was fifteen milligrams, sort of a time-release capsule that stayed with you longer.

Well, on this day I felt I needed the longer one. I'd been out the night before, I was exhausted, and I just didn't think I could make it through the day. So I popped the fifteen-milligram Greenie in that 130-degree heat and about the fifth inning I came into the dugout and said to our shortstop, Larry Bowa, "What did I do the last two times at bat?"

"You grounded out and flew out to right field."

"Thanks."

That was the last time I ever took a Big Greenie. I was so hyped-up I had no recall of the first five innings. After that, I stuck to the five-milligram Greenies like everybody else. We ate them like candy and sometimes at night used them for breath mints!

Why the need? Players would turn to Greenies during a day game after a night game, perhaps during a long road trip, when they simply had no more energy. In those days *you played* because you had one-year contracts without any of the guarantees players have today.

I was the kind of player who pushed his body until sometimes it just wouldn't work anymore. I remember once in Chicago I went out with relatives and drank red wine at seven different restaurants in Chicago, finally getting back to the hotel about 7:00 A.M., knowing I was in the lineup for a day game at Wrigley Field.

I stumbled to the park, popped two Greenies, and went four for four off Rick Reuschel, with *none of the hits getting out of the infield*. I remember I had a new bat that day and didn't put a mark on it. I squibbed one hit over the third baseman's head, another went into the hole between third and short, another high-chopped over Reuschel's head, and the fourth hit behind second base, where the second baseman knocked it down.

Every hit came off the end of the bat and every time I reached first base Reuschel would just look over and shake his head.

Greenies were part of the game. One night eight of us from the Phillies went out for dinner in Chicago and seven ordered dinner. The eighth, a pitcher who shall remain unnamed, said, "I'll wait." Well, we had soup and salads and he just kept sitting there, smiling, saying, "I'll eat in a little while."

Finally, our seven steaks arrived and he asked the waitress for a plate. Then he reached into his pocket, pulled out three Greenies, tossed them onto the plate and said, "Now this is a dinner." Using a knife and fork, he ate all three.

That has all changed. Amphetamines aren't as available as they once were (prescription needed, and so forth), and players apparently no longer feel the physical or emotional need to use them.

I never knew anyone who became addicted to Greenies. They all put their little helpmate bottles away at the end of the season. Everybody knew better, anyhow. We all knew if we took too many we'd become basket cases, so we learned to take them only when needed, sometimes just a half-Greenie. If you took too many you could end up feeling like Silly Putty when they wore off, but many players felt that by using them, they enhanced their performances. It put *mind over body* so you believed you felt no pain, even when you did.

The bottom line: Any time a committed athlete can play a game with intensity, without pain, he's going to do it. He will abuse his body to do it, too, and we did.

Then, however, came the cocaine. I've never tried it and won't. I did try marijuana once but it put me to sleep. I did it because I wanted to say, "Yes, I took it and it did nothing for me." But I don't need to try cocaine to know the results. I only have to look at the addicts to know the answer.

A veteran player from the Mets came up to me last summer and said, "I can't believe it. Nobody on this team uses Greenies. How can these guys get up every morning and know it's the best they're going to feel all day?"

"Times have changed," I said.
"Changed? They've ruined the game!"
And he was only half-kidding.

Nowadays, it's major news when Jose Canseco insults an airline stewardess or is cited by the California Highway Patrol for having tinted windows. And if you call his 900 number you can hear what he ate for breakfast.

So what is normal? Former A's and Giants pitcher Vida Blue got married on the field at Candlestick Park with an honor guard of Giants with raised bats. He refused to do an interview with a TV crew, however, because he "didn't want to turn his wedding into a circus."

In Texas a pitcher named Jeff Russell put lighter fluid on the bullpen ball bag and burned it; and when Cincinnati pitcher Kent Tekulve gave teammate Danny Jackson an eighteen-inch, white plastic inflatable punching bag, it was named "Wham It. The Anti-Stress Device—the low-tech solution to high-tech problems."

Anything that works. When Reds owner Marge Schott called a team meeting last summer and asked advice from players, nobody said a word. Finally, Marge said, "How about prayer? Do you think prayer would work?"

"I don't think God gives a damn whether we hit or not," said Chris Sabo. "If God cared, Billy Graham would be hitting .400."

The simplest solutions are always best. Angels manager Doug Rader has three cars, each with more than one hundred thousand miles on the speedometer, and he has "For Steal" signs on all of them. Says Rader: "I leave the keys in the ignition and nobody takes them."

Pitcher Eric Plunk, before being traded from the A's to the Yankees in the deal for Rickey Henderson, had become a convert from his trademark thick glasses to contact lenses. The only problem was that while adjusting to the contacts he couldn't pick up the signs from catcher Terry Steinbach. Finally, the A's catcher sat down with Plunk and explained his dilemma—that he never knew whether Eric was going to throw a fastball or breaking ball.

"Well, Steinie," said Plunk, "I gotta figure if you don't know what's coming, then the batter definitely isn't going to know what's coming." With that, he picked up his glove and returned to the mound.

Too much knowledge isn't compatible with baseball, anyhow. When Giants manager Roger Craig received a congratulatory telegram during the NL playoffs from The Grateful Dead, he thought it was from a funeral home.

Consider, too, the Bazooka Joe comic strip that Lee Mazzilli keeps inside the sweatband of his cap. It says:

Teacher: "Where are you from?"

Joe: "Brooklyn."

Teacher: "What part?"

Joe: "All of me."

Back in 1986, when there was a rash of hotfoots going around the Milwaukee Brewers' clubhouse, then-manager George Bamberger called a meeting to tell his players the pranks had to cease. While he was addressing his troops, however, catcher Rick Cerone was sneaking up behind him to start a hotfoot.

Last season the same Brewers clubhouse became the scene of a new danger: firecrackers being thrown into bathroom stalls while players were seated on the stool. Finally, manager Tom Trebelhorn decided to take measures.

"I told the players that if the demolition experts didn't cease and desist," said Trebelhorn, "they'd have to start wearing tuxedos on all team flights."

Maybe one day the Russians can improve on our national pastime. Right now they're not so hot. When the Soviet Union's newly formed national team toured the United States last summer—wearing all-new equipment donated by American firms and using one thousand baseballs donated by Wilson—they were humiliated at almost every turn (Navy beat them in the tour opener, 21–1).

What was wrong with Ivan? He was swinging the bat too late, he picked up ground balls like a man trying to avoid a snake, he threw with a stiff and awkward motion. He didn't look as if he was having much fun, either. Maybe it's because baseball hasn't exactly caught hold over there. The first game ever played at seventy-five-thousand-seat Moscow Stadium drew only thirty fans.

Soviet spokesmen, however, insist that baseball is just a variation of an old Russian game called "Lapta," which is centuries old. As one Soviet visitor described "Lapta" at a press conference: "You hit a ball with a stick and then run to the enemy's city, like a base. He tries to hit you with the ball and you are out. There are three outs to an inning. The game is based on your enemy's attempts to deceive you."

Enemy? Deceive? Sounds like a sport invented by Robert Ludlum. By 1992, however, when baseball becomes an official Olympic sport, surely the Soviets will have improved on their skills. Whether they understand that the game is to be played *for fun* remains to be seen. I just hope I'm watching when somebody gives Ivan his first hotfoot.

Meanwhile, I wonder if the Soviets would understand that because of a nail, a pennant might have been lost.

It was a tale of misery for Baltimore pitcher Pete Harnisch, who was scheduled to pitch last September 30 in Toronto in a game the Orioles had to win to keep from being eliminated from the American League pennant race by the Blue Jays.

Harnisch couldn't pitch, though, because he stepped on a nail.

It happened as Harnisch was walking home from the SkyDome on Friday night, September 29, and the nail went right through his shoe into his right foot.

"I saw it [on a board] but stepped on it, anyway," said the disconsolate Harnisch.

"Cleanest city in the world," said pitching coach Al Jackson, "and he steps on a nail."

"The only nail in Toronto," said pitcher Jeff Ballard.

"Imagine if this had happened in New York," said second baseman Bill Ripken. "If this was New York a giant block of cement would have fallen on his head and killed him."

"I told you this was a weird team," said reliever Brian Holton. Was manager Frank Robinson angry with Harnisch?

"No," said astonished F. Robby, "why should I be? It happens all the time, doesn't it? People step on nails walking home from the park all the time."

Instead of Harnisch, Robinson started Dave Johnson on September 30, and although he pitched well, the O's bullpen failed and Toronto won, 4–3, to clinch the pennant.

Harnisch, twenty-three, from Commack, New York, obviously never grew up playing baseball in cow pastures, and had to be as embarrassed about his accident as I was the day I attempted to throw behind a runner at first base.

Playing right field with the Phillies, I made a running catch and could see the runner away from the bag, so I tried for the double play.

Great idea. My foot slipped as I threw and the ball slipped out of my hand and went into the tenth row of spectators. It was classic. I was down in a crouch watching the first baseman and he didn't even jump. He just stood there, looking into the sky as if he were watching an airplane, as the baseball soared high into the crowd.

And when you're standing alone in right field, there's no place to hide.

Like the time last summer when I told the WABC radio audience that somebody "swang" at a ball. Don't ask me how it came out of my mouth, it just did. My only excuse was that we had just been in Texas, where people talk like that all the time, anyhow. Now we were in Milwaukee and after I said it, I turned to the engineer, off-mike, and whispered, "Did I just say he 'swang' at the ball?"

After he nodded yes, I returned to the microphone and said: "Great English, Jay. You're not in Texas, anymore."

Those things happen to rookie announcers. When my WABC partner, John Sterling, had to miss some games late last season because of a death in his family, I had to do my first solo play-by-play broadcast in Seattle. So what happened? The Yankees scored twelve runs on seventeen hits, winning 12–2, and my score-card looked like a garbled computer printout.

This season I want to announce a game from the outfield seats in Yankee Stadium, just as Harry Caray has done from the bleachers in Wrigley Field. Sterling isn't so excited about the idea but I'm hoping we can work it out. My resolution for 1990 is to have more fun in the broadcasting booth and I can't imagine a better place to start than among an audience of rabid Yankee fans.

Just in case, though, we should have one of those seven-second delays like they have on talk shows. But, hey, having a bunch of fans yelling in your ear still can't be as bad as being the announcer for the Arizona Wildcats football team.

How would you like to talk about quarterback George Malauulu dropping back to pass behind the protection of tackle Nick Fineanganofo and throwing to flanker Olatide Ogunfiditimi?

My broadcasting baptism under fire came as host of the cable TV show *Lighter Side of Sports*, which I had to relinquish to North Carolina State basketball coach Jim Valvano last year because of my WABC-Yankee commitments. We're both wacko so the show has continued on its tilted course.

It was fun for me, especially when three-hundred-pound umpire Eric Gregg came onto our studio stage in Atlantic City wearing a tuxedo and looking like a pregnant penguin, and when boxer Marvin Hagler almost had his head fried under one of our studio lights.

For some reason, Marvelous Marvin was apprehensive about being on the show, so to loosen him up, I put on a pair of boxing gloves, burst into the makeup room before the show, shadow boxing and screaming, "Now I've got your black ass." He looked at me and said, "Man, you're crazy," but he relaxed a little.

During the show, though, I noticed that he was sweating profusely. His shirt was drenched and you could see beads of perspiration all over his bald head. Finally, during a commercial break, I leaned over and said, "Are you all right?" That's when I discovered his scalp was almost on fire from the light immediately above his head, which hadn't been adjusted properly by our technicians. Instead of saying something, he had just been sitting there sizzling.

Morganna was a great guest, too, with those size sixty double-D's, and when I warned her about walking up the steps to the stage she said, "Honey, if I fall down I'll bounce straight back, anyhow."

It's about time for me to switch rings. I have World Championship rings from Los Angeles (1981, 1988) and I wear one of them when I'm on the west side of the Mississippi River, but when I'm on the east side I switch to my Yankee ring (1978).

Why do I have a ring from 1988 when I was already retired? You can chalk that one up to the generosity of L.A. owner Peter O'Malley, who sent me a surprise ring after the Dodgers stunned the A's in the 1988 World Series. I had worked for the Dodgers during the off-season as a public relations troubleshooter, speaking at about thirty events and clinics. Others in baseball, I might add, could learn from O'Malley when it comes to loyalty. At last count, former Dodgers employed by the Dodgers included such names as Sandy Koufax, Don Drysdale, Roy Campanella, Johnny Podres, John Roseboro, Claude Osteen, Reggie Smith, Don Newcombe, Manny Mota, Ron Perranoski, Burt Hooton, Phil Regan, Bill Russell, Jerry Royster, Bobby Darwin, Don LeJohn, Camilo Pascual, Lou Johnson, Jerry Stephenson, and Von Joshua.

Same subject, loyalty: Some of my best friends really are crazy.

Consider Dr. Archie and Larry McTague. If they aren't the Odd Couple of Manhattan, they're perennial finalists.

When the Yankees are home and I'm in New York, I "reside" with Dr. Robert (Archie) Laborante and another frequent visitor, McTague. To describe Archie and Larry as pals would be understating their relationship, which began back in the 1950s in one of the Jesuit high schools from which McTague wasn't expelled.

McTague, who ran the popular Upper East Side saloons Mr. Laffs, Tittle Tattle, and McTague's, has surely lost more phone numbers of stewardesses and Rockettes (he once claimed to have fifteen hundred) than most men even fantasize about. Maybe that's why he's now divorced and living with his mother. He has also befriended countless professional athletes over the past decade, including ex-Yankee pitcher Sparky Lyle, whom he met while both were swinging from a chandelier at a party at the Waldorf-Astoria Hotel. And when he hung around with pitcher Moe Drabowsky, their idea of fun was to attach a rubber band to a twenty-dollar bill, then sit laughing at the bar as they jerked it when Yuppies tried to pick it up.

All you really need to know about McTague is that when he was in high school he poured vodka *into his own football team's water bucket* and they won, anyhow, after frequent timeouts. Also, he was once arrested in Japan for snorkeling in the ladies' bath.

Dr. Archie, perhaps the worst driver in all of Manhattan, with violations to prove it, was once mistaken for a drug dealer by NYPD squad cars when he showed up with his black bag at midnight to tend to a patient. How was Dr. Archie to know the apartment building was under stakeout? Although the consummate host, Dr. Arch is also a compulsive cleaner, who has been known to vacuum between the legs of guests at a party.

These are among my New York friends and as the 1990 baseball season swings into gear, it will be good to break bread with them again. With Dr. Archie driving, there's also a good chance of breaking a bone, but at least he can fix it. I still haven't figured out what McTague can do.

It was Noriyuki (Pat) Morita, the Japanese-American actor who grew up near Sacramento, California, and who played karate master Miyagi in three *Karate Kid* movies, who once said during an attack of off-camera honesty: "I can't do karate. It mystifies me in a way, all that stuff about breaking bricks. Why don't they just pick up the brick and hit 'em over the head with it?"

I feel the same way about today's ballplayer.

I never signed a long-term, guaranteed $3 million-a-year contract and what has happened with baseball, economically, mystifies me. And when I hear players say some of the things they say, and see them take themselves out of a lineup because of a hangnail or swollen eyelid, I sometimes feel like picking up a brick myself.

That's what has made this "mission" to uncover all my crazy friends so challenging. I knew they were out there, but truth is truth: Things have changed in baseball. There is a difference and it's *money*.

When I came into the big leagues more than a decade ago we didn't make much money. We roomed together, drank together, chased girls together, and won or lost baseball games together.

Today's player wants to win, too, but also has other priorities. He makes so much money that holding an off-season job doesn't occur to him. He worries more about the *longevity* of a career than the quality of it. He invests and divests, finds only minor discomfort in being disabled, and moves without remorse or second glance from franchise to franchise, always in search of higher wages, warmer climates, and more guarantees.

Yet, in this era of team psychiatrists and rehabilitation clinics, is there no more room for fun?

I visited late last season with three pitchers from the World Champion A's—Rick Honeycutt, Bob Welch, and Dennis Eckersley—and asked them their views on the subject.

Interestingly, they blamed the media for some of the difference in the way players now behave.

Players are more inhibited nowadays, according to the trio of A's, because everything that happens around a club seems to get into the papers or the five o'clock news. Observance of the old clubhouse rule "what happens here stays here" has become as rare as a nine-inning complete game for a pitcher. Many players prefer to remain anonymous rather than do anything that might make them stand out from the herd—that is, jeopardize their contract.

Public image is important. Money is important. Hotfoots are not important. That's the party line.

Yet, when the heavily favored New York Mets fell on their faces during the 1989 season, I remember reading the comments of one Dwight Gooden, who claimed it "wasn't as much fun" around the Mets' clubhouse as it once was.

"My first four years here," said Doc to sports columnist Mike Lupica, "this team was so much fun. There was high-fiving all the time and if people didn't like it we didn't care because we were having so much fun. We were cocky, we were laughing, and we were having fun.

"It just went away and I don't know why. Things like high-fives and rally caps may sound dumb but it's part of what I'm talking about, part of what this team was like when Wally Backman was here, and Kevin Mitchell, and Ray Knight. They were guys who pumped life into us when we needed it. They made us exciting."

A sense of humor helps. I'm not talking about firecrackers under the manager when the score is tied in the eighth. I'm talking about being able to laugh at oneself and the unpredictable situations that develop in baseball.

Consider the Cubs, who clicked with youth last summer and enabled Don Zimmer to win Manager of the Year honors because of their overachievement. Did you happen to look into the Cubs' dugout during the playoffs? Did you *ever* see the manager or any member of the coaching staff smiling? If the Cubs weren't uptight against the Giants, they certainly looked like it and played like it.

Maybe those rumors about the Cubs one day moving their spring training camp from Arizona to Orlando, Florida, are true, after all. Maybe somebody upstairs at the The Tribune Company decided the Cubs might lighten up if they were closer to Disney World. But I've got a better idea: They should take general manager Jim Frey and Zimmer and put them on top of Magic Mountain and leave them there until they learn how to laugh.

Somebody once asked me how I wanted to be remembered in baseball.

Good question for any player or former player.

I suspect I'll be remembered as a guy who liked to have fun and did crazy things like wearing umbrella hats, dragging the infield, and leading cheers, and all of that is true. I did it all to make myself and others laugh, relieving the tension that inevitably builds over the course of a baseball season.

But I worked hard, too—harder than many who had more talent and played ahead of me. I wish I'd had the ability of Dick Allen, for example, who could come to the park, take ten or fifteen practice swings in front of the clubhouse mirror, then go three for four with a couple of home runs.

I didn't have that kind of talent so I took extra batting practice, ran into walls, slid headfirst into bases, and drove myself to be ready even if it was for pinch-hitting.

I played hard. I punished my body and made it fight back. I played a doubleheader every night, even when I didn't play an inning. But I never gave up and when I set my mind to do something, I usually found a way, however unorthodox, to get it done. I may not have been the prettiest, or the neatest, or the best, but I served as everything in clubhouses from team jester to team scrounger, and even came through a few times in the clutch.

Most memorable moment? I guess it had to be the pinch home run I hit off Ron Davis of the Yankees in the 1981 World Series. The Dodgers trailed in games, 2–1, and had fallen behind in game four at Dodger Stadium, 4–0 and 6–3, but my two-run homer brought us to within 6–5 and we eventually won, 8–7, and went on to capture the Series in six games.

The memorable part, personally, was that during batting practice I had predicted to sportswriters that if I got into the game I would hit a home run. After returning to the dugout somebody told me it was time to open my eyes.

Admittedly, playing baseball allowed me to extend a childhood that I'm not sure is finished. Indeed, ballplayers often don't grow up. They talk after their careers are finished about "staying in the game," which, translated, means "staying away from the real world." Ballplayers are treated as royalty in our society and often allowed to get away with things for which others would be penalized.

How, then, do I want to be remembered? I guess I'd want my epitaph to read something like "He played the game hard, knew what it took to win, and could make people laugh." Too long for an epitaph, you say? Okay, just say "Jay was a survivor."

One thing I don't see from the announcing booth is the burning desire by today's players to sacrifice their bodies to win. Perhaps that's also why you don't hear much about players throwing things in the clubhouse after a loss. Oh, once in a while you'll see Don Mattingly or Steve Sax display that kind of emotion, but it's rare.

I don't see players yelling and screaming "Hey, let's go!" to teammates. Why? I'm not sure, and to this observer, it's frustrating. It's not that *individuals* in baseball aren't making great plays because they are. But pennants are won by *teams* and, except from a few players, I don't see the *caring* in some that it takes to win.

It has to be the money. Why else would the game have changed so much? Players who couldn't have afforded briefcases in my day are now carrying portable television sets and stuffing thousand-dollar cellular phones into their Gucci handbags.

But hey, it's their game now and maybe they can have as much fun with their portable TVs and CD players as we used to have in the back of the plane sipping beers and flirting with the stewardesses.

I've already proven to myself during a season-long quest for craziness that it still exists, however masked. Now I'm off on another mission but I don't think I'll write a book about it.

My new challenge: to ride *every roller-coaster* at every amusement park in America. I can't help it. It's a passion. I don't care if they go upside down, sideways, or backward, it's where I want to be. I'm too old to be an astronaut so this is my substitute.

I also have a new hero and his name is Albert Graves.

Albert Graves?

Graves, a former resident of Cooperstown, New York, served under General Abner Doubleday during the Civil War, and when a specially formed committee in 1907 decided that Doubleday should receive credit as the founder of baseball, it was largely because of testimony by Mr. Graves, who told the committee he remembered the general explaining the game to a bunch of kids playing marbles in front of the local tailor shop.

Also, Graves, at age seventy-five, married a thirty-three-year-old woman, poisoned her when he was ninety, and died in an insane asylum when he was ninety-two.

If that doesn't tell you something about the legitimacy of baseball, what else do you need?

I went on a mission to find fun in the game and somewhere along the way, got lost in space.

But I can always be found on page 1,071 of *The Baseball Encyclopedia*, right behind Rex Johnston and just ahead of Stan Jok, who had better lighten up or he's going to end up on page 1,072 with chewing tobacco in his coffee.

As for the fans, this final message: Remember it's just a game, albeit a great one.

And if you're headed toward the ballpark one day and spot a lone horseman wearing an umbrella hat and riding into the sunset, holding the reins in one hand and a lemon meringue pie in the other, that'll be me.

Wave if you love baseball.